Raising the Stakes

Raising the Stakes

E-sports and the Professionalization of Computer Gaming

T. L. Taylor

The MIT Press
Cambridge, Massachusetts
London, England

First MIT Press paperback edition, 2015

For information about special quantity discounts, please email special_sales@mitpress.mit.edu.

This book was set in Stone Sans and Stone Serif by Toppan Best-set Premedia Limited. Printed and bound in the United States of America.

Library of Congress Cataloging-in-Publication Data

Taylor, T. L.
Raising the stakes : e-sports and the professionalization of computer gaming / T. L. Taylor.
p. cm.
Includes bibliographical references and index.
ISBN 978-0-262-01737-4 (hardcover : alk. paper)—978-0-262-52758-3 (paperback)
1. Computer games—Social aspects. 2. Sports—Sociological aspects—Case studies. 3. Sports—Psychological aspects. 4. Internet games. 5. Competition (Psychology). 6. Sports—Computer network resources. I. Title.
GV567.5.T39 2012
796.0285—dc23

2011036911

Contents

Acknowledgments

This book has been many years in the making and I've benefitted immensely from conversations on the subject with a range of people in the game studies and e-sports community. I'm grateful for examples given to me by Christopher Paul, Miguel Sicart, Doug Wilson, and various family and friends about traditional sports or other analogies in games that have helped me think about high-end competitive play. Darryl Woodford provided some helpful input on gambling and alerted me to the closure of the Championship Gaming Series (and thus got me moving on archiving material from the web site before it disappeared). Al Yang facilitated an introduction to an interviewee that proved to be invaluable. Thanks to Florence Chee for attempting to track down some South Korean gaming magazines for me during her final days in Seoul. Special thanks to James Caruso and Mavis Arthur of the JM Production Company for the image from the television show *Starcade* and Melanie Swalwell and The Alexander Turnbull Library for the fantastic image of an arcade game in Wellington, New Zealand. A special shout-out as well to my favorite café, Bruno, for letting me camp there endlessly while writing.

Throughout this project it's been a special pleasure to mull over issues specific to e-sports with the handful of other researchers working on this topic. Of particular value were conversations with Todd Harper, Henry Lowood, Nick Taylor, and Emma Witkowski. Further special thanks to Henry and Emma who, along with Henrik Bennetsen, Matteo Bitanti, and Susan Rojo, were my co-organizers for several fascinating e-sports workshops held at Stanford University and the IT University of Copenhagen. I also benefitted from great critical feedback (either via drafts read or conversations) from Katherine Isbister, Bart Simon, and my colleagues in the games group at the ITU. Without a doubt, careful work by a set of anonymous reviewers also improved the manuscript and those readers have my heartfelt thanks. I'm also indebted to Ida Toft for her assistance with the bibliography and Hanne Albrechtsen for tracking down a variety of articles for me. And without the hard work of the folks at the MIT Press (especially Mel Goldsipe, Katie Helke, Krista Magnuson, and Doug Sery) this book would have been impossible.

While so many people within the pro gaming scene were incredibly generous with their time, I want to give special thanks to Paul Chaloner, Matthias Flierl, Alex Garfield, and Marcus Graham, who regularly helped connect me to other people to talk to and who answered my most basic of queries. The various e-sports professionals who agreed to be involved in our two public workshops were also incredibly valuable in extending the conversation. And though most go unnamed in this text, I'm especially grateful for all the e-sports participants who took the time to speak with me over the years, sharing their experiences and insights.

Finally, I can't give enough thanks to Mikael Jakobsson who, in addition to being the best intellectual sparring partner anyone can have, encouraged me in the day-to-day work of the research over so many years. His continuing insight and support have meant the world to me.

1 Playing for Keeps

As I sit down to polish this introductory chapter with the hope of providing an overview for you, the reader, I am faced with interesting narrative challenges. The first draft of this chapter was written in 2009 amid a global financial crisis whose effects were, perhaps not surprisingly, reverberating down the line to this most niche of activities, professional computer gaming. Though a television show (*WCG Ultimate Gamer*) focused on competitive gaming had recently debuted on the SyFy channel and a new national initiative (the United Kingdom eSports Association) had just elected its Community Council, within the same few months a major global pro gaming team—Meet Your Makers—lost their financial backing and found themselves dropping players. This setback came relatively close on the heels of one of the most well-funded televised league initiatives ever—the Championship Gaming Series, sponsored by outlets like DirectTV and British Sky Broadcasting Group (BSkyB)–shutting its doors in November 2008. For many the succession of events was a powerful blow to their faith in the inevitable emergence of e-sports as a serious venture.[1] People who had staked nascent careers on professional gaming expressed real concern. Many had to go back to jobs outside of e-sports.

Other trends, however, seem to be rising after a period of real upset in the scene. Fighting games (seen as much more accessible to a general audience) are lately being hailed as professional gaming's breakthrough genre. People who had not previously paid much attention to competitive console play were now taking notice of the way the premiere console league, Major League Gaming, has weathered the financial storm. The 2010 launch of *StarCraft II*, a long-awaited follow-up to a hugely popular game by the successful developer Blizzard, brought hope for pro gaming to a new wave of fans and players. And finally, if nothing else, the financial upset of the past several years strengthened calls for the scene to get back to its roots, its passion, and focus on building from the core out. The question I am most directly facing at this moment, then, is whether or not this is a story about a phenomenon in ascendance, a wave of the future for media, leisure, and indeed sports in general, or if we are witnessing a significant downturn in a domain that will pretty much always remain a niche activity for a small portion of gamers.

Of course, such a formulation is a bit of a set-up. Answer in favor of "emerging global phenomenon" and it is hard to not say serious consideration is warranted. Answer in favor of "niche" and perhaps research time might be better spent on larger, more supposedly important things. Indeed, writing a book about professional computer gaming at the same moment in which casual and Facebook games are all the rage is perhaps wildly out of step with our cultural moment. Not surprisingly, I'm going to suggest a third option. No matter which way pro gaming goes, it warrants our serious consideration because it not only represents a fascinating slice of game culture, but it leads us into the heart of questions about the nature and status of play in computer games, the possibilities for (and limitations of) new forms of sport in this digital media age, and the challenges faced by gaming subcultures as they (often ambivalently) find themselves sliding into the mainstream.

This book is intended to be a kickoff contribution into a conversation and a body of research that look seriously at competitive high-end computer gaming. My goal is two-fold: to understand it as a phenomenon in its own right, but also to situate it within our culture at large. While some of the issues that follow will be of particular interest to those in the scholarly game studies community, it is my hope that the work also finds places where it speaks to not only e-sports professionals, but to a broader readership interested in exploring some of the details of this emerging area of computer gaming.

Playing against Each Other

In the last few years there has been a rising fascination with the guys—and in the standard narrative it is always "the guys"—who manage to take video game play to a level most of us never achieve. Whether it is a full-length article in the computer game magazine *Edge* detailing the by-gone era of arcade competition (complete with two-page photo spread reprinting *Life* magazine's infamous 1983 shoot of top arcade players) or any one of the number of independent documentaries produced in the last few years chronicling all manner of high-end competitive play (*King of Kong, Chasing Ghosts, Frag, King of Chinatown, Beyond the Game, E-@thletes, I Got Next*), there is real fascination with the players who transform video game play into something more than a casual leisure activity. These stories draw us in by describing guys who have converted something most of us do for fun into a deeply instrumental and serious endeavor. We see them train: the old arcade players notate the machine's screen with grease pens and tape to help them remember moves while the new cadre of PC gamers attend bootcamps at each other's houses and practice around the clock. We watch them focused on a video screen, battling it out with fellow players, displaying all the emotions we associate with serious competition ("the thrill of victory, the agony of defeat"). While many of these documentaries tread similar ground, they lend important details to what is an otherwise hidden slice of game culture. Taken together, they help build a story in which e-sports are not unique to this current historical moment, but can be traced back to even the earliest days of computer gaming.

Competition between players—and not just player versus machine—goes back many decades. Stewart Brand's 1972 account of the "*Spacewar* Olympics" for *Rolling Stone* magazine stands out in this regard. In the Stanford Artificial Intelligence Laboratory, a number of computer scientists (some of the best in the business) gathered around the infamous PDP-10 computer for a playful, and apparently raucous, evening of *Spacewar*. Brand's description of the event would probably bring a smile of recognition to many contemporary gamers, "Four intense hours, much frenzy and skilled concerted action, a 15-ring circus in ten different directions, the most bzz-bzz-busy scene I've been around since Merry Prankster Acid Tests..." (Brand 1972). From the start, computer game players seemed drawn to not only their interaction with the machine but to the competitive space against one another it could facilitate.

While the earliest days of computer gaming were confined to scientific and university labs (with faculty, students, and research scientists as the prime players), the migration of digital gaming out into the arcade opened new worlds of possibility. As Burrill (2008) argues, arcades are spaces of activity and performance. Building on a tradition going all the way back to pinball and analog arcade machines, *Sea Wolf* in 1976 offered the first high score notation that carried over from game to game (Medler 2009) and, depending on who you source, either *Asteroids* or *Star Fire* in 1979 brought the personalized (typically via initials) high score list to the platform.[2] While some games allowed head-to-head competition, the majority of the contests between players took place asynchronously, via a high score list maintained by the arcade game itself. This simple design decision proved to be a powerful component in shaping arcade culture. Though players would often have close contact with each other at their local arcade, the ability of the high score list to facilitate competition across time was revolutionary. You no longer had to be present to witness someone else's achievements and they did not have to be standing behind you looking over your shoulder to see yours. The machine and its high score list provided continuous competitive play between gamers.

Space, of course, was another barrier of competition to be broken. While you might be the best *Pac-Man* player in your local arcade in some small town, the highest ambition was to be the best in the world. Taking a picture of your local machine's high score list—with you on it—became one way of documenting local achievements for distribution more broadly. In a pre-Internet era, however, the challenges of dealing with thousands of players spread across the country and world were not trivial.

The documentary *King of Kong* (2007) follows the attempts of Steve Wiebe, an avid *Donkey Kong* player, to beat the all-time high score on the classic arcade machine. One of the striking aspects of the story, beyond the personal drama, is the way the struggle, personalities, and final validation of achievement are mediated through the organization Twin Galaxies. Acting as a hub for competitive arcade game play going back to the 1980s and the heyday of old-school stand-up machines, Twin Galaxies served as a repository and vetter of scores within a competitive player subculture. Founder Walter Day was deeply committed to sustaining the scene by using his organization to collect and record top scores, hold competitions (the Video Game Masters Tournament being notable), and distribute information about the best gamers. While Twin Galaxies never made any real crossover into current e-sports, it does provide us one of the earliest glimpses of the ways digital gaming was taken quite seriously as a competitive activity.

The organization was also key in helping publicize high-end play to a broader audience. Even in Day's early promotional activities—securing the infamous *Life* spread or the quirky *That's Incredible* TV show special episode on competitive video games (complete with the winner running to break a paper finish-line tape)—we can see the attempts to nudge this niche slice of game culture out to the mainstream. When you listen to early promoters like Day you hear echoes of the current ambitions, where competitive digital gaming is seen as an inevitable future of sports and play. The feeling is often "The public just needs to see it done right and they'll be hooked!"

One of the most interesting examples of this fascination with competitive arcade play and attempts to bring it to a larger audience was the television show *Starcade*, which ran from 1982 to 1984 (including syndication)

Figure 1.1
Starcade set, with host Geoff Edwards.
Image from JM Production Company.

on U.S. television. Boasting Alex Trebek of *Jeopardy* fame as a one-time host (it was eventually taken over by Geoff Edwards, another familiar face in the television game show genre), the series brought competitors together to battle it out across several different arcade games, accumulating a total number of points along the way.

The episodes (many of which are available online at the *Starcade* archive at http://www.starcade.tv) are terrific fun, examples of both the excitement surrounding this new activity and also the challenges of trying to make it broadcastable and spectator friendly. Throughout the show you can see the producers tweaking the form; shots of the arcade game's screen with the player's face inset and juxtaposed to the game imagery, the host trying to give a overview of how to play the game and perhaps a tip or two (sometimes bemusedly taken by the player), the delightful "everyman" (and sometimes woman) quality of the contestants. *Starcade* is a great glimpse into one of several attempts in the 1980s to integrate a new form of leisure, video gaming, into an existing one, television.

As the arcade scene went bust alongside the rise of home gaming machines like Nintendo's Entertainment System or various Atari consoles, competitive gaming adapted and shifted.[3] Though companies like Nintendo sponsored some live tournaments, for the most part the shoulder-to-shoulder competition with strangers at the arcade waned. Eventually the sofa (and the floor in front of it) became the primary spot where gamers played against their friends and family, and the multiplayer experience began to move into the game world (Newman 2004). The tradition of documenting high scores through photos remained. Companies such as Nintendo collected these by letting people send in snapshots of scores on their television screen, often awarding special certificates or patches for their achievements (Jakobsson 2011). Magazines, including *Nintendo Power* and *Sega Visions*, provided regular printed lists of high scores so players could compare their performance with those outside their immediate networks. As video gaming grew and transformed from an on-site arcade activity to something that took place in the home, its competitive aspect morphed.

While home consoles are a key part of the story of video gaming (Kline, Dyer-Witheford, De Peuter 2003, Herz 1997), it is in the realm of PC gaming that one of the next important nodes in e-sports history is found.[4] We can locate a key breakthrough for pro gaming in the development of first person shooters on the personal computer. Though *Wolfenstein 3D*'s (1992) shoot-outs with Nazis had injected full-out mayhem into an emerging first-person shooter (FPS) genre, *Doom* (1993) and then *Quake* (1996) stand as definitive titles that provided a solid base for competitive FPS gaming to grow owing to their network capabilities.

Developed by id Software's famous team of John Carmack and John Romero, these games played an important role not only as games, but in the development of robust player communities around them. *Doom*, though primarily a local area network (LAN) game for most players, did become available for larger network play via DWANGO (Dial-up Wide-Area Network Games Operation), which, for an hourly fee and dial-up costs, provided servers that players could log into and initiate games from. As King and Borland chronicle, "With *Doom*, and even more so with id's later games, the digital playing field moved from the machine underneath a player's fingers into cyberspace itself, as players increasingly learned to battle each other online" (2003, 89). This turn to multiplayer gaming was taking place not just within FPS titles like *Doom* and *Quake*, but was a growing feature of PC gaming. Internet-based environments—from textual multi-user dungeons (MUD) to games hosted on bulletin board systems (BBS) and national Internet service providers like CompuServe—offered people a way to play, and compete, against each other.

When I spoke with John Romero about this period, his enthusiasm for the multiplayer component of the games was clear. He recounted how, despite the time and hassle it could take to pull off, people were from the first moments hooking their machines together.

Because everybody, you know, they wanted a deathmatch experience, which is super, super intense. Playing against the computer is nothing compared to playing against someone else. And when you are playing at the very beginning when you don't know that much, it's really fun and everyone's laughing and all that kind of stuff but as soon as you start gathering skill, you start gaining a lot of skill, it starts to get more serious and it's more rewarding. (Personal communication, 2010)

Playing against others was the real draw. The value of multiplayer gaming, and the success id Software had with *Doom* and then *Quake* (still a mainstay in the e-sports scene), can be seen as not only rooted in the products themselves but in the energy of the game community and their involvement. Quakecon, launched in 1996 by a group of enthusiasts, became an important home for face-to-face (F2F) competitive gaming. Originally held as a community-driven and volunteer-run event every year in Texas, Quakecon provided avid gamers an opportunity to come together for one big LAN party. Gaming competitions were a part of the event from that very first year, and as Quakecon grew (reaching upward of seven thousand participants one year) it began to draw international competitors.[5]

The influence of id Software on the e-sports scene is perhaps best demonstrated via a now infamous tournament, Red Annihilation, held in May 1997 at the E3 Expo. The grand prize for the *Quake* competition? John Carmack's 1987 Ferrari. King and Borland (2003) note the significance of the event in that it provided a high-profile stage for a growing East Coast/West Coast rivalry. While we often hear a lot of hype about how the Internet makes our offline locations irrelevant, geography does matter in competitive gaming, where ping times and the ability to get to a F2F tournament may pose challenges. The winner of Red Annihilation, a famous Bay Area player named Dennis "Thresh" Fong (who was well established in the DWANGO system and LAN scene), went on to display the car in the offices of his start-up game company, Gamers Extreme. The event has gone down in e-sports history as one of the most famous, for the prominence of the venue, the sponsors, and the prize.[6]

A final piece of history worth mentioning, highlighting the activity level around the launch of e-sports is the Cyberathlete Professional League (CPL).[7] Also located in Texas, former investment banker Angel Munoz launched his influential organization in 1997. It went on to became one of the most high-profile venues for e-sports, covering a range of titles and setting new standards for prize winnings, sponsorships, and corporate partnerships. Munoz described that early period to me as a heady mix of innovation and charting new territory. He spoke about being given a copy of one of id's titles very early on and how it inspired him:

I had a laptop that was, I think it had sixteen colors, which was enough for *Doom* and it had no sound. But when I powered it and started playing *Doom*, it really had a major impact on me. I felt transported to a different reality. And that combined with the fact that at that time I was reading books like *Neuromancer* and *Snow Crash*, it just gave me the sense that I had just previewed what would be a compelling future. (Personal communication, 2010)

The future he imagined was one in which elite gamers, demonstrating their skill, would figure prominently. He said, "At that time all of the press was completely focused on game developers and on games. Gamers were just consumers and there was really no recognition for their talents or anything like that." It was in this atmosphere that he began evangelizing about the notion of the "cyberathlete." Not unlike those early ambitions Walter Day had for arcade players, Munoz envisioned putting a spotlight on the players to "gain recognition and create stars" out of them. His CPL tournaments quickly became the go-to examples for popular press coverage of professional computer gaming and without a doubt he helped launch the careers of many top players. The first CPL tournament, with about four hundred participants, was held in Dallas in 1997 and offered $3,500 USD in cash and prizes (King and Borland 2003). The league continued to host regular tournaments, at its peak supporting hundreds of competitors and tens of thousands of dollars in prizes.

King and Borland (2003) note that the growth of the CPL was closely tied to the rise of *Counter-Strike* (2000), another hugely popular FPS title that was a mod of Valve's *Half-Life* (1998) game. Munoz's tournaments were able to secure some mainstream coverage via outlets like ESPN and MTV, where the novelty and spectacle of teams of young men animatedly competing for prize money by playing computer games held fascination.[8] The CPL in those earliest years became the face of competitive gaming to the outside world. International players made treks from Europe over to Dallas to compete and eventually the league formally expanded beyond North America to have a worldwide presence via local partners in places like China and Brazil. The organization also developed the Cyberathlete Amateur League (CAL), one of the few formally organized outlets for aspiring e-sports players.

Though the CPL embodied many of the aspirational qualities of e-sports it was also decidedly a business, complete with economic ups and downs. In 2008, after a year of decreased activity and many rumors, it was announced that the CPL had been purchased by a new ownership group in Abu Dhabi. The return of competitions was announced, though CAL was shut down in 2009 to the dismay of some who saw it as an important amateur league for developing new talent. As of 2010 no new CPL competitions had occurred. Indeed, over the years the organization has been hit with accusations of unpaid prize winnings, and the property's purchase left some confused about its status.[9] However, despite this somewhat shaky posthumous status, it can't be denied that it and Angel Munoz were an important and influential part of the e-sports scene in the earliest days, helping shape not only how tournaments work but the public face of pro gaming.[10]

While competitive arcade play and the advent of consoles are an important part of the story, it is really in the rise of network gaming that e-sports found its strength. The early Quakecon and CPL events were possible because game culture was transformed by the ability to create shared virtual playfields within computer game worlds. While local area network games are a powerful tool in building an e-sports community, the growth of broader networking opportunities (via early systems like DWANGO and later Internet capabilities) proved powerful. The Internet makes scaling niche activities possible. Even though you may be one of only a handful of players in your town who is interested in competitive gaming, by being able to go online and connect—and compete—against others, a nascent e-sports community is able to form. As support technologies (websites, real-time chat, streaming audio, and video) developed, the community was bolstered outside of the actual game itself. Network play proved to be a fundamental lynchpin in the history of e-sports.

While much has happened since the arcade days and the PC-based competition boom of the late 1990s, it's worth keeping some of these early histories in mind for the ways they shaped the scene's development. They also highlight that contemporary e-sports are embedded in a much longer and rich tradition of organized competitive play. The roots of e-sports in F2F competitions, LAN parties, and avid player engagement are key. While pro gaming is still very much under development and its final form is unclear, the earliest stories about an arcade or Quakecon tournament echo themes we still see today in e-sports: fascination with high-end competition, getting paid for playing computer games, and an emergent formal structuring of gaming as a sport. While our contemporary version of e-sports certainly looks different than an early arcade match, many of the same desires and challenges remain.

Starting in Aarhus

Though not going back to the 1980s (despite my time spent at the arcade then), this project is fairly long in the making. In fall 2003 I traveled from my new home in Copenhagen to Aarhus, the second-largest city in

Denmark. In the course of completing a research project on the popular massively multiplayer online game (MMOG) *EverQuest* (1999) I had come in contact with a type of player dubbed a "power gamer" (Taylor 2006a). Power gaming is a unique style of play grounded in intense focus and instrumental orientation. Very often power gamers are thought of as taking the game too seriously. They can appear to outsiders (and indeed sometimes even to themselves) like people who have converted their leisure into work. This mindset is often deemed odd by fellow players, and some theorists have pronounced it corrosive to play. As the sociologist Roger Caillois wrote about the "contamination" of play by reality, obligation, and professionalism, "What used to be a pleasure becomes an obsession. What was an escape becomes an obligation, and what was a pastime is now a passion, compulsion, and course of anxiety. The principle of play has become corrupted. It is now necessary to take precautions against cheats and professional players, a unique product of the contagion of reality" (2001, 45).

Yet I knew from spending time and talking to power gamers that things weren't so simple; that the line between work and play, pleasure and painful progression, was often blurred. Their experiences couldn't be so easily categorized or dismissed, bundled into the same category as cheaters and set outside the realm of "real" play. Power gamers help us understand something about the nature of leisure, the different orientations people can take to the same ludic object, the creative emergent qualities of play, and the social embeddedness of even the most instrumental player. It's always tricky to try and trace the sparks that lead you down one research path versus another, the things that catch your eye and ear while many other potential subjects simply go by, unnoticed. In this case, my experience with power gamers brought into my field of view another group of players for whom the line between work and play, pleasure and the struggle to progress, repetitive practice and spontaneous play, collided—professional computer gamers.

I was traveling to Aarhus because I had been invited to come watch the World Cyber Games Danish National Final. The World Cyber Games (WCG) were started in 2000 as an international tournament sponsored by Samsung and the government of South Korea (via its Ministry of Culture and Tourism and Ministry of Information and Communications) as a way of recognizing and encouraging technology development and innovation. National finals are held around the world and winners attend a Grand Final in a host city for three days of competition that culminate in the awarding of bronze, silver, and gold medals in a variety of computer games, as well as cash prizes.

Figure 1.2
WCG 2007 Grand Final winners for *WarCraft III*.

The World Cyber Games are unique compared to other tournaments in that they are fashioned as the Olympics of computer gaming. I had read up on the event and was struck by ambitious language describing bringing people together to "lead the development of the digital entertainment culture by promoting harmony of humankind through e-sports and its embodiment in the Cyber Culture Festival" (WCG 2008). And yet, as my first pro gaming tournament experience unfolded, my image of this emerging scene changed shape.

Rather than any high-end venue with fancy equipment and polished marketing, I found myself attending a sort of hybrid event. Half mini-LAN party, half tournament, the venue was an old building on the outskirts of town near the docks. When I arrived Friday afternoon preparations were still under way. Cables were being taped down, machines set up, a frantic search for more power outlets was ongoing, and the sponsor banner lay on the floor. The organizers greeted me warmly and we chatted a bit but they were quickly off hustling to get things set up. The network, the backbone of any gaming tournament, was still being sorted and was one of their biggest concerns. Young people, mostly boys and men but a handful of women as well, came trickling in, all tentatively looking around. Some brought machines to set up in the LAN area for the duration of the event, others just milled around talking with friends, going out for a cigarette, or looking over the shoulder of someone sitting at a machine playing.

The event was a bit of a combination in terms of orientation, being both the national final for the WCG but also co-branded as a Danish e-Sport Union tournament (a newly founded national organization). The space was divided, with the LAN party area in front and the tournament machines in the back, cordoned off by a rope. The LAN section consisted of about sixteen computers, some clearly marked with team names on desktop wallpaper or signs near the computer and others brought in by local gamers. Friday continued to have a very in-progress feel to it even though the official tournament had actually begun and play-offs were happening. When I finally left at ten o'clock that evening things were still being pieced together but, as I learned the next day, matches had gone on well into the early morning hours.

When I arrived Saturday morning music was playing outside the venue and there seemed to be a lot more energy than on the previous day. The opening ceremony was scheduled to take place at 12:30, but matches were already being held in the back room and simultaneously broadcast on a large screen in the LAN area, where seating had been set up for spectators to watch the action. For someone like myself who was pretty unfamiliar with the games at the time, there was a fairly steep learning curve to watch matches. The popular game *Counter-Strike* (CS), which is played with two teams of five all outfitted with weapons and moving across a constrained landscape (the "map," typically holding a variety of buildings, large boxes, oil tanks, and the like) looking for opposing members to kill, was fairly easy to understand at the most basic level without much help. Its last-man-standing mechanic (and an additional layer of play in which one team's goal is to plant a bomb somewhere within the map and the opposing team's goal to defuse it) was easy enough to grasp visually, at least when someone was shot. You see players get killed and remaining ones hide, run, shoot, and attempt to plant or defuse the bomb. As the numbers tick down you can spot a clear end point. Though the intricacies of various maps and tactics can easily be lost on a novice spectator and the aesthetics of the game aren't terribly engaging, the basics can be seen.

Two other hugely popular titles though, *StarCraft* (1998) and *WarCraft* (1994), proved a bit of a mystery to me in terms of tactics and who was winning, despite my finding them much more visually compelling. As complex real-time strategy (RTS) games involving both combat and resources, they can be quite difficult for nonplayers to interpret. Win conditions are dependant on a variety of factors including the deployment of varying types of characters and the management of resources being harvested from the virtual land. In addition, the gameplay takes place over a large map, complete with fog of war, that players constantly zip around on by dropping their camera view into that of various characters they control, all with lightning fast reflexes.

As I watched the matches I could follow a bit simply by the crowd's reaction of cheers, gasps, and groans. This experience of sitting in an audience and collectively watching a match was exciting. I had never had this large group spectator experience when watching a computer game and even though I did not always understand what was happening on the screen, its collective quality was energizing. For the spectators there who actually knew the people competing, it seemed to be an even more powerful community experience. They were following matches with players they not only knew about, but often had themselves competed against or were on teams with.

Saturday night culminated in an incredibly tense final for the *WarCraft III* competition. The match was a very close 2–2 going into the fifth round. In an unforeseen twist the broadcast server, which was piping the video out to the spectator area, broke down, prompting people to go back to the cordoned-off competition area so they could continue to watch. With that technical failure the symbolic power of the rope separating the official athletes from the audience dissolved and people simply crowded around, craning their necks to get a glimpse of the action on the players' screens. The odds-on favorite to win the game ended up losing in a surprise defeat. Despite the spirit of playful competition permeating the match up until that point, the mood in the crowd took a downward turn. Having been

Figure 1.3
Spectators watching a *WarCraft III* match.

seen by many players as Denmark's best chance to take home a medal at the worldwide Grand Final, his defeat also dealt a blow to the nationally rooted ambitions many had.

When I arrived back on Sunday morning I was a bit surprised to see some equipment was already packed up and only a few players remained in the LAN area. Far fewer people were in attendance and I wondered how much last night's tough battle and upset infused this final day. There was supposed to be a closing ceremony around lunchtime but as with other aspects of the event—where matches ran late and technical difficulties proved a challenge—it was hard to get a firm sense of if and when this would actually happen. With the schedule running late each night and the event now winding down, clear closure was hard to find.

The rope barrier that had kept spectators out of the back competition area was now completely gone, having never been replaced after the technical breakdown the previous night, even though a few remaining matches remained. What was once the special tournament area became just a room, filled with empty soda bottles and wadded up papers. Another makeshift divider was being used in the final match area to try and cordon off the two remaining *CS* teams, but for the most part any pretense of formality had dropped and the spectators simply gathered behind the players, watching over their shoulders. The broadcast screen was blank and the audience area was empty.

When the match ended I didn't quite understand if it was the final one of the event or if there were more to come. There were never any official announcements of what was happening next. Throughout the event matches simply started and stopped, moved along by the organizers who would often have to seek out players and teams to tell them they were up. It seemed that the players themselves knew the status of things but an outsider like myself was often left wondering what would happen next. As the day wound down I caught one of the organizers and asked for an update. Apparently the team that won the *CS* match had been the expected winner so there was no real surprise to be had. He played down the final ceremony listed on the program—it would simply be the handing out of a few certificates. As the afternoon drew to a close remaining cables were wound up and machines were packed away. The ending of the event felt more like the morning after a large party where perhaps a few guests linger, but everyone knows the real fun is over. It was hard to reconcile the anticlimactic tone with the fact that it was the national final in one of the most active e-sports regions for one of the biggest professional gaming competitions in the world. Most of the winners and losers had already gone home and I was left wondering if the certificates would simply get dropped in the mail.

In the midst of all this activity, however, I began to see the outline of the pro gaming world in ways I hadn't thought of before. I had gone intending to interview players and see a tournament first-hand. As I began to talk to the competitors, though, our conversations got interwoven with other issues—the way the scene was changing and growing, how some players would act as referees, admins, or informal coaches at other competitions, the complicated mappings of the various teams they had been on, the contracts they dreamed of, or, for the lucky few, had signed. As I looked around I noticed all the other people involved in this event who weren't players but were crucial to its success. The organizers were a couple of older men who were keen on seeing e-sports grow, were building a national organization, and were ultimately interested in finding a way to maintain a business around their gaming passion. They had gotten the contract from the WCG to host this national final but were also launching their own initiatives (the Danish e-Sport Union) with the goal of fostering e-sports locally. The referees and administrators—current players who did not qualify for the final as well as "retired" pro players—spent long days doing everything from keeping the network up and handling disputes to distributing information back out to community members who couldn't be at the event but were participating via the net and various gaming websites. Indeed this invisible online audience was the main one. And I met for the first time a pro gaming team owner who gave me some early insight into the issue of management, contracts, recruiting players, and building a fan base.

This regional event continues to highlight for me some of the attempts, successes, and struggles of the pro gaming scene that we still witness. While much has changed in the years since I attended that first event, there remain core issues and tensions I saw even back then. Young men (and unfortunately rarely women save a few exceptions) competing for high stakes—and peer approval—but still on unsure footing when it comes to their being "professional." Businessmen, sometimes gamers or retired players themselves, trying to nurture a nascent scene of tournaments and leagues. Owners and coaches carving out for themselves some kind of mediating role between the players, teams, and sponsors and trying to create a new career for themselves. Referees and administrators working to uphold standards, make judgment calls, and systemize otherwise-unruly play. And, amid it all, a dedicated groups of gamers and friends collectively creating a new spectator and fan culture as they watched matches, cheered, and debated moves and wins.

As I continued to attend tournaments this cast of actors multiplied. I came to see that the emerging world of pro game broadcasting played a powerful role in not only distributing information to fans, but in interpreting and translating complex game action. Tournament organizers took on increasingly prominent roles. Sponsorship became much more widespread and the number of companies throwing financial support behind teams and players expanded (and sometimes contracted). And while that rough-edged local Danish final represents one small branch of the pro gaming scene, there is another that has emerged in the last few years—tournaments and leagues backed by high-profile investors and partners, often with traditional media distribution outlets, who see huge potential growth and revenues that will come from the emergence of e-sports and professional gaming.

While there has been sporadic journalistic coverage of professional computer gaming—perhaps you saw the *60 Minutes* television show piece on one of the most famous players, Johnathan "Fatal1ty" Wendel—the stories tend to focus on just the players or the team. This is only one piece of the puzzle. Certainly the players themselves are a crucial component to understanding what is happening with this emerging phenomenon, but I will argue that there are a number of important factors, and actors, we should pay careful attention to as well. Professionalization is happening within broader structural, institutional, and social contexts, and includes tournament organizers, broadcasters, owners, referees, coaches, sponsors, and fans. It is also happening in the midst of debates about the nature of computer game play in our contemporary lives and what role, if any, e-sports should have there.

Korean Roots

When you talk to North Americans and Europeans involved in pro gaming about the development of e-sports, it does not take long for South Korea to come up in conversation. Though other Asian countries have launched their own experiments with pro gaming (China being a notable newcomer), for many South Korea is seen as a kind of promised pro gaming land. Quite often infused with a utopic-inflected "techno-Orientalism," tales are told about young men who have ascended to the level of national hero by playing computer games. The stories circle around the rise of a professional scene whose players have fan bases comparable to that of American mainstream sports stars. They hold contracts and sponsorship deals, wear the latest in sport gear from Nike and Adidas, and play in competitions that regularly draw thousands and are broadcast on major television channels.

South Korea is regularly spoken of as the place where your taxi driver plays *StarCraft* and the geeky skilled kid can become a star. As one popular press article titled "Geek Heroes" detailed,

> Mr. Woo of the federal game institute estimated that 10 million South Koreans regularly follow eSports, as they are known here, and said that some fan clubs of top gamers have 700,000 members or more. "These fan clubs are actually bigger in size than the fan clubs of actors and singers in Korea," he said. "The total number of people who go spectate pro basketball, baseball, and soccer put together is the same as the number of people who go watch pro game leagues." (Schiesel 2007)

In Dal Yong Jin's book about online gaming, he presents a more nuanced picture of the celebrity e-sports player in South Korea, pointing out that while there are certainly a handful who reach these mythical levels, "the majority of pro gamers and semipro gamers live a much less glamorous life, confronting hardships such as salaries lower than the national average and 14- to 16-hour days of training for two to three years" (2010, 82).

Yet the allure of playing computer games for a living is compelling for many South Korean youth. With 225 professional players in the Korea e-Sports Association (KeSPA) and 11 pro clubs (owned by companies like Samsung, SK Telecom, and AMD), South Korea is a powerful node in the story of pro gaming, both for the way it paints a picture of what a professional scene that has entered the cultural mainstream can actually look like, but also for the imaginative (even mythical) power it holds for those trying to foster pro gaming in North America and Europe (Korea Times 2007, Korea Times 2004a).

The story of South Korea holds an interesting place in North American and European pro gaming because it is regularly held up as a model for the future of e-sports worldwide. It works as evocative fantasy. The refrain around it often seems to be "If they can do it there, we can do it here!" Whether South Korean e-sports are, indeed, the model for a global future or just a regional phenomenon, we can still benefit from understanding a bit about them. There is something to be said for looking at South Korea's gaming history, though often the details of its success are not explored enough outside the region.

The strength of South Korean pro gaming has its roots in something much deeper than the enthusiasm of the players and pro community. Jin highlights that important structural factors are at work in the rise of the South Korean model "including favorable government policies, a competitive market structure, a swift development of ICTs [information and communication technologies], the transnationalization and globalization of the game industry, and people's mentalities about accepting new technology and online gaming" (2010, 35).[11] Hjorth and Chan additionally signal that the "Korean Wave" of the early 2000s is not constrained to technology and gaming but includes broader "cultural products, especially in the form of television soaps and family dramas" (2009, 6; see also Chung 2009). For example, the complex relationship between Japan and Korea, with struggles over colonization, national policing of cultural influence, and competition, has played a powerful role in the accelerated growth of the South Korean market (Jin and Chee 2009). The South Korean case is situated within a larger intraregional set of relations that go well beyond the scope of gaming. The story of South Korean e-sports highlights the ways culture, larger infrastructural developments, policy decisions, and economic activities have intersected in a fortuitous way at a particular historical moment to support the formation of a new form of leisure and sport.

Game Culture

Most pro gaming aficionados have heard about the widespread popularity among South Koreans of the real-time strategy game *StarCraft*, which has sold more than half of its total copies worldwide in that country alone (Hunh 2008, Jin-seo 2008a). Beyond widely known games like *Starcraft*, however, the annual scale of the games market there comes in at about 5 billion U.S. dollars, or approximately $100 per person, "more than three times what Americans spend" (Schiesel 2007). Dal Yong Jin and Florence Chee note that in 2005 the South Korean online game market alone accounted for "56% of the entire Asia Pacific market share" and that "the Korean online game market is expected to continually grow about 20% annually, reaching $2.6 billion by 2008" (2008). The sheer size and number of people playing computer games in South Korea is a key part of the success of e-sports.

In Florence Chee's (2006) ethnographic work on game culture in South Korea she paints a compelling picture of a population for whom computer games are fairly well integrated into everyday life. She points out, for example, that 54% of the population plays online games. The widespread availability of PC bangs—a kind of 24/7 Internet and gaming café with fairly low hourly rates—helps facilitate a culture in which, "For many young Koreans, their participation in online games represents one facet of a whole community and way of life. The activities surrounding this media ecology determine how its members navigate within their vital orientations and make choices about how they take nourishment, spend money, earn money, and even partake in courtship rituals" (Chee 2006, 232).

Sang-Min Whang (2005), in his research on these game players, similarly discusses the integration of massively multiplayer online games into youth culture. He notes that these games, and the activities within them, become a part of people's daily routines. In this context, playing games and being in spaces in which game culture is fostered is a core part of teen and young adult lives. Playing games, looking over the shoulders of your friends playing, and in general having games as a central cultural touchstone is simply part of young people's everyday experience in South Korea.

Governmental and Infrastructure Support

The foundations for this extensive multiplayer computer game culture lay at least partially in a number of basic infrastructural and institutional facilitators (Chung 2009). Broadband penetration has played a powerful role in the growth of game culture and physical sites for play. South Korea continues to boast strong and ubiquitous high-speed net access, with 89.4% of households connected (Schiesel 2006, Jin and Chee 2008). Domestic net connections have steadily grown over the years, but one of the most important nodes in the story of South Korean game culture is the place of PC bangs, of which there are somewhere around twenty thousand, attracting "more than a million people a day" (Schiesel 2007; see also Hunh 2008).[12]

The growth of the PC bang industry is itself deeply tied to important economic factors with regards to the cost of playing. Huhh (2008) explains that online game subscriptions in these venues are not set up as they typically are in North America and Europe, where individual players purchase a game and maintain an ongoing monthly subscription. In South Korea online games have regularly been handled via "Internet Protocol pricing." In this model the net café holds a site license for a fixed number of network addresses and individual users do not have to buy the game subscription themselves.[13] Their playtime is tied to the machines that have been authorized for access. As Huhh notes, "The charging policy of PC bangs encouraged their visitors to play longer; the more you stayed at a PC bang, the lower the hourly charge became" and while overall costs of this model to the player were perhaps higher than their maintaining a monthly subscription, it offered much more flexibility for the user (2008, 28).

Into this context we see the emergence of additional support mechanisms from the government and industry. Starting in the 1990s, the government recognized the role of games in the lives of its citizens and sought to make developing and supporting the game industry in South Korea one of its initiatives.[14] This cultural basis is also tied to a governmental agenda in which technology would become an important part of the country's economic and development plans. In a report by the Korea Game Development and Promotion Institute, a part of the Ministry of Culture and Tourism, the authors wrote:

> Over 90% of the total population has experienced playing games as of March 2003, with 83% currently enjoying them. The game-playing population will continue to increase as various game contents are developed. To keep pace with such trends, the government has implemented systematic and comprehensive policies to develop the game market into a strategic industry. To this end, the Korean Game Development and Promotion Institute was established in 1999 as a key institution to promote game policies. This institute is in charge of various services to advance the domestic game industry and establish the game culture by setting up a one-stop support system involving all game-related fields, including export promotion, creation support, cultivating talented personnel, and R&D. (2003, 6)

What is striking about this initiative is the variety of ways centralizing the growth of game culture was handled. While we are certainly seeing more and more governments recognize the potential in fostering local game development, South Korea went well beyond the usual initiatives by actually addressing everything from legal frameworks to the creation of more Internet cafés.[15] For example, looking at the following table from one of the government reports on the subject, we can see a wide variety of initiatives enacted to support this development.

This was widespread public policy in action, covering not simply legal changes or support for private investment, but also specific directives taken

Table 1.1
Game Industry–Related Policies

Promotional activities	Contents
Legal and systemic improvements	Enact the Cultural Industry Promotion Law; classification of the game industry as a cultural industry Revise the Sound Records, Video, and Game Products Act: Change from regulation to active support and post management [sic]. Simplify into two grades, i.e., all ages over 18 (Amendment to SVG Act took effect as of September 2001)
Private investment promotion	Expand multi-game places (Internet cafes) Promote professional game investment associations led by private investors
Securing of key points	Designate game specialization complex in each local area for local cultural industry Created game-related cultural industrial complex in Chongju and Daejon in April 2001 to be in charge of planning, creation, production, equipment, exhibition, logistics, tourism, etc.
Operation of Korea Game Development and Promotion Institute	Integrate the game developing companies Develop game technology development and provide information Established the integrated Game Support Center (the former body of the Korea Game Development and Promotion Institute)
Korea Media Rating Board	Publish reports on the gaming industry Operate the Game Academy Established under the SVG Act to classify the grades of game products Classify the game products as all ages and above 18 (Article 20-2) and unavailable (Article 20-3) under the Amendment to SVG Act

Source: Korea Game Development and Promotion Institute 2003.

to foster game tournaments in four major cities (Seoul, Incheon, Jeonju, and Cheonan) and the building of physical game complexes in various parts of the country, including the development of an "advanced arcade game zone" (G2ZONE). Underlying this all is the foundation of the Korean Information Infrastructure Act and intensive government investment in high-tech initiatives (Jin and Chee 2009). These strong governmental and infrastructural supports were joined by the commercial sector also stepping in to leverage an emerging game culture.

Corporate Initiatives

The World Cyber Games (WCG), still one of the largest and most influential e-sports tournaments, began as a partnership launched in 2000 between the government of South Korea and private sponsors, most notably Samsung. It is often dubbed the Olympics of professional computer gaming.[16] It represents one of the oldest and strongest tournaments thus far in global pro gaming. Having grown significantly since its first trial event in 2001 under the name "World Cyber Game Challenge" in Seoul, South Korea, the Grand Final now rotates locations worldwide. The WCG remains one of the more robust tournaments on the pro scene. While I will discuss several aspects of it later in the book, a short introduction is warranted here as it is an important node in the South Korean model of interweaving game culture, government support, and industry investment.

Reaching out to a youth market, and a global one at that, has long been a part of the WCG mission. Strongly informing the collaboration between International Cyber Marketing (ICM, the private organizing body for the tournament), the government (via the Ministry of Culture and Tourism), corporate sponsors, and the Korea Game Promotion Center has also been the promotion of South Korea as a front-runner in digital media and interactive entertainment. As Kim Dae-jung, president of South Korea in 2001, remarked, "I hope that the first WCG will help our nation to become recognized as one of the leaders in game, knowledge industry and IT infrastructure, as well as help the world's game-loving young people exchange information and build friendships" (Sung-jin 2001). Such symbolic and concrete government support around computer games is notable. The country has been explicit in tying leisure culture through computer games to its overall economic development. The level of national support and attention to this initiative is worth considering.

This governmental initiative has been equally matched by serious industry sponsorship. While the WCG has over the years drawn in smaller technology companies as sponsors, larger brands have stepped in to participate from the very beginning, including Coca-Cola, Microsoft, and its longest-running big industry partner, Samsung Electronics. Yun Jong-yong, a Samsung vice chairman, noted in 2004 that "Every year we pay more than half of the total cost of the WCG, but we are not doing it expecting an immediate rise in sales [...] Mostly teenagers, more than 1 million people who participated in this event from over 60 countries, will remember our brands for the rest of their lives" (Korea Times 2004b). Samsung's strong corporate representation in the event can also be seen in the makeup of ICM, where positions like president and CEO have been filled by Hyoung-Seok Kim, longtime Samsung executive involved in overseas sales and marketing, or Jong-Yong Yun, co-chairman of the World Cyber Games Committee and vice chairman and CEO of Samsung Electronics. In the North American and European tournament world it is very rare to see this level of top-tier corporate (not to mention executive) support for e-sports, either from government or industry.

Beyond large scale international events like the World Cyber Games, South Korea boasts a vibrant national league culture strongly supported by a variety of corporations who sponsor teams. From mobile phone companies to financial services, computer gaming teams and leagues have received support from organizations beyond the narrower band of tech companies and computer peripheral makers we generally see tossing their hat into the ring in North America and Europe. As Kim Byung Kyu, a senior manager at Shinhan Bank noted, "We're not just the sponsors of this league [...] We're the hosts of this league. So we have a bank account called Star League Mania, and you can get V.I.P. seating at the league finals if you've opened an account" (Schiesel 2006).

Linking a national pastime, computer gaming, to creating new customers for a business has been an important factor in corporate support for South Korean e-sports. This has been particularly powerful in the mobile phone market where major companies such as KTF, SK Telecom, and Pantech sponsor their own popular and well-regarded teams, seeing them as valuable advertising outlets.

> Analysts say the mobile phone-related companies have jumped onto the gaming bandwagon to jazz up their image by exerting a strong pull from online game fans, who are typically in their teens and early twenties. "The game fan demographic attracts handset makers and wireless operators since the young fans are also the mobile phone outfits' main customers," Hyundai Investment & Securities analyst Han Ik-hee said. (Schiesel 2006)

While North American and European organizations still primarily draw sponsors from computer-related companies, South Korean sponsors have found a viable overlap between a desired youth demographic and the larger game culture.

In the popular Pro League alone eleven companies participated in "spending around $1.5 million per year on average" supporting Korean e-sports (Jin-seo 2008a). Apparently executives and advertising managers—not just of mobile companies but other lifestyle products—see sponsorship of professional computer gaming as a good investment, an opportunity to reach the huge numbers of young people spending money on services and products. Often citing return-on-investment ratios of 500%, sponsors have come to value the promotional opportunities that pro gaming offers South Korean businesses.

> SK Telecom, which operates T1 club, agrees on the high effectiveness of e-sports marketing. "It seems that fans want to thank the company for making the T1 team," said Cho Man-soo, manager of the T1 club. "It's not just a brand awareness. It's more like loving the team, loving the company. They have loyalty to the company." [...] SK Telecom manager Cho said that it estimates its promotional effects through media coverage to be 15 billion won ($16.5 million) and that is only counting traditional offline media such as newspapers, magazines and cable and satellite TVs. (Jin-seo 2008a)

It's not simply private corporations that are piggybacking on the role of game culture in South Korea. The Korean Air Force also got into e-sports with their sponsorship of Air Force Challenges e-Sports (ACE), a profes-

Figure 1.4
Members of the ACE team.
Image from ACE Airforce Team.

sional team for the military branch (conscription for males is still active in the country). As Jin-seo (2008b) notes, "The Ace [sic] has been the only place where young professional gamers can continue their career while completing the mandatory military service—an inevitable choice for most players because their peak time as a gamer overlaps their military conscription age."

Following on their heels the South Korean Navy announced its own *Starcraft* team, Aegis. As one article described it, "The Korea e-Sports Association (KeSPA) said it expects to see gamers in Navy uniforms playing in *Starcraft* pro competitions in the second half of this year. The order to create the team came from Chief of Naval Operations Admiral Song Young-moo, a Navy official said, after it was concluded that a gamers team could be an excellent low-cost publicity move" (Chosun 2007).

KeSPA

One of the best examples of an organization that unites the government and corporate efforts to foster e-sports is the Korean eSports Association (KeSPA). Launched in 2000 with the approval of the Ministry of Culture and Tourism and managed by top corporate executives within the technology and gaming sectors, KeSPA is involved with the ongoing regulation and organization of South Korean players and various tournaments. Though I will discuss KeSPA in more detail later, it is worth briefly mentioning here as it has historically formed an important part of the South Korean scene.

While most countries struggle with ad hoc affiliations and have no broad policy decisions helping them develop e-sports regionally (and no mechanisms to enforce them even if they did), KeSPA has been actively involved in everything from maintaining player statistics and rankings to managing broadcast licenses and organization details for tournaments. Its power as a regulating organization, though often contentious, has been important in stabilizing a fast-growing scene in which the boundaries between amateur and professional are still shifting.

Media Outlets

This vibrant competitive gaming culture is also supported by a wide variety of media dedicated to covering and broadcasting South Korean e-sports. With television stations, online broadcasters, publications (online and print), and a huge number of websites for the emerging sport, pro gaming in South Korea gets ample media attention and distribution. According to some estimates teenagers watching computer game competitions outnumber those watching baseball, a popular sport in South Korea (Korea Times 2004a).

Given the ways gaming has entered mainstream television culture, and indeed the attention to promoting players, the synchronicity between industry sponsors and target demographics is apparent. Media outlets are adopting some of the frames we find in traditional sports coverage. While games are certainly a key artifact, the focus on players provides a frequent narrative hook. As Hyong Jun Hwang, the general manager of OnGameNet (a major cable channel for e-sports) put it, "We realized that one of the things that keeps people coming back to television are the characters, the recurring personalities that the viewer gets to know and identify with, or maybe they begin to dislike [...] In other words, television needs stars. So we set out to make the top players into stars, promoting them and so on" (Schiesel 2006). The crafting of a fan and spectator culture for computer games takes place in a variety of venues. Websites are certainly one of the key outlets for the production of a pro gaming scene, with places like FighterForum, Gom TV, Pandora TV, and Hana TV offering robust online coverage of players and tournaments, including everything from replays to interviews and photos.

In addition, television channels OnGameNet and MBC Game provide regular coverage of computer game tournaments, as well as maintain their own fairly extensive online presences offering interviews, fan hubs, and video on demand (VoD), which are captured replays of matches—a mainstay of the competitive gaming scene. With primetime viewership in the millions, it is not a marginal market (Jin and Chee 2009, Whang 2005).

This large audience is not simply watching raw footage. South Korean e-sports media have paid careful attention to developing game commentating, ongoing player and team narratives, and visualization to help viewers get into the games. While North America and Europe have experimented with bringing professional tournaments to television, South Korea has been a strong front-runner in integrating the consumption of game tournaments into mainstream media. In this regard it represents a fascinating emerging model of spectatorship in a medium that is often thought of as singularly interactive and not spectator friendly.

Transitions and Changes in the South Korean Scene

The fascination with South Korean e-sports that one finds in the North American and European pro gaming world is not unwarranted. The South Korean model is one in which the interweaving structures of government support, technology infrastructure, broad industry sponsorship, strong organizational institutions (like KeSPA), legal and market accommodations (such as IP pricing in net cafés), and a mainstreamed game culture have created a powerful milieu where professional computer gaming has thrived for a number of years. As HanbitSoft (the company that brought *StarCraft* to the country) CEO Kim Young-man put in 2007, "Korean online games has extended its ideals from being a toy to becoming part of a cultural enterprise as the market becomes larger everyday" (Jin-seo 2008a).

Though there have been some signs of downturn and stagnation in the South Korean pro world—Hanbit was looking to sell its team in 2008 and OnGameNet's viewership has dropped it from ninth to sixteenth in overall cable channel rankings—we would be remiss to not keep the South Korean e-sports model in our minds as we proceed (Jin-seo 2008b, Jin and Chee 2008).[17] It helps situate broader structural features that the growth of a new form of play, and sport, can require. E-sports has clearly established itself there as a viable leisure and professional activity, weaving together a cultural inclusion of video games with elite competition and spectatorship.

Researching E-sports

As is perhaps apparent from the previous discussion of South Korea, the domain in which e-sports circulates is a decidedly global one, which provides interesting challenges for an author setting out to write a book dealing with its emergence. My field site for this work thus encompassed a range of countries and tournaments, all involving not only a set of globalized e-sport practices but a variety of activities and meanings simultaneously situated in very local contexts. Given the scope of the potential domain I had to make some hard choices and face up to real constraints in the work. While I was able to make one trip to Seoul, got a chance to visit the offices of International Cyber Marketing (organizers of the World Cyber Games), and talked to someone from KeSPA, the research in this book is primarily drawn from my experiences in the European and North American scene and it should be seen through this lens.

Given that constraint I have, however, attended a fair number of tournaments over the years, ranging from several WCG Grand Finals (one in the United States and one in Italy) to very small invite-only tournaments like the Arbalet Cup in Stockholm. When possible I would with permission "shadow" a player or team, a tournament commentator, or an organizer or administrator, simply following along and taking in the range of their activities and conversations during an event (where language permitted). Generally while at tournaments my days began with early start times and often ran late into the night. This typically lasted for several consecutive days. During such events I'd have numerous informal conversations with the range of participants you encounter at a tournament. I became a fairly avid amateur photographer as a way of documenting the field, and most of the images in this book are drawn from my own collection.

I've also had the privilege of running two separate day-long public workshops on e-sports (with collaborators Henry Lowood, Emma Witkowski, Matteo Bittanti, Henrik Bennetsen, and Susan Rojo) where we invited ten to twelve working e-sports professionals (players, team owners, tournament organizers, commentators) for extensive conversations about their work.[18]

In addition to this fieldwork, I've conducted a number of formal interviews over the years with everyone from commentators to players to team owners. In several instances I was fortunate enough to visit the offices of a team, tournament, or league organizer and interview several members of the staff on site. At other times interviews were conducted tucked in a corner at a tournament, at a café, via email, or online through Skype. Aside from a couple instances in which I've interviewed a very public figure whose identity could not easily be hidden, I've chosen to anonymize my respondents. I must admit I struggled with this decision since this book is as much a historical account as a traditional case study and indeed, it might benefit some interviewees professionally to be clearly represented here. But given that some of the issues at hand were fraught, or dealt with conflicts, I've decided the overall protection of people's privacy outweighed the benefits of any single person's individual identification.

As with much of my previous work I have also used the online construction of the e-sports and pro scene as a valuable resource for understanding what is happening. This includes following blogs, reading forums, watching videos, and listening to podcasts. The rise of professional computer gaming cannot be understood without a full accounting of its online components and I consider the material I've gotten from these venues key in documenting it.

This project has not always been an easy one. As is perhaps apparent from the various events I've gone to over the years, the research has been long in the making. The first event I attended was in 2003 and as I finish this manuscript it is 2011. In large part this has been due to two factors: the scope of the project and the vastly changing nature of the scene over these years. In most research you go until you reach a kind of saturation point. You start hearing the same things in interviews, seeing the same things in the field. Because I ended up not simply doing a study of one particular league or team, reaching this point has taken much longer than if I had focused more narrowly. The dynamic nature of the field has kept saturation always just out of reach. Leagues, tournaments, and teams have radically altered in just these past few years. Several major outfits that at one time seemed to have real longevity and stability suddenly folded, often leaving people scrambling to find new gigs and make sense of what was happening. It has also been an incredibly experimental decade for e-sports, with mainstream media attempts ascending and receding, financial fortunes rising and falling. It has additionally been a decade in which the real rise of computer gaming in our culture more generally has occurred, a shift from being seen as just for geeks to something for the mainstream. Truth be told, I have probably only still reached partial saturation. There is simply still too much happening in professional e-sports to call the fieldwork complete, the case nicely wrapped up in a tidy single volume. So this is, with eyes wide open, as much a conscious claim of provisional saturation and documenting things where they are at now, as anything. It is my hope that other researchers' accounts of various aspects of the scene will help fill in gaps and broaden the story.

This work has also been challenging in terms of my own relationship with the field. Unlike my prior research on virtual worlds and massively multiplayer online games, I never felt myself become a natural inhabitant of the e-sports community. If you, the reader, have noticed the omission of the term "ethnography," you have spotted a key break in my own practice. By virtue of the games played (I have never been a FPS player and RTS games come with some work), its often misogynistic culture, and its deeply insider nature (which is largely only broken by being an avid player and fan), I was always fairly outside what I was studying. At live events I always felt my otherness. I was a noncompetitor, a woman, and a bit older than most attendees. That the people I have interviewed over the years were as gracious as they were given these invisible boundaries is something I'm very grateful for. From a methodological perspective this outsiderness, of course, has a double nature. Things that were otherwise obvious for the insiders generally weren't for me. When claims were made about how one game was naturally easier to watch than another, for example, I felt the unspoken assumptions all too clearly. I perhaps sensed the gap moments and breakages more acutely because I often lacked any easy internalized interpretive schema. Yet my otherness also sometimes kept me at a distance from the people I encountered. I recall reading with some envy about the mundane hanging-out time Michael Kane, author of the book *Game Boys* (2008), spent with the e-sports teams he was writing about, or the easy conversational rapport he had managed to achieve when at a bar with the guys after a match. These kinds of moments remained elusive to me. For a variety of reasons, some I'm sure I'll never know, access of the sort I'd been used to in my prior ethnographic work was always a struggle. While some would suggest marginality should be maintained in fieldwork (Traweek 1998), I am ultimately quite ambivalent about the degree to which it occurred in this project compared with my own prior ethnographic research.

I should perhaps come clean about another aspect of my otherness in relation to this subject—I am not a big traditional sports fan. I came to e-sports not because it resonated with my own experience with baseball or basketball, but because it hooked into my curiosity about what I've in the past called instrumental play. My interest came from being a gamer, not a sports fan. Again the nonnaturalized aspect made me ask the "dumb" questions but, I would hope, those were often useful interventions for the research. The downside, of all this otherness is that I've probably had to work three times as hard to make sense of things that might otherwise easily come to mind if you're a sports or FPS fan. And I've surely overlooked some key links or examples that will immediately spring to mind as fans read this book.

Far too often in research we leave hidden the difficulties of our work, the things we struggle with. Our efforts reside in some isolated box that we end up writing around, and young scholars can find themselves hitting walls no one ever told them about. I certainly did earlier in my career. In this work, rather than hiding from the struggles it took to complete it, I want to put them on the table as part of what shapes the book you hold in your hands. The story, and history, I am constructing here, are—indeed can only be—partial and deeply informed by my own position. Ultimately a complete story of e-sports will unfold through a collective production of various works on the subject. My modest hope is that this book provides an early contribution—both in terms of its analysis but also by just laying down some basic documentation—to what will hopefully be an ongoing collection of research, including perhaps not only game studies, but fields like leisure studies or even the sociology of sport.[19]

Structure of the Book

Much like the way North American and European participants turn to it, I use the South Korean case study above as a referent point in the framing of this project. It reminds us to not only take a look at the players, whose stories understandably so captivate us with their vision of what the future might hold for play and work, but to take into account larger structural mechanisms and other activities (teams, leagues, broadcasters) as central mechanisms in the formation of a pro culture. The South Korean pro gaming scene prompts us to consider the ways structures and actors beyond the sole computer game player have influenced and shaped a professional game culture. Whether it is through sponsorships, team management, broadcasting, or a myriad of other factors, fully understanding professional computer gaming requires a larger, more sociologically informed eye to fully make sense of it.

In this regard the remainder of the book will pick up on such angles in the hopes of painting a larger picture of this emerging, albeit precariously situated, slice of game culture. This chapter has sought to lay out some basic structures and provide an initial setup for understanding the pro world, giving an early glimpse into a tournament and juxtaposing it against the South Korean model.

Chapter two explores debates about whether or not computer game play can indeed be considered sport. This question is something that players and the pro gaming community themselves regularly wrestle with. Mapping the contours of the debate provides useful insight into how participants understand the nature of play, sport, and even work. Drawing on the language of sport, and e-sport, is a powerful rhetorical tool for legitimating elite computer game play within the community. Beyond the more philosophic or phenomenological issues around sport are fascinating issues that arise with the regulation of matches and rule sets. At the heart of this discussion is a consideration of computation's role in constructing play, something that goes well beyond the domain of just e-sports. I recount several stories of contentious and widely debated instances in high-end tournament play in order to discuss the complex nature of rules and how the professional community is negotiating computational boundary making, human action, and agency.

Having tackled the nature of rules and sport, chapter three examines the most commonly heard angle into pro gaming, the players themselves. The focus in this chapter is less on telling individual stories of particular players and more on presenting an overall picture of the development of an e-sports career. Rather than assuming one seamlessly advances to elite status, the analysis here takes a more sociological approach in asking how someone becomes professional. The model suggests that the career path from amateur to professional is quite bumpy and often unsuccessful. It is also heavily dependant on being actively socialized into a professional identity by a range of actors and forces. This chapter tracks the ways players regularly start in the world of LANs and online play as they move into professionalization. One of the central questions arising in this study is that of the line between work and play, certainly not unfamiliar territory for any serious sports player. An examination of how hobby gets transformed into work, a consideration of "serious leisure," and the complicated nature of professional play are all themes in this chapter.

Also in this chapter I explore how gender is being constructed in the pro scene, with debates concerning the viability of women as top competitors. And rather than simply equating the issue of gender in games with women and femininity, this chapter looks at how masculinity is being formulated in e-sports. Hegemonic masculinity constructs a very particular model of the "ideal man." It intersects the notion of an athlete in complicated ways. Yet how this construction of masculinity (in which whiteness also plays a role) aligns, if at all, with what is often seen as a fairly "geeky" pastime is important in thinking about gender and e-sports.

Chapter four moves from focusing on players to focusing on the enormous amount of work sustaining the pro scene, what we might think of as the business of e-sport. Leagues, teams, owners, referees, competitions, sponsors, and a variety of other infrastructures are explored. This chapter gives the reader a picture of the range of actors behind the scenes and also helps tell the story about the kind of money involved. I present several institutional models for organizing e-sports and how competition is actually managed by some of these companies. Discussion of sponsorship and contracts, as well as skirmishes around issues of intellectual property and e-sports, is in this chapter.

Chapter five tackles the crucial issue of the possibilities for spectatorship and fandom in pro gaming, two angles rarely considered in game studies in general. Competitions and tournaments go back to early LAN days and I present an overview of the main competition venues (with a particular emphasis on offline matches). Though often quite unknown except to the most diehard fans, game journalists and commentators are introduced as providing powerful explanatory work for audiences. Breaking down the components of fan culture, this chapter discusses how websites, forums, podcasts, video on demand, and a variety of media help foster a growing community centered around the pro scene. This section looks at tournaments and events from the eye of a spectator and addresses some of the remaining big challenges in this domain.

Chapter six concludes the book with a discussion about the latest developments on the horizon and the role of globalization in e-sports. In particular, it notes the high degree of commercialization we are starting to see in the North American and European market. It provides a glimpse into the emerging state of pro gaming in countries new to the domain, such as China, and the rise of professional console gaming. I turn a final eye toward the mainstreaming of e-sports as it grows and provide some consideration as to future possibilities for the professionalization of computer game play.

While the story of professional gaming may at first glance strike some as a niche past time, it leads us into the heart of many questions we ponder in the face of computer gaming's growth as a mainstream leisure activity. It asks us to confront our notions about what play, work, and sport are. We must consider what the nature of our activity is exactly when we are looking over the shoulder, or at the television channel, of another gamer playing. We also find ourselves in the thick of a debate about the nature of rules, computation, and emergent play. High-level competitive gaming also leads to debates about the relationship between the construction of gender, sport, and competition. Ultimately, thinking about e-sports helps us analyze the transition many groups face as they struggle to convert their leisure time and playful passions into serious play, where the stakes are high, reputations built, and money gained (and lost).

2 Computer Games as Professional Sport

If I were to ask you to imagine a sport, your mind would probably turn to football, tennis, baseball, cricket, or any number of other traditional sports we regularly encounter. If you are a watcher of the Olympics or other large-scale competitions, you might also think of things like gymnastics, diving, track and field, perhaps even marksmanship. But probably most of you would not conjure up the following:

Figure 2.1
Song "Stork" Byung Goo, *Starcraft* world champion.
Image from Global Gaming League Wire.

Yet images such as this, and players such as "Stork," push us to reckon with what comprises the heart of sports. Is it an issue of physicality? Of exertion, skill perfection, or some other alchemy of action and an individual human's striving and drive to excel? Over the years the scope of what constitutes a "real" sport, and indeed meaningful athleticism, has been debated.[1] Well before computer games entered the scene, enthusiasts, regulatory bodies, and athletes debated the merits of counting everything from equestrianism to snowboarding as a sport. Were you to go online now with a few simple search terms, you could find heated debates about whether or not poker, chess, or darts should be considered a sport.

It is in this context that computer gaming now finds itself sitting, often uneasily, between digital play and sport. As mentioned in the previous chapter, in South Korea spectators watching computer games can outnumber those watching traditional sports such as baseball. Hwang Hyung-joon, the general manager of OnGameNet, one of the major South Korean computer game tournament organizers and broadcasters, has argued that, "It is the Pro *Starcraft* league that can be called a sport, like the pro baseball league or pro basketball league. The league has all the requirements to be called as a professional sport. Competitions, winners and losers, and fans. It is a matter of how popular the league can be among the people" (Korea Times 2004a).

Such an argument is a tremendous leap for many outside of e-sports culture. Athleticism is still primarily seen as overt demonstrations of physical activity and skill. The revered moniker of "sport" gets reserved for the coordinated and formalized activities around these skills. Long-standing debates about what constitutes a "real" sport intersect deeply held notions about masculinity (and femininity), class, and culture. The field is littered with examples of negotiations, compromises, and transitions. Only the most naïve, and ahistorical, would suggest the coveted legitimacy of sport is bestowed objectively, outside of any deep cultural values about what constitutes meaningful human and social action.

The debate about the status of computer gaming as a sport, however, is not confined to the margins or to those who do not play computer games and question their value. Indeed, if you look within the avid community of computer game players and e-sports aficionados, you find regular conversations not only about if computer games can be thought of this way, but indeed whether or not particular titles and genres warrant such inclusion. Whether it is the hardcore computer game player who doesn't see a connection with what he or she does when playing a real-time strategy game and what they identify as a traditional "jock" culture, or the dedicated e-sports player who draws a line between titles that facilitate "real" e-sports play and those that can't, all across game culture players are wrestling with how to understand the scope of their often passionate and committed engagement with these digital artifacts.

In this chapter I explore some of the ways the practice of computer gaming *as sport* is constructed. Rather than provide a checklist of factors and then see if e-sport matches up as athletic or "sporty" enough, I will look at the ways it is constructed as such in everyday play (both practice and tournaments). Fundamental to my approach is to not render a definitional judgment myself, but to document how it is understood as sport, and produced as such, within the community itself.[2]

Materiality and Pro Computer Gaming

Much of the conversation around athleticism and sport is, understandably, rooted in notions of materiality and embodiment. Computer games can prove elusive artifacts when we try to discuss the material world in relation to them because so much of our attention drifts to the space on the screen. The media aspect of computer game play may prompt an argument suggesting they cannot be easily aligned with a notion of sport (Hutchins 2008). The virtual worlds and simulations we encounter there, often with fantastical or near photo-realistic imagery, can focus our gaze in ways that may sometimes block attention to the outside world. It is all too easy to fall into an analytic mode that obscures our corporeal bodies, which are implicated in our play. Those bodies interact with a range of technologies and physical artifacts that mediate our play in digital spaces and so to fully understand computer game play we need to attend to both its embodied and material qualities.

Within computer game studies there is now growing (although still fairly small) attention to each of these notions, and connecting up with it is helpful for discussions of e-sport (Bayliss 2007, Dovey and Kennedy 2006, Lahti 2003, Swalwell 2008).[3] There are two approaches via which we can talk about materiality and e-sports: the ways the corporeal body plays an active role in skilled performance and the assemblage of that skill and expertise as produced through a network of bodies and technologies.

Embodied Play

When we sit at the computer or with our game console and engage in play, we orient our bodies in a variety of ways. They are situated in relation to the input devices (keyboard, mouse, console controller, steering wheel and accelerator, microphone), the physical space (table, chair, sofa, floor), the visual space (television, monitor, the room around us), and the aural space (via headphones or speakers, but also in relation to the ambient sounds or voices of other people in the physical room). While the most intense moments of gameplay can prompt us to talk about feeling as if we have forgotten our bodies (gamers often talk about being in a "zone" or stumbling out of a kind of altered state in play), it is actually in those moments we are most *fully inhabiting* a body that is commingling with the ludic system (including rules, mechanics, aesthetics) as well as the technology via which gameplay passes through us and back into the system through our actions. As Dovey and Kennedy note, "Gameplay involves us in a set of relationships with material objects that must be handled skillfully and appropriately in order for play to take place—gameplay is a tactile and kinesthetic experience" (2006, 107). This circuit of play is constructed not outside of our material embodied existence but through it.

Watching elite players one can see the way highly competitive play has inscribed itself onto, and into, their bodies. Top RTS players exhibit a stunning amount of skill in the number of commands they can carry out via mouse clicks and keyboard strokes (resulting in upward of two hundred actions per minute). The perceptual acuity of first-person shooter players—where their knowledge of game maps and weapons meets interpretive work in elaborate eye-to-hand coordination—can leave the average player's head spinning if they face them in battle. Racing competitors can exhibit surprising nuance as the circuit between the foot on the "gas" pedal works in concert with the hands on the steering wheel and the visual display rendered on the screen.

We can also see the broader ways players' bodies are enlisted. Tense shoulders, focused visual attention, "on point" posture, complex cognitive engagement, and stillness in the body except for the key interface points (eyes, hands, and even feet) all speak to the ways the body is not only always present in computer game play, but indeed the ways the mastery of the body is crucial in pro gaming, much like in traditional sports. This is probably one of the most vexing aspects of games for many amateur players. While certainly a large part of success in computer gaming is learning all the ins and outs of the game and the advantages of various options (player classes, weapons, etc.), plus knowing the field (the map, the terrain), without a doubt this knowledge must be embodied to have any meaningful impact. You may know what you should do, but your reaction times and your ability to carry out in concrete ways the strategic decisions you make are key. Language like "flailing" or "button mashing"—where the link between what you see and want to act on runs up against the actual ability to act—highlights how central control of one's body is for computer gaming. At the topmost level of pro gaming, embodied skill must be naturalized to the degree that it is unconscious in order for true mastery to occur. This is not dissimilar from traditional sports. In the same way that basics like dribbling or throwing a ball have to be ingrained into the very physicality of the sports player, computer games similarly require a deep internalization of moves, and their mastery, for the highest-level play to occur.

In Emma Witkowski's work (2012) on the subject she has made the astute argument that we can identify three powerful vectors of physicality often associated with sporting bodies and correlate them to pro computer game players: human movement, the balanced body, and haptic engagement. As she argues in her study of elite *Counter-Strike* players, they demonstrate a remarkable amount of sophistication and nuance that is located both within individual embodied practices, but also within larger team contexts. She writes,

> In Counter-Strike, "sporting movement"—needing to see as we move—is achieved by engaging players physically through aspects such as maintaining a controlled body whilst quickly navigating the 3D environment, by moving the character proficiently with reference to the team (through intercorporeal agility such as "knowing by body" the practiced team tempo), as well as by being executed in the muscles and tendons controlled by hands and fingers and in the subtle control of breathing. (14)

This complex coordination that weaves cognition with physical-technological skill is achieved through constant and rigorous practice. In the same way traditional sports shape embodied action, elite computer game play also inscribes itself on the body of players, refining over time the most nuanced yet complex circuits of action.

We should also not forget the toll that can be taken on the body at play. Pro gamers will mention headaches, eye strain, and exhaustion at long days on competition or time spent on the road. Over the course of a multiday tournament players talk about the real physical challenges they face having to marshal serious focused attention during matches despite often operating on little sleep, erratic schedules, and back-to-back high stakes performances. While I've not heard too many stories of things like carpal tunnel syndrome, perhaps that is more owing to the age of the players than anything and we may eventually see the physical costs of intensive sustained elite play.

Body-Technology Assemblage

As we can see from the outset, the deep linkage between the corporeal body and technology is always already present in e-sports. One result of this is that it provides an excellent opportunity to understand the assemblage at work in making up computer game play. Yet before turning attention to that, I want to linger for a moment on the relationship between the body and technology in sports because, while it is perhaps all too easy to think of traditional sports as more "pure" in this regard, it would be far from accurate. The sporting body has always been tied up with technology. It is only in a fairly abstract conjuring of idealized athleticism that we might imagine an isolated "natural" body confronting nature in a test of skill. Contemporary traditional sports regularly demonstrate this complex relationship not only between various technologies on the field (be it new innovations in gear or equipment), but in the regimens of practice and body modification undergone in sports medicine, physical therapy, and advanced training. And none of this mentions the ever-shifting sands of performance-enhancing drugs. Whether it is a debate about the legitimacy of a new Speedo swimsuit, the use of high-altitude tents for training, or the allowance of a golf cart in a major tournament, traditional sports constantly negotiate the integration and boundary-monitoring of technologies and ongoing constructions of "pure" human agency.[4] Though this boundary work may be more apparent in e-sports, it is not unique to it.

Nicholas T. Taylor, in his 2009 work on a *Halo 3* team in the Major League Gaming series, cautions against erasing the materiality of computer game play at the competitive level. Drawing on Latour (2005) and inspired by the work done by Giddings and Kennedy (Giddings 2007, Giddings and Kennedy 2008) in thinking about the role of nonhuman actors in computer game play, he wisely notes that we need to pay careful attention to the variety of nonhuman agents that structure and inform competitive gaming activities. In his study he highlights the ways mundane factors like the length of cables connecting XBoxes to TVs, controllers themselves, and even seating arrangements, play an important role in not only how competitive play unfolds in a given setting, but how it is "produced, in similar ways, across different regional, national and linguistic contexts" (Taylor 2009a, 195). Todd Harper, in his detailed study of the fighting game community (2010) similarly highlights the role of technology in play, discussing the adoption of specialized "sticks" versus out-of-the-box console pads. While we should be cautious about overstating the homogenizing power of artifacts (versus understanding their contingent setting in local practices), we can certainly pay attention to the kinds of recurrent material issues that arise within the pro gaming world.

I was particularly struck by this point at that first competition I attended. As I watched players sit down to either practice or engage in a formal match

Figure 2.2
Player at the WCG 2007 with his keyboard carrying case.

I saw them go through a kind of ritual with the space. They uniformly would pull out of their backpack or bag their own keyboard, mouse, and mouse pad.

Any peripherals provided by the tournament organizers would generally be tossed to the side and the player would begin the process of plugging his own equipment in. When competitors sit down and set up you often see them quickly move their mouse back and forth across the mouse pad to get a feel for it, to reconnect the embodied action interfacing with peripheral to the digital space. They test the speed, making sure the surface of the mouse pad accommodates their movement in just the right way. Perhaps unsurprisingly the sensitivity of one's mouse is a very personal, but crucial, affordance for play. Weighted mice, where small bits can be swapped out to actually change the heft and movement, have been developed. Sometimes players take the mouse apart and pull out the ball, blow out dust, put it back together, and go through the motions of quick movement testing again. They may cover the mouse with a tissue while they warm up, to keep it from getting too sweaty before the actual match.

Mice, which we often think of as simple input devices, can radically alter gameplay, especially in conjunction with mouse pads. One player I spoke with described how mouse dots per inch (DPI), sensitivity, and mouse pad size worked to shape action. To quickly achieve the needed full 360-degree views, players would use high sensitivity levels but often risked overextending the view if they were too quick. Over time, mouse pads got larger and indeed you'll now see huge ones at tournaments. As one player put it about this shift, "That definitely changed because once a little bit larger mouse pads started to be created, people could cut their sensitivity in four and become a completely different style player where they would just walk in, looking every way slow, and once a flash would pop in front

Figure 2.3
Standard XBox controller on the left and the controller pro *Street Fighter* players use on the right.

of them they're able to swipe really fast and turn from it without twacking out." The link he is pointing to here, between technology (mouse sensitivity settings), material configuration (mouse pad size), and actual style of play is rarely considered when we talk about computer games.

I have seen pro *Street Fighter* gamers go through similar processes. Unlike most average players, they generally do not use the standard console controllers for their game but have purchased specialized arcade-style input boxes (typically called "sticks"). When they plug them in and synch up with the game you can see them quickly hitting buttons and moving their character around—warming up not only their avatar but their physical body as well. For expert play to be achieved, the nuanced circuit between corporeality and virtuality must be completed.

Generally tournament machines have discarded peripherals (sitting on the floor or stowed away by organizers) and most serious players use their own gear. One of the most famous players in the world, Johnathan "Fatal1ty" Wendel, markets his own brand of specially weighted, customizable, mice that are promoted as ideal for tournament and serious play.[5] These practices are so common in the pro scene that tournaments not only

Figure 2.4
Unused equipment, WCG 2007.

accommodate them (bringing your own devices is allowed, with some minimal restrictions) but players clearly talk about the physicality of their play when discussing, for example, actions per second.

Sound, or more specifically, headphones, also plays a role in constructing the material (albeit auditory) space of gameplay. Very often sponsors will provide headsets for teams, but finding the right pair for a tournament context can be challenging. One player said, "It's kind of tricky because sometimes you get these really good quality headsets that cancel out all the noise but then sound is really bassy and you can't hear your teammates yelling at you. So you try and find headphones that you can kind of hear a little bit outside. But then you go to these big events like DreamHack and you can't hear anything again. And on top of that, when you have a sponsor, you have to be using their equipment, so you only have about two or three different headsets to choose from."

I also noticed even at my first tournament that tables themselves would sometimes be augmented. Players would pull out a roll of heavy-duty duct tape from their backpack or grab one that might be laying around and lay a piece down on the edge of the table near their mouse hand to prevent rubbing or snagging. While high-end tournaments (like the WCG Grand Final or CGS with its ready-for-television sets) often have well designed or at least solid, sturdy tables and chairs, many competition setups are made from rough thrown together tables (which may give splinters) or simple folding tables. One top player described how important these basics are, saying, "We get so upset when we go to a tournament and they have the tables set up poorly. Because there's five of us and so a lot of tournaments will try and do like, three tables for like 2-2-1, and then you have one guy that's far off on another table. Some tournaments try and space it out evenly but then you're sitting between two tables and you have this giant crack, your legs are up against bars. So if they don't have enough long tables it affects you." He went on to mention similar problems with poor chairs and how he will sometimes bring a towel from his hotel room to use if the chairs are too low. On the competitive circuit (including boot camp practice venues) players often do whatever they can to optimize not only their interface with the machine, but the actual seating space itself.

The computer and monitor also play a key role in matches. It perhaps goes without saying that computer quality has a significant influence on play. A poor computer can not only alter, but hinder, the game and make for a strange playing field. One player noted the frustration that can occur when a poor machine causes lag—a time lapse between when the action is taken and when it is registered in the game. Shots get screwed up and your action becomes out of synch with the network. He contrasted this to traditional sports, noting, "When you're playing a video game, there's a chance for net code errors. When you throw a basketball to someone there's no chance for the space you're playing on [a basketball court] to glitch and to angle a little differently you know." Yet as Emma Witkowski notes,

> Basketball courts, as with most pitches/fields of play (i.e. cricket, football, etc.) are often "glitchy"—hence "home-court" advantage. Knowing how the rim will bounce a shot off it is something all players "play with" during warm-up, which sometimes even reshapes one's shooting for that day in order to accommodate "the glitch." Some players are even coached to only shoot off of the backboard due to the unknown quality of the rims that will inevitably be met in play. (Personal communication, 2011)

There thus remain many variables altering how a field of play operates for any given session, and we should be careful to not overlook the small yet important details expert players deal with, nor to idealize the physical field. Experienced athletes not only have ways of talking about the variability and adaptation required, but indeed the dynamic nature of a sports field is an expected factor to be dealt with. While traditional athletes will suss out the nuances of a particular court or field during warm-up and adapt to changes that emerge over the course of a game (for example from rain or wear and tear), elite computer gamers similarly produce sophisticated perceptual adaptations and work-arounds in their own glitchy situations. Gamers regularly are calculating on the fly and adjusting to accommodate the digital world interfacing with their own embodied action.

What may be a surprise, though, is that the monitor itself is also quite important in the gaming situation. Older-style cathode ray tube (CRT) monitors, while bulky, provide much better performance for FPS games than do the newer flat liquid crystal display (LCD) monitors dominating the consumer market right now. It's no surprise, especially when monitor producers are sponsoring an event, that it is the newer screen technology that players must use.[6] The effects of this run from changing gameplay and game-feel to how practice happens. Gun recoils feel slightly different on different refresh rates. Gun spray precision can be affected, for example. As one player described it, "So you have to use more, what we call like, burst fire and tapping. So you have to kind of, it actually makes me aim better because I know I have to focus more. I don't know what it is about the technology but you have to be more precise. CRT's give you a little bit more leeway." Things like flash grenades will be rendered differently on a CRT versus an LCD (taking longer to fade on an LCD), thus changing both how they are used and how players adapt to them and strategize their use. And while LCD monitors are increasingly the norm, some players will still use CRTs at home but then swap to an LCD a few weeks before a tournament if they know that LCDs will be used.

Beyond these very concrete material conditions of play is another set of factors that are one of the most commented-on issues in competitive gaming—network connections and ping times. In online multiplayer games the amount of time it takes for your and your competitors' machines to communicate with the game server is central to fair play. If one of you has a poorer connection (higher ping time) it is going to show through lag in executed moves, what you see on the screen, your feel for the action (gun recoil), and your general ability to act and react. One of the common refrains, for example, in discussions comparing North American to European e-sports concerns the problems ping times cause. One player I spoke to emphasized how much high ping times restrict practice opportunities, saying, "In America we can only play against other teams in America. We find a server that's centrally located, we'll play with like fifty ping and there's really only between four or eight teams that are even worth practicing against and even then you get bored with playing the same teams and it becomes pointless, they already know what you're doing. And you also are competing with them a lot in tournaments so you don't want to give away what you do."

He went on to note that this fundamental infrastructure difference allows European teams to practice against a much wider range of competitors. He also suggested that it fosters a different practice culture. In his opinion, the range of teams you could play against and good network conditions promote a more dedicated and serious practice atmosphere. Top teams hit chat channels to schedule regular practice sessions where four maps at a time would be played (versus a more ad hoc/one map norm). North American players who come to Europe to compete or attend boot camp regularly echo this line. They often remark on the culture of skilling up, undergirded by the network configuration. As the player commenting on ping times and practicing put it, "Because the Internet here [Sweden, where he was for a tournament] is amazing and they've all the top teams in the world to practice against. They're constantly getting better and we're constantly playing catch-up."

Ping time can diverge into favoring or disadvantaging different play styles, though, too. A player who takes one angle at a time (one who "wins with their keyboard") may not feel the ill effects of a high ping time as much as one who is always on the move, reactive, swiping their view back and forth. As one player noted, "So when I'm playing with really high ping and I can't get myself out of tight situations because I can't hit the shots, it causes me a big problem because I have to like, make a quick change to my play style and play very passive and make moves only when I really notice it and not as much of the time." Within competitive multiplayer gaming the structure of the network, and how it facilitates machines talking to each other, is central to how the action unfolds and the styles of play a gamer can actually use.

As we can see by looking at these examples, professional computer game play is deeply interwoven with material, embodied practices. Though it is easy to fall into speaking of computer game spaces as simply virtual and of leaving the body behind, in reality we are continually working through, and with, materiality when we engage in digital play.

This complex relationship between technologies, athleticism, and human action is something we see in not only e-sports, but in classic sports such as basketball and swimming. We might further complicate the conversation by considering the way sports such as Formula 1 racing or perhaps even cycling provide us with concrete examples of the required co-construction of athleticism with machines. We can certainly think of a number of other sports where there is no action without the corporeal-technical circuit. Within this framing of contemporary sports, e-sports and the athleticism embodied in its competitors certainly finds a familiar home.

Ultimately we can see how action is not simply determined by the structure of the game itself but shaped and tweaked as it moves beyond the parameters of the software. Player action is produced via a complex matrix that involves not only the corporeal body, but the technology, specific contexts, and the games themselves. This means that computer game play evolves over time and is not a static form. It becomes expressive, dynamic action.

Rules, Negotiation, and Play

While embodied, skilled action forms a core definitional point when we talk about sports, we also need to turn our attention to the formal contest of skills to help flesh out our understanding. Competition, and for the purposes of this part of the discussion, the rules governing it, become a core area of consideration. Computer games pose some interesting challenges when trying to understand how they migrate into professional play.

Most people can probably recall instances, perhaps even experienced with some regularity, of playing a tabletop or sports game in which some point of contention around the rules came up. Perhaps someone made a move considered illegal by others or the group is unsure what occurs next in the procedures of play. In these moments play will often (though not always) be paused to haggle over a point of procedure, rule books will sometimes be consulted (albeit quite rarely in friendly games of sport), or some on-the-fly rule will be made up that satisfies everyone (or most everyone) playing. If the group playing is a mix of those familiar with the game and first-time players, there will often be just some (occasionally hasty) verbal description of the rules provided to the new people and perhaps a follow-up clarification to get things moving again.

Literature on gaming and play outside the digital context regularly highlights these kinds of negotiations, unspoken or ambiguous boundaries of action, and the general malleability of any given contextual gaming moment. Linda Hughes, in her fieldwork dating back to the 1980s on children's games, presents us with some of the most astute material one can find on trying to reconcile formal rules and actual play. As she writes, "Rules are assumed to be of many different types, multilayered and hierarchical, referencing very different antecedents and outcomes. They are assumed to be subject to constant negotiation and reinterpretation in the course of everyday life" and that while people tend to "assume game rules are at all times explicit and foregrounded," in fact, by observing players one finds that "the degree of rule explicitness may constantly shift, and such phenomena are high contexted and indicative of social relationships among gamers" (2006, 515).

Game designer Stephen Sniderman has similarly picked up on themes of indeterminacy, negotiation, and games as open systems. In his 1999 article, "Unwritten Rules," he discusses the variety of ways games escape from an imagined state of perfect knowledge to one in which play is always grounded in specific contexts that complicate the range of known and possible actions with regard to rules. The myriad of unwritten rules, ambiguous scenarios that call for adjudication (either by a formal referee or the participants themselves), human factors and norms, traditions, and varying "house rules" all complicate the idea that game rules can be clearly specified and bounded prior to play. As he puts it, "No game or sport is played in a vacuum. All play activities exist in a 'real-world' context so to play the game is to immerse yourself in that context, whether you want to or not. In fact, it is impossible to determine where the 'game' ends and 'real life' begins. As a result, knowing only the recorded rules of a game is never enough to allow you to play the game" (2006, 480).

Given the ways context and negotiation are involved with game play and rules, digital games are particularly interesting owing to their nature as computational artifacts. On the one hand, they are commonly thought of as bypassing some of the normal work of play, with its debates around rules, permissible actions, and the scope of the game space. Computer games can seem to, by virtue of their nature as software objects, settle such questions by encoding their logics in the very structure of the game's software, and perhaps in its hardware. In this model of computer game play the machine steps in and acts as the ultimate referee. We, as participants, are seen as not needing to read rule books, haggle over interpretations, construct house rules, or perform any of the other typical activities that support gameplay. The computer simply takes care of it all for us. It provides the play space, the rule sets, and even keeps track of the score. While other layers of rules are sometimes introduced to nuance this model, within this framework there remains a core sense that the computer is centrally relied on for the lion's share of rule governance.

This view is perhaps best summarized by Ernest Adams and Andrew Rollings in their book *Fundamentals of Game Design*:

> Unlike conventional games, video games do not require written rules. The game still *has* [emphasis theirs] rules, but the machine implements and enforces them for the players. The players do not need to even know exactly what the rules are, although they do need instruction about how to play. In most video games, the computer sets the boundary of the magic circle because player actions are meaningful in the game only if the machine can detect them with its input devices. The computer also determines when the player reaches the goal. It adjudicates victory and defeat if those concepts are programmed into the game. (2007, 18)

While Adams and Rollings are primarily speaking to game designers and addressing pragmatic issues of making games, David Myers, long-time game studies scholar, argues for a formalist approach in understanding gameplay, one which posits a framework in which authentic game action is best understood, and indeed formulated, by a strict adherence to the internal rules of the system as enacted by the software. In *Play Redux* he suggests that computer games are a particularly powerful artifact via which to revive a formalist approach. He argues that because they allow such a clear view ("more measurable and more determinable") of the heart of the game system via their code, they can be particularly helpful in unpacking the nature of games and play (2010, 5). This approach, one that lays core definitional properties solely within the realm of computation, leads him to conclude that "Thus, to avoid any confusion over what the rules actually are, we can define rules-breaking play—and any so-called bad play associated with it—as play not explicitly allowed by the rules *as represented by the game code* (emphasis Myers, 19).

This move animates his now infamous "Twixt" experiment in which he sought to play the MMOG *City of Heroes* solely according to the computational rules as he interpreted them, not taking the social rules, community interpretation of the system's structures, or specific culture of the game into account. Though he labels the research a "breaching experiment," for many he played with (or against) it felt more like an act of griefing, wholly out of touch with the way on-the-ground play is a complex negotiation of structure and culture. While he rightly notes the regulating power people have in these environments and the degree they will go to in policing (see also Taylor 2006b on this), his own experiment simultaneously dismantles his formulation of how actual play works. Yet an abstract definitional commitment (in other words, rules can only legitimately be located in systems and/or code) leads him to mostly rue the condition of the playful individualist in his summary analysis of the incident.

While it is certainly important we find good ways to talk about the work computation does in facilitating digital play, often on the behalf of human actors in handling rules, it is crucial we don't overstate how closed the system is or overreach in ascribing power to the formal system as encoded in software. Miguel Sicart (2011) has suggested that this turn toward a new formalism—often located in a commitment to procedurality with its focus on system rules and structure embodied in a computational system as the locus for the production of both action and meaning—mistakenly sidelines the actions and interpretations of actual players (see also Wilson 2011).

Players, and their situated practices and meaning-making, are core components we cannot overlook. While it is easy to identify simple cases where software does all the work of managing gameplay for you (for example, a quick five minute game of *Tetris* on your phone), a significant portion of digital gaming writ large is constituted through a much more complex handling of rules, a negotiation between system and user, human and nonhuman actors, given structure and emergent practices and meanings.[7]

One method of problematizing an overly simple version of how rules function in games is to attempt to parse out different types of rules and situate their roles accordingly. Perhaps most notable in this approach is Katie Salen and Eric Zimmerman's book *Rules of Play*, which posits three different types of rules: operational ("usually synonymous with the written-out 'rules' that accompany board games"), constitutive ("underlying formal structures that exist 'below the surface' of the rules presented to players," that is, the "formal structures [that] are logical and mathematical"), and implicit (the "unwritten rules" of the game dealing with "etiquette, good sportsmanship, and other implied rules of proper game behavior") (2003, 130).[8] This framing has some real value in helping meaningfully highlight the work players do in creating the actual conditions for their gaming.

Though Salen and Zimmerman do pay attention to the role of culture and player intervention in gameplay experience, they nonetheless still hang onto an orientation that at a deep level disentangles contextual use from rules. As they note, "in the chapters concerning RULES [emphasis theirs], however, the focus is not on the visual design, narrative content, cultural history, or social use of games. Instead, it is on game rules: the formal structures of a game" (2004, 134). The formal identity of the game is fundamentally understood not via any consideration of implicit rules ("we can immediately eliminate implicit rules as a possible answer" [134]) but primarily via constitutive and operational rules. In both these categories the strong signal is that they are disconnected from the agency of the player or the specific context of a given play moment. For example, they speak of operational rules as the sort "written out as instructions for players" or constitutive rules as, via their underlying mathematical structure, "exist[ing] independently from the player" (132). So while on the one hand their framework gives us a platform from which to talk about the work players do in managing their own play, theoretically there is still an orientation that sets this work somehow apart from the base conceptualization of the game, which seems to be primarily rooted in either the work of the designer or operationalization via the machine.

Computer game studies continues to wrangle with the relationship between computational systems, rules, and player agency. While there is often a willingness to put social processes in the theoretical mix, when it comes to the definitional move—be it how rules are generated or where they reside—often harder lines are drawn. One can be left with the overall impression that there is a core computational system at work, one created by a designer, which provides constraints shaping ludic action. What the game is can be understood, in this model, fundamentally through its designed rule set.

This formalist approach has been flagged by long-time game designer Greg Costikyan (2010) as overly narrow, noting the rise of a "disciplined, systems-oriented design philosophy that is today the conventional norm in our field." He argues this mode can limit what we think "games are, what they are capable of doing, and how they achieve an effect on players." Richard Gruneau has suggested a double nature presented by the study of rules and play. He highlights that although play has an "aura of unreality" that we tie to its abstract form, the specificities of this form are in fact deeply tied to the social and cultural.

> [W]hile one of the purposes of rules is to separate play from reality, the very act of rule construction has the effect of embedding play deeply in the prevailing logic of social relations and thereby of diminishing its autonomy. For this reason, the study of play is haunted by a fundamental paradox. Play gives the impression of being an *independent and spontaneous* aspect of human action or agency and at the same time a *dependent* and *regulated* aspect of it [emphasis his]. (2007, 37)

Formalist and systems-oriented design often overlooks this double nature, focusing primarily on either an abstract rendering of game autonomy or rooting any dependence to the agency of the formal designer. There is also a curious relation between the dream of total computation and what is ultimately at the heart of games, contingency, which is, as Malaby puts it, essentially "that which could have been otherwise" (2007, 107).[9] As he points out in his consideration of games (riffing on a formulation from Dibbell 2006), they are exactly unlike things like income tax software because "They are about contriving and calibrating multiple contingencies to produce a mix of predictable and unpredictable outcomes (which are then interpreted)" (105). It is perhaps this odd pairing of computation and semicontrolled indeterminacy that has mistakenly led some down a wrong path when it comes to understanding rules in computer games.

There are a number of studies that signal that digital gameplay in the wild is not nearly so tidy when it comes to delineating machine versus human rule structures (or designer versus player) and the unfolding of actual play experience. Todd Harper (2010) gives a number of examples in which house rules and conventions (often situated in an arcade) shape fighting game play, including nuanced judgments around the use and informal prohibition of particular game characters and moves. Mikael Jakobsson's 2007 article on a console game club and their competitions for the game *Super Smash Bros.* shows how the gamers enact a dynamic set of rules to facilitate play that go well beyond the formalized ones set by the game.[10] Through his fieldwork with a console gaming club in Sweden, as well as his analysis of the broader scene around the popular Nintendo title, Jakobsson provides interesting examples of the ways the players negotiate the formal rules of the game for their specific play purposes. He writes, for example, of the tensions that occurred when West and East Coast American players began to encounter each other at tournaments.

> While the West Coast players saw the randomness of different items and stages as an essential flavor of the game, the East Coast players tried to strip down the experience to the core of game. They all agreed, however, that certain restrictions to the original design were necessary in a tournament situation and items like the hearts and apples were never allowed. In the light of how differently the game has been played by different players, in different places, and at different times, it becomes clear that the constitutive rules actually play a very small role in defining the game. (6)

The question of the role of constitutive rules (the abstract core mathematical rules of a game) as described by Salen and Zimmerman is provocatively highlighted in Jakobsson's work as itself subject to negotiation. In the case of the "Smashers" in his study, such tweaks (including on-the-spot ones at a given event) facilitate play.

We can see similar negotiations in MMOGs, where players regularly make their way through divergent play structures and practices, often even having different goals in mind. In my previous work on this genre (Taylor 2006a and 2006b) I sought to highlight the complex negotiation around what counts as appropriate and fair play for online players and how they often interact with software to construct strong norms and rules governing their activities well beyond the fixed system the game software provides. MMOGs regularly prompt user discussions on if, for example, taking advantage of glitches in the terrain to one's advantage is cheating, or if using additional third party helpers constitutes rule breaking. As games increasingly allow for modifying the actual game software, new vertices of this debate arise. For example, in the online multiplayer game *World of Warcraft*, which allows users to modify their interface ("mod the UI"), we find that players regularly discuss the appropriate boundaries of action and "fair rules" as the use of these bits of software alters what they can and can't do in the space. It is not unusual to find players discussing whether using a piece of software that assists them in healing, for example, crosses the line of fair play (Taylor 2006b).

The issue of rule breaking and cheating in computer gaming is complex and has been discussed in depth by Mia Consalvo (2007), who highlights not only the diverse ways players approach the subject, but how game companies themselves straddle an ambiguous line when it comes to what the system does or doesn't let players formally do within a game.[11] As she notes, the work around play, the contextualized nature of "winning," and nuanced systems to facilitate play all speak to the ways users construct diverse and contextualized systems of interpretation and use with game systems. Research by other scholars such as Kücklich (2009) or De Paoli and Kerr (2010) similarly suggests a more complex relationship between player agency and code than is typically formulated when it is imagined that a computer game simply hands over rules that everyone seamlessly obeys. Analysis of cheating in computer games regularly highlights the contingent nature of rule systems among varying player communities.

Within research on role-playing games (both offline and online) we can find similar trends in the ways player communities explicitly discuss and debate what they consider appropriate forms of play, even to the point of working around and tweaking, when possible, constitutive rules. For example, work done by researchers such as Copier (2005) and Mortensen (2008) shows the dynamic and emergent community-based structuring of play that occurs even within computer worlds. They have found rich player practices organizing game, and nongame, interaction. We can find similar creative moves within the offline role-playing scene (Stenros 2010; Stenros and Montola 2011). This work has provided a frame for understanding rules and experience in role-play that puts at the center of the game the players themselves, suggesting, as Markus Montola notes, that role-play is fundamentally "qualitative and non-algorithmic" (2009, 25).

I've thus far focused mostly on research within digital games. Work by play studies scholars such as Hughes has highlighted the complex ways actual play is interwoven with situational rules negotiation. But what about how traditional sports deal with them? Surely that space represents a much tighter formulation of rules, ones less subject to discussion or interpretation? Not quite. As Gerald Griggs notes about the construction of rules in sports,

> However, it is well known that, in reality, there is much more to "playing by the rules" than just defining and following the constitutive rules—known as "formalism." In practice, a shared understanding about the importance of regulative rules insists that participants are generally considered to be both "playing according to and in the spirit of the rules." This distinction has been termed the difference between "formal and informal fair play." (2011, 97)

He goes on to note that what is judged to be fair play is deeply contingent on how "different groups, ages, levels of performance and nationality, depending on existing social and cultural norms" meaningfully reckon with their activities (98). Scholars within sports studies regularly argue that participants often have nuanced readings of rule violations, some being more permissible than others. These judgments are generally made in relation to a model of the overarching ethos of a game or its "spirit" (D'Agostino

1981, Loland 2002). Work like this regularly highlights the limits of thinking of constitutive rules as the core identity of a game or the central guide for action.

To be clear, it is not that rules don't matter in sports. They absolutely do and their existence is crucial in sustaining the game. But as I have written before, whose rules in which situations? Rule systems are perplexing because their force is derived from being granted (by the players or institutional governors of play) an authority to speak to the conditions of the game, and yet in the actual situation of play we see that it is a kind of provisional force. At times we reassert our agency and intervene upon the given rules. We accept them to be guiding principles... until they aren't. We follow them easily... until we don't. I want to tread carefully here because I am not arguing that the moment-by-moment experience of a game is riddled with stops and starts, anxieties and insecurities about what the rules are. Generally it isn't. Large chunks of any given game session are seamlessly managed and arbitrated by rules, both formal and informal. But there are constant and discrete moments in games that remind us that ultimately rule systems are dynamic, interpretable, and incomplete.

Rules change over time, adapting to cultural and ethical shifts, new forms of technology, developments in the institutional organization of the activity, and new understandings of everything from athleticism and aesthetics to reformulations of gender. They are contingent and dynamic, existing in conversation with our cultural moment. Rules are not fixed, but are evolutionary systems that grow alongside the ongoing construction and performance of play. The long view of this is probably not so contentious—most people can certainly recognize shifts in a favorite sport over the years. Think, for example, about changes to ball handling, permissible equipment, or allowing women to compete in a particular sport. But are rules fixed within any specific gaming moment?

Any formal gaming situation contains some, at least rough, sketch of a rule system. They are a needed component in producing a shared gaming experience. In high-stakes competitions these systems may be more fully articulated, though this is not necessarily so. But rule systems are also always subject to interpretation. Their meaning and their ideal enforcement are contingent on situated and shared understandings. Griggs's reminder about the spirit of the game is instructive here. Communities of practice have nuanced and sophisticated ways of constructing their play that often require insider knowledge to understand the core areas of value, dispute, regulation, or contention. For example, players may shade their use of a rule set given newcomers to a particular match or a change in environment (for instance, if the turf has gotten wet and muddy). Athletes regularly have notions of good sportsmanship that guide conduct and rulings.

Even when formal referees are introduced, we see complex handlings of rules. Only in the most straightforward moments do the formal rules completely guide play. Perhaps one of my favorite considerations of this subject is Bruce Weber's recounting of learning to be a baseball umpire. The complexity of the work sports referees do, and the judgment calls they constantly have to make, is beautifully detailed in his book *As They See 'Em*. As he notes, "Anyone who thinks a strike is a strike is a strike ought to recall that the strike zone is like the fulcrum of a seesaw. It sits at the swivel point of baseball, between pitching and hitting, between offense and defense, and if it isn't precisely situated, the game is thrown out of balance and one side is left up in the air" (Weber 2009, 169).

The very act of *constructing* a strike zone is one of the umpire's most important jobs. The job of the umpire is "not so much to enforce the rulebook as to represent it [...] in truth he's much more of an arbitrator, keeping the most contested area on the ball field from being taken over by one side or the other" (Weber 2009, 172). Weber's discussion of the contentious introduction of various technologies to both take over some of the work of umpiring and validate umpire decisions only highlights the push and pull between human and nonhuman action. His account of learning to be a professional umpire chronicles being socialized into an expertise that can deal with the complex and nuanced handling of rules, ones which require a sophisticated interpretive touch.

In some games interpretability is not a problem to be solved but a core part of the game, a kind of bedeviled pleasure. Soccer or football's offside rule actually relies on a nuanced judgment call about the will and intentionality of the player in question. The factors in judging an instance to be in violation of the rule can be subtle. The power of the rule, even if highly debated, has now been leveraged as a tactic in the form of the "offside trap" in which one team sets up another to force the position and judgment call. Whether it is in the formulation of the strike zone (which is entirely situational based on the specificity of that particular player) or the adjudication of the offside, we see the ways rule systems are not simply always already present, but are situated and contingent systems.

Certainly the longer a sport is formally established, the more organized and officiated play is, and the higher the stakes (often financial) are, the narrower the gap between emergent play and what is anticipated in the rules becomes. Well-established sports move toward ever increasingly stable systems (Loland 2002). But there is no final point of completion in that process. Harry Collins, in his useful discussion of rule systems, expertise, and computation, draws on several examples from traditional sports and notes that, "we found that even in those cases of very well-established sports, with highly codified constitutive rules, played at the highest standard and with the careful planning that befits world class events, the rules were not adequate in themselves to cope with unforeseen circumstances" (1990, 93). He recounts a move made in the 1986 World Cup for which there was no corresponding rule, thus requiring an emergent on-the-spot judgment by the referee in alignment with a call about the spirit of the game.

The history of sports, including professional ones, is littered with moments like this. Chuck Klosterman describes a shift in American football, one now taken for granted, that speaks to the situational and evolutionary nature of actual play—the forward pass.

> Previously, it had been unclear how referees were expected to enforce a penalty for forward passing—there wasn't a rule against passing, much as there isn't any rule against making your slotback invisible. How do you legislate against something no one had previously imagined? When an illegal forward pass was used by Yale against Princeton in 1876, the ref allegedly decided to allow the play to stand after flipping a coin. Action had evolved faster than thought. (2009, 151)

This gap is never completely erased—rules must always be interpreted and enforced by specific communities situated within particular, historically located sets of ethics and concerns. Loland situates a critique of rules formalism in sports, noting that "rule interpretation is a logical necessity" (2002, 6). The shared context for interpretation is key. When people are in disagreement and don't share an underlying interpretive schema things can break down. There may be a formal rule, tucked away on page 137 of some rulebook, but it only becomes embodied and takes force, assuming legitimate authority, when participants collectively recognize it as such.

If we take these notions of the dynamic and interpretative components to heart, we must also conclude that rule systems are never totalizing. They are incomplete systems, made real only through the interpretive work of the participants (at times broadly construed to include formal institutional actors) and never fully developed. Collins writes, for example, of the "new interpretations" that are called upon, "even in highly ritualized, fully consensual, and long regulated sets of activities" (1990, 84). He goes on to point out that this is not a case of a rule system simply being "deficient" as is commonly thought, but that a perfect state of rules is simply unattainable given it would be a "complete description of the past of *every possible future*" (1990, 92, emphasis mine).

Because play takes place in the contingency of human action (and in the case of computer gaming, amid complex technical systems that are themselves actually fairly dynamic actors), rules also never fully sum up in advance the possible or legitimate realm. Often they are incomplete systems because people simply do not know all the rules associated with their activity. The experience of knowing just enough of the rules to start play is all too common, especially for novices. Partial knowledge of rule sets does not impede play and in fact is a very normal condition of it, at least at the nonprofessional levels. For those that do know the full rule set (be it expert players or referees), we still find such players provide valuable interpretive work in applying them or in the confrontation with emergent practices. Expert players "discover" new moves and tactics all the time and these must be reconciled against rule sets. New technologies change what is possible, shifting the way a game unfolds, and this must be evaluated. Durable rule sets are evolutionary; the stability is not in any particular rule, but in the ability of the entire system to adapt and be in conversation with situated human action (Suchman 1987).

These factors—dynamic, interpretable, nontotalizing—pose important challenges, and limits, to the role of computation in gaming. Until computers are able to act as sophisticated *social* machines, ones that can understand situated action and participate in shared ethical schemas, they will never fulfill the idealized scenario in which the computer fully takes over the regulation and operationalization of play. Collins notes the limits on computers saying that, "So long as they are not members of our society, I argue, they cannot imitate our intelligent activities" (1990, 18). The algorithmic nature of computation, and the way encoded rules in computer games align themselves to this modality, highlights the limits of thinking about the computer as the core framer and arbiter of game play. Jesper Juul writes, for example, about the kinds of rules that can be specified by a computer program and notes they are fundamentally algorithmic. He argues, "For something to be an algorithm, it has to be usable without an understanding of the domain. As such, what can qualify as an algorithm—and therefore what can be made a rule in a game—hinges on a decontextualization [...]" (2005, 82). Yet this very decontextualization is exactly that Collins identifies as a limiting feature of computation. Algorithmic rules will only ever provide us with the barest outline of potential, not actualized, play.

This is terrain that must be traveled carefully. My intent here is not to erase the importance of technological actors, including their embodying morals, ethics, and values. Nor is it to underplay the often autonomous agency we confront when nonhuman actors become co-conspirators in our playful experience (see, for example, Taylor 2006b and 2009 for more on this). Technologies matter and this is not a reductionist argument about human agency. As I discuss in a number of places in this book, professional e-sports, and gaming in general, are made of an assemblage in which nonhuman actors figure in key ways. There are certainly ways in which our technologies even participate in the production of culture. But generally speaking they are not dialogic and interpretive actors, whatever productive qualities they may hold. We need to reckon with any subtle layers of situated action and interpretation human actors engage in that computers currently can't.

Collins's broader consideration of artificial intelligence and action is instructive here because he presents us with a way of understanding varying forms of action and unpacking where some confusion comes in with regards to imagination about what computers can do. Rather than leaning primarily on Dreyfus's (1972) valuable intervention into the debate, which suggested embodiment was crucial to understanding intelligence (one which a number of contemporary artificial intelligence researchers have taken to heart), Collins picks up another thread and that is the social context of meaning and action. He and Kusch argue that there are two different kinds of action: polymorphic and mimeomorphic. The shortest version of the difference is that "Mimeomorphic actions are actions that we either seek to or are content to carry out in pretty much the same way, in terms of behavior, on different occasions. Polimorphic [sic] actions are all the rest" (Collins and Kusch 1998, 31). Polymorphic actions are deeply situated in social contexts, and are carried out based on the specificity of given situations.

Despite their being socially situated, polymorphic actions are not devoid of rules. As Collins and Kusch clarify,

> Polymorphic actions are 'rule-bound' in the sense that it is usually clear when they are being done the wrong way. For example, there are wrong ways of doing even so ill-defined a thing as going for a walk. One way to do it wrong in many societies would be to brush against others on the sidewalk. Though polymorphic actions are rule bound, it is not possible to provide a recipe for doing them the right way that could be followed by someone who did not already understand the society in which they are embedded—there are too many context-dependent possibilities. (32)

This is a key point. Far too often when consideration of the social is interjected into the conversation it is seen as some disavowal of rules or norms. This is absolutely not the case. The social is deeply involved in a production of order. But the position Collins so usefully presents for us is that this form of rule-boundedness is not easily distilled. It is only meaningful, interpretable, via a shared cultural understanding. Until computers are able to share our cultural and social mileus, polymorphic action will elude them.

What is particularly helpful in Collins's framework is that he provides us with a way of understanding some of the confusion that arises when we analyze computer game play. While polymorphic action is squarely in the human domain, we nonetheless, along with machines and computers, *also* engage in mimeomorphic action. Indeed, there are likely fair chunks of game playing behavior that we might think of as ludic mimeomorphic action. At other times what looks like mimeomorphic action is, in fact, polymorphic. And indeed sometimes polymorphic actions have within them mimeomorphic actions.

> For instance, swinging a golf club in part realizes the higher action type "playing golf," an action that is not mimeomorphic. Playing golf includes actions such as negotiating with the caddie, estimating distances, judging wind conditions, considering one's opponent's strengths and weaknesses, "gamesmanship," and so forth. All of these are polymorphic actions (though they may each contain components that are mimeomorphic actions). (Collins and Kusch, 51)

The trick is we do not, indeed perhaps cannot if we follow Max Weber's (1949) injunction, know which kind of action it is simply by looking at it. Interpretive schemas are central. Far too often in computer game studies we have not made these distinctions or have simply assumed that since the action looked machinic it fit a computational framework and indeed could perhaps be seamlessly governed by such a system. In fact, the terrain of human and nonhuman action is much more complex. At times nonhuman actors (be they software or not) step in and do admittedly complex work within our play spaces. But humans are also themselves constantly negotiating hybrid systems where technology and culture intersect. At this point, computers simply don't have full access to the cultural realm and as such, are locked out of some aspects of our experience.

Dreams that computation can fully step in, interpret, and regulate play misapprehend the complexity of human action. Players, theorists, analysts, and designers—anyone with an interest in the state of computer game play—must recognize that the humans involved in this domain remain important arbiters in what counts as "good" or "fair" play. Computer gaming is rife with robust discussions about the "spirit of the game" versus the "letter of the law" that we also see in sports. Computation can't solve this because it is a conversation rooted in nuanced sociality. It should also then not be surprising that our larger massively multiplayer or broad network games are riddled with disputes and disagreements about cheating and fair play. Having a shared frame underpinning the gaming moment is key. My argument is not meant to simply reduce things down to a privileged position for humans. Humans that do not share a cultural context or epistemological frame encounter many of the same blockages in carrying out, and understanding, polymorphic action as machines do. And certainly far too often we have overlooked the significant role nonhuman actors play in our gaming, to the detriment of our analysis. Perhaps at some point computers can find a way to share cultural ground with us, or at least debate it to reach common understanding, albeit with sustained disagreement (which is what some humans certainly try). But until they can act as sophisticated cultural actors and interpreters, we have to make sure to pay careful attention to the labor the humans bring to the (computer game) table. To overlook that side of the story is as much a disservice as forgetting the other.

Finally, though game rules make up a special category of rules, we should remember that rules function in complex ways in all aspects of our life. Rule construction and violation are a normal part of human activity well beyond games and part of the work we do as social creatures is constantly create, weigh, assess, accept, and refute various governing structures we encounter. Iszatt-White discusses, for example, rules violations within industrial settings. These were spaces where, given the potential severity of the hazards at hand and thus the elevated stakes, one would think such activity would be quite minimal. Such sites, where much more is often at stake than in mundane everyday play, are particularly interesting to consider in relation to professional e-sports. As she notes, "Where there are rules there will, almost inevitably, be rule violation, and this in turn has implications for management in terms of achieving a balance between rule following and heedfulness" (2007, 452). She found that often workers' "actions appeared to be prompted by constant attention to the environment and risks within which they were working, rather than by a conscious intention to comply with a rule. If asked, they would often describe their behavior as being 'common sense' in the light of the environment in which they worked" (455). Workers were thus always evaluating and refining, based on their situated contexts, their adherence to formal rule structures.

While games perhaps call for much more explicit orientation to artificial rule structures (indeed this is part of their pleasure), we can see even in this example that when faced with rules, people regularly operate within the bounds of situational knowledge and generally understand their activities in relation to specific contents, not simply abstract rules. Iszatt-White also nods to Charles Perrow's theory (1984) of the "normal accident" in which technological systems are not exempt from, and indeed have expected, "unpreventable and inevitable accidents." Dynamic responses by humans are thus always already implicit in such systems. Weaving in conversations about technology's indeterminacy is likely to prove useful in our consideration of computer gaming. The computational systems that make up our digital play are not exempt from the more nuanced understandings of rules or technology we have in other domains. While games certainly ask for us to adopt special conditions vis-à-vis some notion of a "magic circle" we step into, as we know from studies of nondigital gaming this circle is malleable and porous. Overlaid with what we know about rule operation in daily life and about technological indeterminacy, we can clearly see the need for a more nuanced understanding of how ludic systems work in the face of concrete human action.

Pro Tournament Rule Structures

One might think that the negotiations described above are applicable only to a particular subset of play or genre and that the serious domain of pro gaming, where large sums of money, prestige, and even national honor are often at stake, would surely represent a sphere in which the rules of play bear a one-to-one correspondence with formal computer system rules and constraints that are well defined in advance of competition. I argue, however, that rules negotiation is a consistent feature of multiplayer computer gaming, even at the professional level. Part of the work the pro community does is not only try to rhetorically legitimize computer game play as sport, but actually establish structures and procedures to handle the dynamic context of play itself. Such an argument not only problematizes often unspoken assumptions about how computation governs contemporary play, but highlights the need to look at the grounded practice of any given game scenario to fully understand the action taking place there.

In the case of pro gamers, one of the first places rule discussion and formation emerges is in the more casual or local scenes players operate in. Players are regularly socialized into the norms of a game by their friends or via the other players they meet in the game (Taylor 2006a). There are a variety of levels at which this happens. In the competitive e-sports scene it may be the ways players learn informal rules about sportsmanship and behavior (for example, language conventions in the game space or values of fair play) or what maps and settings are used and their importance. Very significantly, players also learn norms and practices about what constitutes cheating, both on a particular server but within the larger e-sports scene.

Formal tournaments operationalize many of these bottom-up community practices. It is important to note just how much is not contained within the game itself and needs to be specified within tournament rules. For example, if we look at the published rules for the World Cyber Games Grand Final we find they actually break things down into several categories: basic player regulation and game-specific rules. Basic player regulation rules cover a number of issues, including:

- Age restrictions (tied to Entertainment Software Rating Board (ESRB) ratings and/or any national requirements)
- ID and passport requirements
- National tournament guidelines regarding team size
- Previous year's grand medal finalists automatically advancing to the following year's national final
- Player substitution guidelines
- Equipment guidelines for players (regarding bringing their own gear)
- Declaration of photographic ownership rights of players by the WCG.

While these rules generally pertain to the tournament structure, the various rules issued for the different games speak to the way actual competitive play is negotiated between the game artifact and a specific situated instance. Most of the rules documents run between five and ten pages and carefully specify many aspects of gameplay. These include:

- Technical specifications of the tournament machines including information about processor speeds and the model of the monitor
- Rankings, tournament structure, tie situations, knockout stages
- Time issues (match duration, delays, etc.) and disconnections
- Map, track, stadium selections
- Game settings (difficulty level, character selection, speed of play, fog of war, etc.)
- Guidelines for if a match is on stage (versus a closed tournament area), which can include things such as clothing restrictions and guidelines, communication with the competitor, discretion of WCG to change monitor settings, audio settings, and the like.

• General prohibitions on activities that jeopardize "fair play" (stating no cheat programs or map hacks allowed, also no intentional disconnections).

While many of these rules are about setting up the conditions for play, quite significantly the actual moderated use of the game software itself forms another crucial part of rules construction in pro play. It is quite typical that a range of actions that are technically possible in the game are actually disallowed in tournament play. For example, some of the tournament rules for specific games from the World Cyber Games 2009 include:

Starcraft

• Flying Drone: A Zerg user uses a drone bug to make it fly around right after the match starts. (Zerg's drone is a ground unit and should not be able to fly around. This breaks the game balance, so it is not allowed.)

• Terran Building Crushing: Destroying or making ineffective interceptors, cocoons, air units, dark swarms, antimatter disruption web, etc. using Terran building's ability to float and land.

• Lurker Burrow Bug: Intentionally burrowing a hydra that is changing into a lurker under a building.

• Zerg Unit Grouping Bug: Making multiple units look like lesser number of units using Zerg's burrow.

Counter-Strike

• Binding Duck to scroll wheel is NOT permitted.

• When defusing, the player must be able to see a part of the bomb.

• Silent C4 installation is considered illegal. This offense may result in a warning or loss of all remaining TR rounds at the sole discretion of the board of referees.

• Use of map bugs in play (e.g., map swimming, auto aim, etc.) is NOT permitted.

• Use of unfair but available scripts (e.g., silentrun, attack+use, centerview script, norecoil script, etc.)

FIFA

• The players must kick off with a backward pass at the beginning of each half and after every goal is scored.

• The players are not allowed to shoot the ball directly onto the crossbar from a corner kick in order to get a chance for a header when the ball rebounds.

• It is not allowed to score a goal from one's own half of the field.

• It is forbidden to make a throw-in directly into the opponent's penalty area. Should a player throw the ball directly into the opponent's penalty area he shall be warned. Should he persist, he shall be disqualified from the tournament. Any goals resulting from a throw-in into the opponent's penalty area will not be counted.

• There is a bug in FIFA 09 where the ball sometimes enters the goal from the top of the crossbar or from the top or side of the net, and FIFA 09 (PC) considers it a goal. Should such bug occur during a match, the player should take note and, at the end of the match, call a referee to confirm the bug with the use of the in- game replay. Should this bug be confirmed, it will be removed from the final score.
• "Long balls" (Q+A, Q+W, etc...) are allowed in specific cases. To understand when a long ball is allowed or not, have a look at the following image:

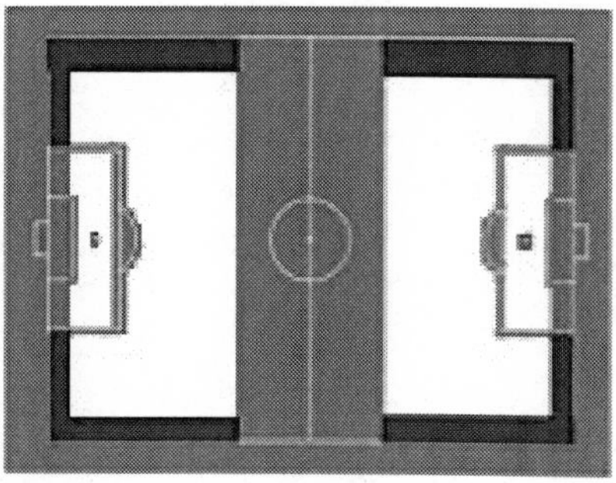

Figure 2.5
FIFA boundary image.
Image from World Cyber Games.

Long balls are allowed when done from inside the green area or when you are in your own half of the field. Long balls are forbidden when taken from one's yellow/blue area and are directed into the opponent's yellow/blue area. The image above is for explanatory purposes only. In order to allow the referees to make the appropriate call, a patch will be used to detect forbidden long balls. (World Cyber Games 2009 Rules)

This kind of detail is not unique to the WCG. Most long-standing tournaments and leagues have developed fairly robust additional rulesets and guidelines well beyond anything that comes via the software itself. As we can see by this selection, there is a wide range of behavior and interaction with the computer game that gets regulated completely outside the software itself. You may also begin to sense from reading just these few examples that in pro competitions there is also a referee who will be making judgments about players' performance and adherence to game rules. Sprinkled throughout the rules are mentions of intentionality, specific conditions of enforcement, or discretion by the on-site referee. The actual conditions of competition at the professional level with respect to rules are thus a complex mix of bottom-up community-driven norms that become formalized rules, combined with a tournament's own variety of rules, folded into the discretionary action of on-site referees (who often confer with each other and the players, and use playback options). It is a far throw from computational devices plopped down into a tournament and smoothly adjudicating play.

Tournament rules thus hold a dual position whereby they are both emergent processes in dialog with the specificity of the given event, but also are always reflecting (and in turn constructing) local and grassroots conventions. A number of local conventions have been adopted by tournaments. For example, the community has put in a lot of time weeding through various maps or configurations and has through experience often honed in on the best for competitive play. But even with years and years of revision and polish for some games, breaks and gaps still occur in the webbing of rules and these can be particularly instructive.

Two Stories from Seattle

I must admit, I was not initially attuned to this aspect of gaming in the pro scene. I unreflectively assumed that surely at the pro level I would not see the kinds of ongoing and complex negotiations around the rules of play that I had witnessed not only in various tabletop gaming sessions, but also within the domain of my research into massively multiplayer online games. I knew of squabbles at local LANs or various skirmishes that occur online when people play, but my fieldwork at World Cyber Games Grand Final in Seattle in 2007 brought fresh light to this issue for me.

A large portion of my time at that year's event was spent inside a part of the tournament area that had limited access for other spectators. It is quite typical at the WCG that most of the matches are actually held in spaces that attendees can't access (something I discuss in more detail in chapter 5). Those who are allowed in—typically other players, team managers/coaches, press, sponsors—still generally have to remain behind some kind of barricade to prevent any interference with the players. I was fortunate enough that several of the referees I had met previously consented to let me into the *Starcraft* and *Warcraft* tournament area where I sat, stood, and watched games for hours a day, often chatting to the refs as the events progressed.

During one of the key *Starcraft* matches I began to hear murmurs that something was amiss. In the middle of a tiebreaker round between players Song "Stork" Byung Goo and Vakhtang "Ex" Zakiev, Stork was spotted using a move that was illegal in the WCG Grand Finals, the "observer bug."

In this move one player's observer unit is placed directly above an opponent's turret while it is being built. When the turret is complete, the bug prevents it from attacking the observer unit hovering over it, thus allowing one player the benefit of being able to view what is happening in their competitor's portion of the map. In a game where opponents operate with incomplete information about the other player's actions ("fog of war") and have to do battle across a large map and among a myriad of factors, knowledge of an opponent's development and strategic deployment of units, including continued access to an otherwise hidden game state, can provide an invaluable advantage.

Interestingly, however, none of the official referees spotted this happening. It was actually Nick Plott (also known as "Tasteless," a former high-end player himself and very well-known American *Starcraft* commentator who works in South Korea) who, sitting among a group of spectators that included other players, journalists, sponsors, and managers, spotted the move and notified the refs.

Simultaneous to the onlookers' growing awareness of what had happened, however, iP.Ex surrendered and signed off on the official form

Figure 2.6
Real-time strategy games match area, WCG 2007.

saying Stork won. The ensuing rules discussion highlighted the contingent nature of computer game play, even at the professional level. On the formal level of officiating the referees were conferring over the replay, analyzing what had happened and discussing among themselves both a verification of offense and a decision about how to handle it. They were also juggling a number of rules at work that ranged from iP.Ex signing off on the match to the bug use itself.

The rules discussion, however, was not simply taking place confidentially between the referees, but was actually being debated among all present, including the players themselves. The tournament area quickly became a hub of activity with reporters, fellow teammates, players, and other interested parties turning to one another to discuss the issue. As word began to circulate outside the area more people showed up. As Lucas Bigham notes in his *Got Frag* article on the event, "A few moments later, several members of the South Korea media caught word of what had happened. With cameras in-hand and close to a dozen people trying to get Stork's attention, the tournament area for *Starcraft* had turned into a mad house. Stork was asked to sit down with a reporter to answer several questions while at the same time the referees were still trying to decide what to do" (Bigham 2007).

Various stakeholders sought the ear of the refs to try and persuade as to the most appropriate course of action. At the same time the players themselves made their case, to each other and to the referees directly. Some weighed in saying that no matter what had happened, iP.Ex had signed the form that Stork won and so the rule applying to the finalizing of a game applied first and foremost. Others suggested that Stork's use of the observer turret bug constituted a clear violation of the WCG Grand Final rules and, as such, warranted either his total elimination from the tournament or at the minimum a replay of the match. Still others tried to interject that in Stork's home country of South Korea the observer turret bug is actually allowed in some tournaments so he could not really be blamed for continuing the practice in this venue. This argument is not entirely watertight as the ban on the move is actually upheld in some South Korean tournaments and not others. It is additionally complicated by the fact that that frequently national playoffs for the WCG Grand Final may themselves use some locally based rules. It is thus possible that someone might compete under one rule set to qualify for the Grand Final, but another to play in it. Given the range of potential rule situations any given player might encounter, it is no surprise that community members had ample room for debate.

Figure 2.7
Turret bug debate.

After much discussion and negotiation a replay was decided on by the referees, citing the rule that said the offending player should be given a loss and/or a warning. The head referee, Armin Sayedi, was quoted as saying, "This is really a sensitive situation because of the tiebreaker. The rules say to give him a loss and a warning. My opinion is that it did not affect the game that much. I would not offer a loss to Stork. Ex wanted the decision to be fair to him and this was the fairest option for both players" (Bigham 2007). Stork subsequently re-won the match and advanced in the tournament.[12]

While the tumultuous scene became a widely discussed event at the tournament, other games were not immune to their own set of rules struggles. Two other notable incidents occurred during this Grand Final competition, both involving prohibited moves and accusations of their use. The first incident involved a match between the Swedish national winners, a team called Fnatic, and the South Korean eSTRO team. In the midst of excitement over eSTRO's surprising upset against Fnatic (culminating in their elimination from the tournament), murmurs began to circulate that eSTRO had been using the prohibited "duckjump" move.

The duckjump move (also known as silent running, double duck, or Begrip movement) allows a player to move at a running speed in a way that also masks the sound by repeatedly hitting the crouch key. Audio can be a crucial signal in helping players gain tactical advantage—this is no minor bug. It also has the effect of altering hitboxes, thereby making some shots unexpectedly difficult (St-Jacques-Gagnon 2008). Though Fnatic's manager Sam Mathews eventually spoke to the referees about the issue, rather than any full review of the replays it was decided that since Fnatic had signed off on the loss (much like in the *Starcraft* incident I previously recounted), the issue was closed and their elimination stood (Vikan 2007).

While this incident was wrapped up fairly quickly, a second one also involving *Counter-Strike* went on much longer. While attending the Meet Your Makers (MYM) versus eSTRO match I began to see referees conferring and an increasing number of spectators milling around and murmuring. Watching pro matches in this kind of environment can be quite difficult, where you are unable to see all the screens and generally lack any meta view of the game or have any commentary feed. So it was only by asking people I was standing next to what was happening that I began to hear that eSTRO was contesting MYM's win, saying MYM had been engaging in the duckjump move. The irony that the same team that had previously been accused of this move was now accusing another winning team of it was not lost on many. Despite *CS* matches at this level often having several referees positioned behind each team to watch for such violations, no definitive judgment could initially be rendered.

What ensued then was several hours of the referees and various stakeholders reviewing replays, debating with each other what actually happened, and discussing what could be done. As the time dragged on people became increasingly frustrated. Team members, managers, and even press weighed in with their opinions. If the ear of a referee could be caught to make their case, it was. Jonas Alsaker Vikan recounted the incident,

> The administrators standing behind the teams were consistently unable to identify the duck-jump incidents as they happened. The teams that lost though were hot off the trails of other complaints and filed their own. Hours of demo scrutinizing followed and flip-flopped decision-making turned the tournament into a parody that will live on in infamy. And the pressure took its toll on them too, as the fatigue set in the decisions became more irate. (2007)

Figure 2.8
Typical *Counter-Strike* match set-up (though with makeshift wall to block competitors seeing each other's screens).

Figure 2.9
CS rules discussion.

What happened next is one of the more unclear, and contentious, parts of the incident. Most accounts (and rumors) suggest that it was decided that MYM would keep the win and advance but that decision was altered forcing a new one map play-off.[13] This final deciding round concluded with eSTRO winning, thus sending shockwaves through the crowd.

Not only had the indeterminacy of the rules violation caused tumult, but the inability of the referees to decide the issue expediently and convey those decisions clearly to everyone, including spectators, raised serious flags for many at the match. Whether or not it was true, the perceived intervention by nonreferees into what was essentially a rules and procedure issue was deeply corrosive to the endeavor as a serious sporting event. In many ways the incident highlighted not only anxiety about rules in pro play, but the underlying relationship between these events as competitive sports and as consumer entertainment marketing venues.

The sense that rules and their implementation were up for debate with some frequency and straddled the line between predetermined and emergent proved to be a regular topic of conversation throughout the tournament. Even the spaces where the matches took place seemed to materially reflect the contingent nature of play.

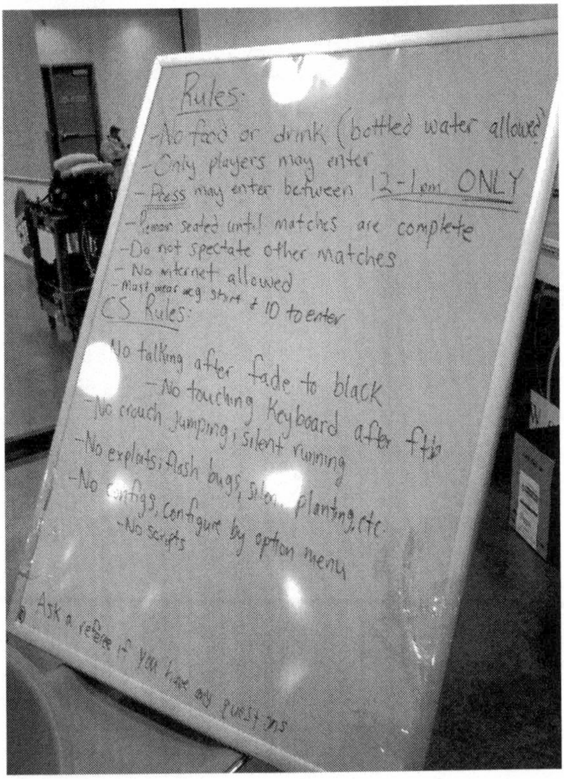

Figure 2.10
Whiteboard eventually put outside tournament entrance.

This whiteboard appeared a day into the tournament and for me is a great example of how rules get handled over time in real scenarios. Given what had been happening in the tournament someone felt compelled to distill some key points to better govern the space. The rules notated on the board occupy a range of domains and address different levels of play. On the one hand the makeshift sign notes practical details like the prohibition of food and drink and who is allowed in the space. But we can also see a second section for *Counter-Strike* only that includes a mix of obvious admonitions (such as "no exploits") to the contested silent running prohibition. Both sections are interesting because they reflect not only a reassertion of rules known and agreed upon in advance, but also try to address emergent issues that were presenting themselves at the event. As became very apparent to me during the course of this tournament, the nature of rules and their enforcement in computer game play, even at the professional level, was not nearly as "given" as it may seem. They were regularly haggled over, people struggled to verify if and when they had been broken, and certain ones rose to the top to be reemphasized. It was not nearly as tidy a picture as one might expect.

Post-Seattle Discussions and Aftermath

These two events—the *Starcraft* match and the *CS* tournament—were often framed in the pro gaming media as aberrations and simple cases of bad refereeing that needed to be protected against in the future. A number of stories were written about the WCG that year with titles such as "World Cyber Games 2007 International Disgrace at the Grand Final" (Ali 2007) and "Counter-Strike: World Scandal Games" (Vikan 2007). Causes for the problems were located in everything from basic flaws in the tournament rules to, in the case of *Counter-Strike*, a long-time valuable head adminstrator, Laurent Genin-Satoh, not being present to oversee the tournament and the event being much worse off for the loss of his expertise (Vikan 2007).

One the one hand part of this postmortem analysis helps us understand the powerful role human actors still play in pro gaming. Referees are valuable parts of the competitive scene and the breakdowns in Seattle highlighted for many how essential skilled refereeing is to facilitating play. On the other hand, I also want to pull back a bit from sole causality stemming from the absence of one or two people. While I am sympathetic to wanting to locate the blame for these incidents in a singular reason like the loss of skilled and knowledgeable refereeing leadership, as I review my event fieldnotes for other tournaments (both before and after this one) I cannot help but notice that rules discussions, often handled via on-the-spot arbitration, are not uncommon in the pro scene. Perhaps one of the most common reasons for this is that technologies will glitch out and immediate decisions have to get made about how to proceed. I've seen monitors go black and then pop back on in the middle of matches. Games crash in finals where one team loses valuable assets they have accumulated in earlier rounds. Cameramen bump into players as they edge around for a shot. Players make a disputed move (or, more often then not, appear to) and referees step in to review footage or hear arguments. While the Seattle tournament was extreme for the way it distilled many examples of rule-boundary work in one weekend, these ongoing negotiations are simply part and parcel of professional play.

What was also quite interesting is that the on-the-spot tournament debates were later expanded into larger community ones. Forums and comment threads offered places for vigorous (and often vitriolic) discussion of what happened at the event and who was at fault. For many it was not a simple matter of bad refereeing. While a fair number of the remarks stayed at the level of name-calling or simply dismissing teams, other comments tapped into the deeper issues at stake concerning the state of rules in the game and standards of professionalism. For example, one commenter (using the name Khonsu) touched on a few games, writing,

> StarCraft: Those guys were just playing the game the best way they knew how. The illegal exploit I don't agree with it being illegal at all. I fail to see how the mechanic breaks the game. All it does is add depth. As far as bracket abuse, this is all a part of the game. Like it or not Stork was playing the game which best guaranteed himself, and his team success. If we don't want to endorse these kinds of actions then a different tournament structure must be considered. Counter-Strike: This is why I had [sic] the game and community so much. Banning something like crouch jumping which again is a mechanic built into the game, which does not break the game, is childish. Furthermore supporting a game that is broken from mechanics like boosted bomb planets [sic], phantom bomb plants, Flashbang Bugs, 16bit Smoke, Wall Clipping, etc...is retarded. With all the problems the game has, it is obviously not suitable for tournament play. Possibly CSProMod will change my opinion on that however CS1.6 and CSS are NOT [sic] tournament worthy games. (Ali 2007)

A later respondent, Kennigit-TL, followed up on the *Starcraft* issue:

> The Turret bug is banned in every major Korean league. WCG is originally (and will is) a Korean event and it has always been banned. The issue lies in the fact that the official rules look for an intentional exploit of the bug. When Stork then said that he had no idea about the bug, no one wanted to step on any toes—Samsung, inter-

national sponsor of WCG is also his team's sponser [sic] (Samsung Khan). Obviously he would have taken the match either way but it's still very fishy.

@Khonsu, I have to agree with you [sic] points on starcraft. The foreign players admitted to fiddling a bit with their performances to force 2 koreans into a match up. While I agree with you on the glitching as a gameplay mechanic (it is accepted in open arms with pushing through mineral walls(the fact remains that if it had a [sic] been a foreign player who had done to T/O bug he would have been disqualified instantly. (Ali 2007)

Within player communities there is regularly discussion about the relationship between the system and forms of legitimate action within the game. Very rarely is the software-as-given the end point of any argument. Questions of deep play, context and continuity, and overall balance within tournament settings get brought into the mix. Experienced competitors will often identify systemic problems they see as preventing a more idealized form of play for a particular title. The code is considered insufficient (or perhaps outdated) for the fullest realization of the game's play.

For others the issues of honor and sportsmanship were key. It is not unusual to hear this idea linked to a broader notion about what constitutes fair play and what can be expected of competitors. There is often an argument that standards must be upheld either to legitimize e-sports more generally or to maintain a healthy gaming environment. Two commentators (using the names Handicapable and Forresthu) weighed in on this angle, writing,

"Throwing matches" in ANY form of competition, any game, any sport, is shameful. Lifetime bans are handed out for this in physical sports. E-Sports are a special exception because you don't like the way the brackets are set up? No thanks. (Ali 2007)

They should have given stork defloss even though he had the game won with or without the bug. It is just unprofessional behavior to use bugs intentially [sic] and a defloss would have sent the right message to wcg player not to abuse bugs. (Bigham 2007)

This concern with digital gaming sportsmanship echoes findings by Moeller, Esplin, and Conway (2009) in their research about online sports game play. They found that player communities had developed robust ways of identifying behavior ("cheesers, pullers, and glitchers") whose sportsmanship was debated. Such discussions highlight the ways game communities evaluate play, taking into account system affordances, but rarely stopping there.

While the power of any single experienced referee can certainly smooth over a bump or two, WCG's 2007 Grand Final brings into the spotlight regular issues around rules and the possibilities for implementing them in any formal way. Indeed, the WCG itself and a number of other tournaments have addressed these bugs directly. In a particularly interesting example of engaging the community, Thierry "Tee" St-Jacques-Gagnon, the WCG's Grand Final Chief Referee for *CS* 1.6, made a public post in which he reflected on whether or not duckjumping should be allowed in future competitions. He noted the history of why it was disallowed in the first place (it was seen as an unfair advantage along the lines of other exploits) but also admitted that the WCG was taking heed of many players' opinions that it was a legitimate form of play. He also noted that, indeed, the move was not banned in a number of other leagues. He then proposed three options the WCG could take going forward: keep the old rule but fix the dispute mechanism, get rid of the rule and allow the use of the move, or finally have the WCG create its own mod for the tournament that would allow a form of the move (fast but not silent) and also fix other bugs (St-Jacques-Gagnon 2008). He asked readers to give him direct feedback. Within a month the WCG announced that they were altering their rules for the 2008 tournament and the duckjump would be allowed, though with the provision that it could not be bound via mouse or keyboard. And the 2009 GosuCup (sponsored by the *SC* Web site *GosuGamers*) made the decision to allow the use of the observer/turret bug in matches (Olsen 2009).

These discussions surrounding the Seattle WCG were not unique to that event but indeed are part of larger ongoing conversations about rules in various games. Forums and editorial articles regularly review rule sets for upcoming tournaments or discuss how a particular game is posing challenges or needs some tweaking in how competition rules are handled. The community itself weighs system rules, constraints, and possibilities against what it sees as necessary for optimal competitive play. It rarely accepts systems as given, instead situating them in complex and dynamic ways to sustain the form of play they want and value.

Monitoring and Managing Competition

Given that computation does not hold the singular power to adjudicate pro matches, it is worth spending a few moments talking about how regulation happens at tournaments. I've thus far discussed how rules get developed and amended, debated, in a competition setting. But there are additional components involving the on-the-spot management of actual tournament competition: players themselves, referees, and administrators.

Players and Self-/Community Regulation

After the Seattle event I began to use that incident to query players about how they experienced things like rule enforcement or notions of cheating. Was what I saw an anomaly in their minds? Their answers often surprised me and I still wrestle with how to situate their impressions of how a tournament unfolds with my own. My experience of watching tournaments is to see frequent moments of small breakdown and repair—game crashes, computer and monitor troubles, and at times un-uniform conditions of gameplay. As I spoke with players it was not that they did not also recognize these, but seemed to situate them as simply part and parcel of play, nuisances that had to be tolerated. The glitches and hiccups of a tournament were just life in e-sports. But they also suggested that a fair amount of community governing is happening in tournaments during these moments and that major issues would be caught by the players themselves.

I have found this sentiment particularly strong in the *Counter-Strike* community, where a very old game is played by a fairly small group of people who, at the most elite levels, all know each other pretty well. When players sit down to prep for a match they configure their settings to accommodate their preferences. Some things people are allowed to tweak (like mouse sensitivity) and other things not (binding certain actions to a key). One player remarked that some tournaments will formally oversee this process but others won't, leaving it to a kind of honor code. As he put it, this was not a problem since "the community's gotten so close now, everyone trusts each other" and that it is a handful of the same teams playing so "no one's going to expect the top team to cheat." He clarified though that this wasn't always the case.

> I remember people at tournaments used to, players from the other team would walk over and be like, 'Can I check your video settings?' and make us all like open it up and then we'd go and check theirs. So it was like mutual, you know? But I haven't done that in a long time. It's just, you're newer to everything, you're all paranoid. Like now, I know everyone here. At these tournaments, they're competitors and honest people and they're good at what they do and I trust them, you know. I feel like I don't need to go check. I feel like it's rude actually, if I went to go and be like, 'Can I check your settings?' I'd really feel like that's pretty rude.

A teammate of his also spoke about how at mid-sized and small tournaments you had much more player regulation taking place. For example, in describing how teams negotiate map choices (via a system of vetos and agreement) he said, "We have the ref there, doing that the first time and after that we just like, kind of figured, okay, why would we ask him to come, we can just do it ourselves. [...] if there's a dispute obviously it's going to come down to them but you don't really need them because there's rarely ever any problems." This surprised me given what I'd seen over the years at tournaments. Indeed the day after my interview with this player I saw his machine not launch the game properly at the start of a match. He several times unsuccessfully tried to get the attention of an admin for assistance, only to have it finally sort itself out and allow him to continue play. This kind of glitch is not unusual to see in tournaments.

Thinking about the gap between my view of things and his is instructive, though. His formulation of what counts as a "problem" speaks to the expected imperfect conditions of play competitors have gotten used to. It suggests a more normalized version of contingency, and an expected adaptability on the part of those involved.

There are those problems and glitches that people smooth out or deal with on the spot, and then there are the sorts that bring the entire tournament to a halt. The first sort are so normal that they are nearly invisible to the players themselves. Systemic issues of fair game administration and how players step in to manage their own tournament competition become an important factor in understanding how professional play is currently constituted. Perhaps because of the kind of expected, indeed normal, irregularity you find in competitions, self-regulation, particularly at the highest end, is not unusual. To have formal methods to manage it is simply not, at this point, scalable. In the case of the player I mentioned whose machine was acting up, you would have to add another layer of oversight and management to handle such things: row admins (a person watching over each seating area), more referees, team coaches (who aren't players) to signal for help, or technology monitoring the virtual playing field. For many e-sports tournaments this kind of infrastructure support is simply not possible so self-regulation remains an important component of the professional scene.

Referees and Admins

The kind of player regulation one sees at some of the mid-sized and smaller tournaments is often contrasted to the more formalized management of play at large competitions, with an official ref who runs through a set checklist. Beyond the work the community itself does to regulate matches, there are several formal roles that have developed over the years to attend to rules and the smooth operation of gameplay at tournaments. There are a couple terms used for the people who manage a tournament's matches—referee and admin. The language is a bit unclear at times. In larger tournaments you will sometimes see a distinction between the two, with admins taking care of the technical infrastructure of the event (software, servers, etc.) and referees solely dedicated to handling rule enforcement, disputes, or judgment calls. In smaller venues you will very often see one person or set of people handling all of these duties. The distinction isn't always entirely clear. "Admin" is the more common term used in the community and "referee" is something slowly being adopted, in part because it carries important symbolic weight (not unlike the black and white striped shirts you sometimes see them donning at high-profile events).

Either way, refs and admins do important work in tournament events (or online matches) in helping manage competitive play. In my experience people who are familiar with the challenges of running tournaments know how invaluable these people are. They typically act in several domains: validating the "field" of play (making sure machines are configured according to tournament requirements), adjudicating potential cheating violations, and handling unexpected or ambiguous game situations (software and hardware glitches, unclear player actions, interference, and the like.).

Field validation is a key issue and ongoing challenge in e-sports. Tournaments will have specified settings that the machine and the game software must run for official play. As previously mentioned, some parameters may be customized by the players but there will be other variables that are fixed for the purposes of the match. Referees and admins are responsible for ensuring the equitability of the playing field that is constructed via the game's software and hardware. Beyond simply making sure the game is set up and operating as required is a concern for cheating. This can occur via a couple methods: software modification/hacks and illegal player actions.

As you can imagine, given the number of parameters that could be adjusted, not to mention the hackability of software, concern for the integrity of the game is always important. While technical anticheat software is often in operation during matches (particularly online ones), it regularly still falls to a human to make a judgment call. As a community manager for one of the largest and most successful leagues put it when discussing the necessity of actual people making the call, "You will never have a 100% anticheating tool. You always will have cheats that will not be detected by the tool. So that's the reason why we still have the anti-cheating team which control it by their experience and with their tools, because no tool is 100% perfect." This league has their own software they use to help manage play but even they recognize the limitations of a solely technical solution. As his colleague further clarified, "It's impossible to find every cheat because it's a competition for itself. We are making our anti-cheat [and] they are programming their anti-anticheat." The skill involved in sussing out cheating is actually fairly nuanced and relies not only on technical tools, but being aware of what new tricks and hacks may be springing up in the community, having a sense of who the players are (including knowing who to keep an eye on), and the kind of deep contextual knowledge of the game and play actions that are only built over time.

Beyond technical cheating methods are cases where players are engaging in illegal actions and moves. These require a very sharp eye to pick up on and, especially in the case of team games, covering that massive field of play (ten viewpoints for a single *Counter-Strike* match, for example) can be enormously challenging. Referees rely quite a bit on an adversarial model of governance whereby players or other stakeholders will police each other and each other's teams for violations. These are then taken up by refereeing staff and reviewed, typically by watching replays and talking to the involved parties.

Much like in traditional sports the basic call of a violation or acknowledgment of some problem in play is only the first step in handling the situation. The ref or admin must make nuanced decisions about how to proceed. While competitive matches typically have very detailed rule sets, the penalties for violations still generally leave a range of discretionary latitude to the referee including everything from calling for a rematch to declaring a winner or kicking someone out of the tournament. As one admin put it, "Of course you can use your rule book and can make your decisions with the rules. But of course it's a lot of touch and instinct. So it depends on each case. We try to talk to the users and it's like in soccer, maybe you see something, maybe you see something not, maybe you can solve it without any card."

As was argued by a number of people after the Seattle WCG, this "touch and instinct" is not something everyone has and putting on a referee shirt is not enough. I want to linger on this point a bit because I think it speaks to the level of professionalization referees and admins are themselves having to undergo as e-sports develops. This job is still also very much in a hybrid space where sometimes the people acting as refs and admins are as much fans as anything, with the newest ones sometimes even a bit starstruck to be near famous top players. They are typically drawn from the community itself, often players who were unable to progress up the ladder to the most elite matches. Unlike in, for example, baseball, where two official schools handle all the training for aspiring umpires (via a pretty rigorous program), pro e-sports refs are a self-trained and self-governed group, often standing betwixt and between player-fan and referee identity.

While the role is very much in-progress as an emerging profession, the work administrators and referees do within e-sports has been important to the scene being able to sustain high-end tournaments. As pro gaming grows they help mediate a transition where community and self-governance may not always be enough. They also provide crucial setup and interpretive work, filling in gaps between computation and actual play.

Gambling and Money Games

Despite the regulatory work happening in e-sports, notable significant breakdowns have occurred. In April 2010 stories emerged that several South Korean players were suspected of throwing *Starcraft* games. Though outlets like the BBC picked up on the news, it was in major e-sports hubs such as Team Liquid that the story unfolded over several months. As South Korean press releases, articles, and forum posts were translated, the tale was pieced together across community sites. Rumors and speculation were rampant for several months with e-sports journalists and fans alike trying to make sense of what was happening. When the smoke finally cleared eleven players, including the immensely popular Jae Yoon "sAviOr" Ma, were indicted for colluding with private illegal gambling outlets (throwing matches, leaking information, and acting as middlemen between the gambling organizations and other players) (Hyun-cheol 2010). The amounts they received for their cheating—between 2 million and 6.5 million won ($1,700-$5,700 USD)—are relatively small given the massive risk to both their own reputations and the stability of what is essentially a national pastime (Si-soo 2010). All were permanently banned, via the regulating arm of KeSPA, from ever participating in the professional circuit again (MrHoon 2010).

The image frequently evoked was that e-sports now had its equivalent to the 1919 Black Sox scandal in which Chicago White Sox players intentionally lost games for money during the World Series. For some this equation was a kind of perverse sign of legitimacy: e-sports had arrived. For others, especially avid fans of the *Starcraft* pro scene with its strong roots in South Korea, it was simply a devastating scandal and loss of confidence in their favorite players. Personally I've been surprised it has taken this long for such an incident to happen (or at least come to light). The lack of widespread systemic regulation and the growing stakes lend themselves too easily to abuse in e-sports. Combined with some cultural affinity in the scene to betting and gambling (be it poker or "money games") the terrain was ripe for abuse.

Perhaps one of the most integrated e-sports gambling traditions resides in the fighting game scene where "money games" are an important subsidy for players. Given that fighting games are only recently emerging into professionalization in a way that secures sponsorship and team funding, informal betting on matches at tournaments can provide players a way to defray the costs of participation and, if they are lucky, earn a little extra money on the side.

The formalization of gambling in e-sports is still fairly undeveloped. While many countries heavily regulate gambling (including within traditional sports), the Internet has made enforcement of such prohibitions tricky. Online bookies have sprung up everywhere. Few have integrated betting on e-sports matches though one, XLBet.com, has been letting people place money on *Counter-Strike, Warcraft,* and *Starcraft* matches for several years now. While it's not clear to me how many e-sports fans actually use this kind of site (I suspect only a select few who have the disposable income), there is a nascent culture of gambling within e-sports.

Growing Pains?

One of the questions that lies at the heart of the discussion about the development of computer games as sport, and the contingency and indeterminacy that we find in the scene, is whether or not what we are witnessing is simply the growing pains of a new sport coming into its own. This line of argument would suggest that all of these debates, discussions, and messy scenarios are just what happens when a new phenomenon emerges until norms and practices get settled. It would posit that there is some end point at which things get finalized and such negotiations and critical issues drop off. While it is certainly true that over time communities (be they players, refs, admins, sponsors, managers, or the complex combination of those) form powerful norms and practices (everything from communication conventions between participants in a tournament like "gg" for good game to standard maps used in most tournament play), to imagine there is a moment in which rules and their negotiation is complete is mistaken.

My intent here is not to suggest that the pro gaming world is completely underdetermined when it comes to rules and norms within tournament play. There is broad consensus on many aspects of how a game is handled at the highest levels, especially for titles like *Counter-Strike* that have been around for more than a decade. There are strong social norms and practices that have developed over the years. In many ways the written-out tournament rules that are produced for matches actually reflect the hard work of the community over time to iron out the bugs in using these games for highly competitive play. What I do want to highlight though is that rules formation in computer gaming is an ongoing process and occurs in dialog with emerging technologies *and* techniques. As machines, screens, and even mice change, the actual performance of play adjusts. Often this adjustment involves players finding new ways to perform, new tactics and approaches, even to games they've been playing for years. All these adjustments require rules, which are also a component of play, to shift accordingly. While the Seattle examples are extreme cases, they help highlight the degree of social labor that goes into negotiating computer game play at the professional level.

Within tournaments and even in more casual practice, there is a fair amount of rules negotiation—discussion, and debate over the scope and extent of rules, haggling, appeals to noncomputational referees, and indeed the general practices we see take place in analog games and sports. Rule construction and negotiation regularly takes place across time (including into the gaming session) and involves a number of actors (including nonhuman agents). This matrix includes the periods during:

- practice time and noncompetition play
- regional qualifiers
- finals
- postgame analysis

and among:

- the originating game software and its actual users (be they the players or other stakeholders)
- players and teams as they engage in practice competitions with each other

• tournament and competition organizers/stakeholders (including sponsors or funders) and players/referees/other participants both in advance of matches and at times during an event
• cross-tournament "conversations"
• referees and players at the actual moment of play in a tournament
• technological actors such as software mods made for specific competitions
• competing technological actors such as the game software and broadcast media.

By unpacking the construction and negotiation of rules not only across a period of time but among a number of actors, we can begin to complicate the notion that computation serves as a totalizing agent—a penultimate game master, if you will, in computer game play. The professional gaming scene offers a particularly useful field site for this investigation given assumptions about how rule sets might work in high-level (moneyed) competitive play. Ultimately what we find is a mix of technologies, emergent norms and practices, interpretive judgments, and much debate and refinement of rules governing computer game play. The complexity of action, rules, structure, and competition that we see in traditional sports is certainly echoed in this digital domain.

3 Professionalizing Players

Periodically the mainstream media's eye will turn to e-sports and crank out an article that leaves its readers either scratching their heads in bemusement or daydreaming about becoming the one who is profiled. For example, an *ESPN.com* article about a Major League Gaming (MLG) match opened this way:

> Victory smells like Red Bull. Maybe it's body spray. The hall is alive with the sound of small arms fire: popping pistols, thumping shotguns, staccato assault rifles. The crack 'n' whistle of sniper rounds; the sudden, terrible boom of exploding frag grenades. There are breathless *ooohs!* and frustrated groans and the urgent irritating bleeps of depleting deflector shields, squawking reminders that you are absolutely, positively about to die, or worse yet, get *pwned*—that is, blasted and humiliated by some 14-year-old kid wearing a Pokemon Breeders T-shirt. (Hruby 2007)

The *New York Times* has done their share of similar articles over the years, such as their piece on a nine-year-old *Halo* player named Victor M. De Leon III, also known as Lil' Poison (Lambert 2007).[1] And perhaps the ultimate feature on a pro player has been the *60 Minutes* 2006 television show segment exploring the life of certainly one of the most well-known players out there, Johnathan "Fatal1ty" Wendel.[2]

In most of these popular press pieces we can find similar fascinations and highlights. The age of the player is frequently a kickoff point, the piece marveling at young people engaged in serious endeavors. But this seriousness is also positioned against videogames, which are still typically seen as entertainment and perhaps even a bit frivolous. Add to the story face-to-face competitions with actual prize money and you tend to get a tale about a cultural oddity in the making. Outside the e-sports world these stories are simply one of many offerings a reader finds on any given day, novelties to talk about that week. But within e-sports these stories can circulate as legitimizing and aspirational tales, signs that professional gaming is reaching the mainstream.

As I mentioned at the beginning of this book, though I've since gone on to look at institutional and structural issues around e-sports, my own interest in pro gaming also started with players. They are a natural entry to the story because they personalize the activity, providing us with an embodied picture of high-end competitive play. They offer a familiar narrative for the entire endeavor. Without a doubt they are important to understanding e-sports not only for the specialized nature of their play but also for the ways they are more generally transforming leisure. Intensely serious competition, and the people who perform it, is captivating.

Much like the power gamers I've previously written about, pro gamers help us understand not only instrumental and focused play, but illuminate broader assumptions about computer games and the limits those assumptions sometimes have (Taylor 2006a). As with power gamers, pro gamers do not simply appear out of thin air but are created not only through their individualized efforts but through a broader social process. The possibilities and realization for professionalization include everything from being socialized into highly instrumental play by their peers to institutional influences, economics, relationships with technology, and larger cultural factors around things like gender and play. The transition (and its frequent failure) from average player to professional, and what it means to inhabit that space, is what this chapter will focus on. Rather than assuming that a gamer seamlessly advances to elite status, the analysis here takes a more sociological approach in asking how someone *becomes* professional—how they, and their play, are worked over and transformed. The model suggests that the career path from amateur to professional is quite bumpy and often unsuccessful. It is also heavily dependant on being actively socialized into a professional identity by a range of actors and forces.

From Fandom to LANs and Beyond

With the shift from the arcade to the home, the space of video game play moved. For many the time with digital games is spent seated at desks playing PC games or on sofas with consoles and TVs.[3] Our passions and our gaming fandom often remain tucked away inside domestic spaces. But not always. If we spend time on forums posting and reading about games, we port our enthusiasm into a public sphere. If we have mobile devices (Sony's Playstation Portable, Nintendo's DS, game-enabled phones, and the like) this boundary between private and public also becomes blurred. And if you're like me and listen to podcasts, you often bring your game-playing self out into the world as your headphones link you to other fans talking about their favorite game.

Perhaps the other biggest jump in undomesticating our play (or at the minimum complicating the interiority home play offers) occurs with the widespread network capabilities of our games. While computer games have always tapped into our local friendship networks—be it sharing the sofa while we play a console game together or sitting next to each other at our desks and handing a keyboard back and forth—networked multiplayer functions in games shift our solo play into a communal activity. From the earliest days of PC gaming this desire to connect to others and play head-to-head or cooperatively has been present. The old work-around of dragging machines to each others' houses has been significantly supplanted via online networked capability.

The multiplayer aspect of e-sports is central. What is, of course, interesting is this need not be so. One could imagine things having unfolded differently such that the challenge of e-sports was constructed as a player versus machine competition. Early battles between chess master Garry Kasparov and IBM's Deep Blue computer harken to this path, one where the contest was focused on human versus machine intellect and skill. And yet e-sports has developed as a decidedly player-versus-player activity, and has been since its beginning. When you attend tournaments it is the energy of players competing face-to-face that animates.

This inclusion of other players is a key shift. A number of popular e-sports games (*Warcraft, Starcraft, FIFA*) need not actually be played with other people. You can play a single-player version and go head-to-head with the game AI. But what you consistently hear from pro players is that at some point this was no longer enough for them and that playing against other people became the meaningful challenge—both personally and socially. Playing against others typically starts by simply playing your friends, either in person or via the net. Setting up friendly, albeit competitive, matches among your social network is a long tradition in game culture. For pro gamers they typically find that over time they come to be the strongest player in their own friendship circle and hit a wall where they are no longer getting the challenge they once did, and still desire. Very often pro gamers talk about a point at which the rest of their friends had moved onto the next title but they persisted with one, focused on mastering it and other players. Their desire to compete in that game propelled them to find new outlets for play. As one player described the transition to me,

> The thing is, when you play CS for fun, at home, like, it's for fun. But then when you start going to tournaments, you just want to win. It kind of changes, because

you don't try to have fun anymore, you just try to get better. It's the same as sports, where like first you play with your friends outside your house and you have a little fun, and then you join a team and there's like, okay, I actually want to win. I don't just want to just play, I want to win. It kind of changes. You just play for the competition. Like competition and travel is what I've been playing for for years. I never really think about the money because you don't really make that much. You could get like any random job probably make about the same in the end. So I mean, just the competition. You get the same adrenaline rush when you're winning games as in real sports.

For pro players this focus on competing against others goes to the heart, and beginning, of their stories. As you talk to them you hear repeated trajectories that move them from their local circles onto larger playing fields. Unsurprisingly most players start in their own, or friends', homes. They pick up a game, often on the recommendation of a friend or family member, and find it captivates them. They will devote hours upon hours to mastering it, endlessly fascinated by the intricacies of the system, its characters, its weapons, its properties. Figuring out strategies and tactics become core play activities.

If you are a dedicated player and your local network has moved on to another title, or you no longer get any challenge from playing against your friends, you will broaden your base of competitors. This is a shift not everyone makes. Many average and casual players may never hit the online functionality of a game and seek out new people to compete against. Pro gamers are different in this respect. Testing their skills beyond their network of friends and family is fun, is a challenge, is where the real action is. The move to playing beyond their immediate social network is an important developmental step in the life of a pro gamer.

Very often this transition is facilitated because a player has been grouping with friends and playing casual matches against other teams or clans. Through this involvement with others, built over time, they come to know other players outside their immediate network. They are often even identified by other players as the strong person on the team. Online player stats are a component in building gaming profiles and reputations. It is not unusual for a gamer to start with their offline friends and family but, as their play progresses, get "picked up" by another clan whose members they only know online.

The widespread inclusion of network functionality in games has altered the traditional trajectory of play for those moving into professionalization. In the past the LAN party was the primary venue for head-to-head competition. Players would take all their gear—PCs, monitors, peripherals, sometimes even chairs—to a single location and meet up with other players face-to-face. Linking their machines over a local area network (LAN), they'd create on-the-spot game servers for their favorite titles and play matches repeatedly (typically over the course of a weekend).[4] As games have come to foster the continual availability of multiplayer competition via the Internet, players now have many more opportunities to hone their skills beyond their local friendship networks. Pro gamers have typically spent hours upon hours playing in online matches before they ever get to a tournament. They will build reputations online and come to have a network play community complete with regulars, grudges, and deep insider knowledge about one another's styles.

Despite developing skills online, face-to-face competition remains the gold-standard for e-sports and the community even has a term for people who only ever compete online, "LANdodger." Experienced pro gamers will often recount the visceral shifts of going from being the best of their friends to playing online to actually turning up at a F2F event to compete for the first time. Players' first F2F tournaments are typically within driving or train distance of their hometown, though the increasing use of online qualifiers is broadening this so that one's debut tournament may be a fairly significant regional or national one. Nervousness, stage fright, jitters, self-consciousness, difficulty focusing, and even fear are common descriptions of what it feels like to make that shift from being "king of your bedroom" to meeting your online competitors and facing them in person. Successful players do not entirely shed these pressures but understand that mastering their own internal and bodily reactions is a core first lesson (completely understandable to anyone who has had to publically perform) in making the shift from amateur to professional gamer (Witkowski 2012). Rachael Hutchinson highlights the way having spectators can affect gameplay, writing that "the presence or absence of audience may make the player feel vulnerable or overconfident" (2007, 295). The management of anxiety, tension, anticipation, and one's overall emotional state are an important component of the embodied experience of high-end play and, like all athletes and performers, a crucial skill advanced players develop.

Components of Pro Play

This mastery of one's body and visceral reactions in the competitive environment is just a single component of a set of skills professional gamers must learn. Top fighting game player and game designer Dave Sirlin has written a book called *Playing to Win* in which he details his own list of what makes an elite player: "Familiarity with tournaments, deep knowledge of the game at hand, love of the game, mental toughness, mental attitude toward winning, losing, improving, technical skill (usually dexterity), adaptability, knowledge/ability in other games of that genre, yomi [akin to 'knowing the mind of the opponent'], and appraisal" (2005, 111).[5]

Sirlin's examination of top-level play is echoed by two studies done on *Counter-Strike* players. Rambusch, Jakobsson, and Pargman (2007) found in their conversations with *CS* players that participating in e-sports tapped into both individual skills and one's ability to function on a team. They note the ways experienced players draw on not only cognitive skill, but facility with technology and the social context of teamplay to become top players. Reeves, Brown, and Laurier conducted an in-depth analysis of *CS* play sessions, paying careful attention to the construction of expertise in the game. They argue for the centrality of several areas in understanding skilled play—"the highly localized and manually dexterous 'ways of moving' around that virtual terrain; reading terrain 'at-a-glance'; tacit coordination with and awareness of other players; and, crucially in this case, exploitation of appearances by enemy players" (2009, 213). Though they argue that these tap into what any skilled CS player would know, they also provide a foundation for understanding what professional players also have to master.

My own observations and conversations with players confirm much of this. Because of the professional nature of the players I've looked at we see several additional nongaming skills that also emerge. If we were to break down the various areas that professional play requires it would include embodied skill and mastery, technical facility, game and systems mastery, tactical and strategic thinking, skilled improvisation, social and psychological skills, and, at the top-most end, career and institutional savvy. Being able to weave together competency across a range of areas is what separates casuals, amateurs, and short-term professionals from those who manage to create multiyear careers within high-end computer game play.

Embodied Skill and Mastery

As I discussed in chapter two, this aspect of computer game play is far too often overlooked when analyzing our engagement with digital games. But as we've seen in the discussion of physicality and sport, and its relation to e-sports, professional players are actively engaged as embodied actors when they are practicing and competing. Whether it is in mastering one's own reactions to the experience of competition or the nuances of embodied performance as it intersects video game play, understanding and managing yourself as an embodied actor is a central challenge for any professional gamer.

This is perhaps one of the trickier areas to unpack since so much of our experience of embodiment operates at the visceral and unspoken level. Comportment is constructed through a varying series of nuanced and minuscule maneuvers. Indeed, at the most elite level these have become so internalized, so naturalized, that explaining them and verbalizing them can be a challenge. Yet they remain a core foundational property of elite play. Lowood observes that, "The criticisms leveled at RTS games of reducing strategy play to mindless mouse-clicking misunderstands the denigrated 'clickfest' or 'button-mashing' by missing the connections between mastery of syntax and strategy, both invisible on the screen" (2007, 94). I would certainly extend this to all genres. Christian McCrea, for example, recounts the experience of witnessing a *StarCraft* match between famed player Lim "Boxer" Ho-Ywan and his competitor Hong "Yell0w" Jin-Ho that "altered my experience of games entirely" (2009, 180). He develops the notion of deep play from Clifford Geertz (1973), suggesting a level of nuance, stakes, and sophistication we don't normally associate with computer gaming. Focusing on the way embodied skill, perfected through training, can play a role in computer gaming is a crucial first analytic step in understanding pro play.

Sudnow, in his 1983 book *Pilgrim in the Microworld: Eye, Mind, and the Essence of Video Skill*, gives us one of the most compelling analyses of digital game play around. Despite it being rooted in early arcade and console play, he nonetheless unpacks the impressive cognitive work players undergo in becoming experts in their games. As he himself skills up he makes visible the work of play, recounting how he marked his video screen with tape to help him train timing and positionality, how he would daydream strategy and practice in his imagination, how he had to train his gaze and reflexes, ultimately how his interaction and skill with the game was embodied in hands, eyes, ears. It's a beautiful account of the complexities of skilling up in digital games and the stories Sudnow presents echo into our current high-res gaming world.

Technical Facility

This embodied nature of play is in relation to technological systems. Far too often in game studies we have not paid attention to the way our relationship with technology and our technical skills have a role in shaping our gameplay. Dovey and Kennedy have written, for example, about technicity—the "particular kinds of attitudes, aptitudes and skill, with technology" (2006, 113)—as central to game subjectivities. As I signaled in chapter two, the technological components of computer gameplay are central in how they are constructed as objects of high-end play. We should not be surprised that technicity plays a role in the development of the professional gamer.

Very often we black-box this side of things when talking about playing with computer games, but the ability to manage and customize user interfaces, build your own PC to optimize and save money (and thus perhaps allowing you to play at all), troubleshoot technical problems (including hardware, software, and networking), apply patches to software, set up home networks, and in general speak assuredly (and thus with legitimacy) about technical matters within a gamer subculture is crucial in the production of professionalism. When talking to pro players, the adeptness and naturalness with which they integrate detailed technical facility into their embodied action and cognition is evident. Whether it is a discussion of networks or simple ease around technical objects (not being afraid they will break something, for example), the technicity of pro players is apparent. What is particularly important about Dovey and Kennedy's formulation (2006) is that it does not bracket these abilities off as just mundane "skills" but notes they way they are enlisted into a larger production of subjectivity. Being able to engage with your machine and software at a detailed level for the purposes of play or competition is not simply about functionality, but part of a "preferred subjectivity" at work in the scene.[6]

Game and Systems Mastery

Even from the first moments a player installs a game they are engaging it as a system with embedded rules and, typically, win conditions. A large part of play, especially in the earliest moments, is simply understanding how the components of the system work, how they interact with each other, and how you can master them to advance in the game. Games played at the professional level also typically have some kind of world, and maps, that need to be learned. This can involve not only knowing how the terrain is laid out, but understanding glitchy spots in the game, places that can be exploited or need to be avoided.

In my work on MMOG power gamers I argued that they were the slice of the player community that would with intense focus methodically explore and test components of the game, pushing it, and themselves, to the utmost (Taylor 2006a). This form of instrumental play, in which gamers will dynamically set goals and create scenarios that allow them to refine their skills while exploring the contours of the system, is core to professional play. Professional players are certainly a form of power gamer.

They have deep knowledge of the system side of their games. They know its limits and the places to best exploit it (within a rule structure) for competitive advantage. As previously discussed, tournament rules are typically an ongoing conversation between systems, he deep situated knowledge of pro players, and the requirements of competition. If one of the foundational components of competitive play is mastering and working with embodiment, then systems mastery forms another cornerstone. Knowing a map, what various characters or classes can do, and weapons, as well as understanding the physics of a system and knowing basics like commands, macros, and shortcuts all form a part of game mastery.

Tactical and Strategic Thinking

It is safe to say that all players, amateur and casual included, are engaged with both embodiment and system mastery. Even if you are just sitting on your sofa you will be working to get your body in synch with the game controller, coordinating your senses and the input. You'll also from even the earliest training levels be learning about the system and how to play to win. If you were to go head-to-head against a pro they would certainly outshine you in these areas but the one you would likely feel most trounced by was their acute sense of tactics and strategy.

This is a particularly interesting category to try and understand for the more casual player because for those of us who are not professional we may not even be able to *see* the nuance and skill of the pro. I've certainly had the experience of watching a soccer game and seeing a real fan gasp and cheer at a play while I simply sat there dumbfounded about what was going on, having not seen anything notable. High-level computer game play can also be like this at times. In a flash the game is over, some wild move has been made and you've perhaps missed it. And yet the complex strategic and tactical skill pro players bring to the table is one of the biggest things that separates them from us.

Pro players will have, over hours and hours of practice and competition time, built up arsenals of moves and strategies. Sometimes these are formalized by teams as set patterns that get called out during a match, not unlike traditional sports teams who have well-practiced playbooks they draw from. Other times it is simply a vast unarticulated internal catalog of tactics that have become so naturalized they are initiated without thinking. This naturalization is typically a sign of real skill, that the time lapse between recognition of a situation and skilled response is a split-second.

This ability is born from long hours of practice. Pro players will often run scrimmage matches to work on moves, try out new "counters," or explore new characters and tactics. Players sometimes think of this attention as a form of "research." The ideal situation in many cases is to play others just a bit above your level, as they push you the most. The goal is to have internalized a tactic or counterstrategy at such a deep level that its quick execution feels natural, is second nature, and happens without cognitive overload.

It is worth pausing a moment to highlight that this is not unique to computer games. I could have written these things about strategies and tactics for traditional sports as well. Those within e-sports often make this connection. But for those who don't know much about computer games it is worth highlighting the kind of complexity of action this form of play requires. Too often the depth of computer game play is still not recognized by the mainstream and gamers can seem little more than button mashers. The flip side of this simplistic coin is that their activity is portrayed as so much of a novelty that it gets rendered nearly mystical. But, at the core, skilled computer game players are engaging in a kind of familiar complex strategic and tactical mastery, a sophisticated form of cognitive and physical work, mediated through technology and perfected through hours of play with others.

Skilled Improvisation and Imagination

While you and I could probably sit down and have a pro gamer teach us a solid chunk of basic tactics to play our favorite game, what also divides top players from the rest of us is their skilled improvisation. No competitive game unfolds according to a fixed script. Elite play is interwoven with opening moves, set and known tactics, and a high dose of improvisation. Pro gamers have gotten to the point where they have mastered the basics, built a core repertoire of advanced skills, and are able to maneuver dynamically based on the actual play situation at hand. Henry Lowood, drawing on his experience as a referee for a WCG *Warcraft III* match presents a riveting tale of how during a edge-of-your-seat game a top player, Manuel "Grubby" Schenkhuizen, executed a winning, never-before seen-move.

> Grubby had performed. He grasped an instant opportunity, made a preposterously rapid decision in the real-time heat of battle, and applied masterful knowledge of game syntax and 'micro' (the term used by players for micro-management of individual on-screen units) to carry out his game-winning performance. (2007, 14)

What is important here is not then just improvisation but imagination. Top players are willing to think, and move, beyond the bounds of conventional play. There is a deep provocation at work here, one that challenges standard rhetoric about computation and action. Computer games are far too often thought of as totalizing systems with fixed scripts, producing predictable play. Routine, and the constraint of action, are often thought of as inevitable products of computer game play. Yet the world of pro gaming is rife with improvisation. As Lowood (2006, 2007) suggests, these players are creative performers within their domain. They are moving around a system looking for new nooks to take advantage of, or are strategizing some creative approach for a new counter to an established pattern. While the average player may master set moves and become good at picking up new strategies in the community, pro players are constantly trying to be front-runners in innovating new play options. They perfect new approaches, often keeping them secret (as much as possible) until an important tournament "reveal" to give them a distinct advantage. The terrain of pro play in any given title shifts over the years in relation to the emergence of new imaginative tactics and strategies. Computer games allow for, and indeed at the top end require, like all sports, skilled improvisation *despite* their computational structures. Action is both expressive and dynamic.

Social and Psychological Skills

So far a fair amount of what I've detailed could be easily framed as individual in emphasis. Pro players, however, are deeply embedded in communities of practice and social networks. Tactics are learned through social interaction. From the moment a novice player steps into a server to game with others, they are also being socialized into community norms and expectations. Pro players develop values and skills that intersect this social context. It can range from mundane things like how you behave before, during, and after a match (the limits of trash talk or an appropriate disposition if you win) to learning how to play the psychological side of competitions (using that trash talk to psych another player out or picking an opening strategy to throw a competitor off). Knowing the conventions of varying contexts (tournament rules, national or cultural norms) is also invaluable for top players.

There is another aspect of psychological skill involved in advanced play and that is the ability of elite performers to quickly develop a mental model of their opponent and in turn work out what kind of game they are playing. One of the players I interviewed has been playing *Counter-Strike* since he was a preteen and is now on a top pro team. He often spoke of things like intuition and mental games as being important components in elite play.[7] For example, when discussing how easy it was to take down lesser players he said,

> Some of these people haven't even like, breached the mental game of *Counter-Strike* and they still had this picture of it's like 'you run around the corner and shoot this guy here.' They don't understand why someone is able to [kill them] consistently [...] When you finally breach that barrier about really mentally defeating somebody, playing those tournaments is so easy and its so different because everyone's just playing straight on the game. They don't even realize sometimes how you're faking them. Because you're kind of abusing their natural instincts. Because if you already understand what that natural instinct is, [for example] if you make a footstep in the right direction, most of the pro players have already thought out what the other guy thinks when he does that. [...] They think they're faking you. But really, you already knew they were going to do that. So the second they start running back, instead of drawing into their fake, you just come out and kill them. And they get surprised constantly. Because you understand the basic level of how most people think.

Part of what he is suggesting here is that elite play is not simply about knowing tactics, or even being able to improvise, but adeptly creating a mental model of your opponent and adjusting your play accordingly. At the best moments you are using their own play against them (they try and fake you, you know they are, you take advantage of that insight). You may even use your opponent's likely model of *you* against them. As another player put it, "I know this guy, he thinks I'm so good that I won't even think of doing this so I'm just going to do it." Sometimes you are building a model using real data from having watched replays or prior competitions (one player equates it to a pitcher knowing who his hitters are), sometimes you are building based on the smallest bits of information. Ultimately using an opponent's play style and mental models against them certainly represents a kind of second-order psychological game skill.

In addition to these skills is the basic learning curve (sometimes failed) that players on teams have to undergo to become a good member. Learning your role, how to work together as a team, how to listen to directions or give them, how to handle criticism and arguments, and other basics of being a member of a squad of people forms a crucial skill for team-based pro players. You can be the best fragger in the world but if you can't work on a team you won't find yourself building a long-term career. Sometimes you hear players talk about how they may not be the best player out there but have worked hard to be a solid member of a team, contributing to the overall success. Experienced and more mature players often find themselves in positions to mentor newer players. This can range from teaching new skills to doing nuanced work that involves putting them in their place to help integrate them into the scene. Teamwork becomes not just a central skill, but a core pleasure for many of these players. As one put it to me, "It's just, at this point if we didn't have a team none of us would play. It's not the game that draws us to it anymore, it's just the competition and the team aspect really."

The work that is involved in playing something like *CS* is, for nearly every player I've spoken to, something they equate with teamwork in traditional sports. One top player put it this way,

> Everyone in this game, it's like you cannot do anything by yourself in this game. When you're playing against a top team, you can't just go somewhere by yourself and expect to get something accomplished. So it's a five-man operation. Everyone has to be on the same page. You throw one grenade in the wrong spot and you could get everyone killed. We spend like three hours on the server just going over our strats and making sure everyone knows what to do. Same way you practice soccer.[8]

Beyond the social skills involved in-game, pro players also need to be able to handle mundane things like traveling with a group of people, sharing hotel rooms, interacting with tournament organizers and admins, being responsible on the road (including basics like bringing your sponsor-branded t-shirt to wear), and increasingly presenting a public face to spectators and fans. As one put it, "I have four personalities I have to deal with every day. So it's not just in the game, we're in a hotel room together all the time. So if we're not getting along, we're not going to play well." In the same way the F2F tournament can highlight for the novice player the unique pressures of event competitions, the lived reality of the "road work" of a career e-sports player highlights skills you need outside of the game.

Career and Institutional Savvy

There is a component of social skills I would place into a much broader category—attention to one's career and a more meta-level savvy about the scene. Perhaps of all areas this is the one that divides those who build multiyear careers in e-sports and those who don't. All things being equal, knowing how the *professional* game is played is crucial to success. The most successful professional computer game players in the world (in terms of building a sustainable income over several years) are the ones who have paid some attention to the career aspects, including building a recognizable name/brand for themselves, having a public reputation, dealing with contracts and sponsorships, changing teams as needed to maintain a stable playing trajectory, and in many cases adapting their play to fit the evolving nature of the competitive scene.

Given e-sports players do not (at the time of this research) have agents who are doing the work of navigating various institutional opportunities (and thickets), the best professional players are not only working on perfecting their play, they are often acting as their own managers. This is impressive when we think about how young many of them are and how this may have been their main occupation, their first paid job. It is perhaps also not surprising then how slim the top-most layer of longer-term professional players is. When combined with the range of other skills required—embodied, technical, game, strategic, improvisational, social, and psychological—adding in career and institutional savvy makes for a serious set of competencies for anyone, much less a young adult embarking on a professional career still deeply marginal in mainstream culture. The risks are high, though. Signing contracts with minimal negotiation (and no legal representation), no long-term planning, and often little financial consideration is the norm. Top players who are crossing national boundaries to work for a team often get entangled in marginally legal practices (such as using tourist visas to stay in a country despite being formally employed, for example). With little outside and mature guidance, successful pro players have to not only be on top of their game, but keep a sharp eye on navigating the often murky world of e-sports employment and finances.

Work and Play

All of this is not possible without extreme dedication and hard work. Certainly professional computer gamers fascinate many of us because of the way they seem to transform objects and activities of leisure into a very serious endeavor. While we may play a game for a few hours a week or a weekend afternoon, pro players will have clocked hours upon hours practicing and competing. While we may shift from game to game, picking up new titles or dabbling in demos we download, pro players (although they are still very much gamers and always checking out new things) can exhibit dedication to a single title for years and years. In the case of games like *Starcraft* or *Counter-Strike* they are also playing games that came out over a decade ago. In a culture where progress, technical or otherwise, is valorized and chased after, this can be immensely perplexing.

Of course, if we step back from the specialized niche of computer games we can find myriad examples of people who have transformed their objects of leisure into an occupation. Play becomes work, work becomes play. Traditional sports are populated with men and women whose passion for playful activities that they likely discovered in their youth have been honed over time such that they can make a living at it.[9] Of course, it's not always a good living. Nonetheless they pursue their goal of being a professional athlete. The notion of converting something you love into something you can do as a vocation holds an almost mythical status in our culture, a goal only the luckiest few attain. And yet when it comes to computer games and their highly intensive play, alarm bells often go off.

There's been a fair amount of hand-wringing about the breech in boundary lines between work and play. Concerns over the "grind" nature of some game genres (MMOGs lead list of culprits), the overly repetitious nature of a game mechanic, the leaking of gameplay into "real-world" economies, or the "gamification" of our everyday lives have all at least partially anchored their concern in a fairly dichotomous model of how play works. A heavily policed model of the "magic circle" has far too often led to the claim that when play is touched by the outside world, when it takes on meaning beyond the specialized game system, when it *matters* to anything other than the play experience itself, it becomes corrupted, and corrupting.

Unfortunately such a hard-line position is simply not tenable, neither empirically nor conceptually. Actual players, be they pro or not, recognize the messy nature of play, the way it can occupy a "both/and" relation to work or obligation. When we watch an amateur basketball player go down to their local court and spend hours dribbling a ball and shooting we know that somehow neither simply "play" nor "work" adequately captures what they are doing. We understand that playful pleasure is often wrapped up in sweat, exertion, hard work, repetition, frustration, even anger. We don't hand-wring over these athletes, question their motives, worry that they are somehow denuding a pure sense of playful freedom and exploration.[10] Yet somehow when the eye is turned toward computer game players exhibiting all the same exertions—repetition, frustration, work-like devotion—there is often a pause. Somehow computer game players are not accorded the full measure of complex human experience and meaning-making that even the youngest traditional athletes are. Far too often an almost moral panic of "play becoming work" gets evoked. This is at the expense of understanding not only the nature of computer game play, but also its emerging role in our culture as both object of leisure *and* serious occupation.

It's important to note that acknowledging the play in work and the work in play of e-sports does not mean that there is not at times ambivalence for some as they move into a professionalized sphere. As Gillespie, Leffler, and Lerner argue, "cultures of commitment may problematize daily life for participants" (2002, 298). Players often have to sort through what it means when a hobby transforms itself into something else and some feel that attempting to professionalize their play comes with a cost they can't bear. Perhaps it means they no longer play with friends or that they have to practice even when they are tired or "not into it." Sometimes travel schedules or the constant close contact with teammates while on the road can be draining. For some the commercialization of the scene gives them pause and they feel the distance from their earliest gaming experiences more acutely. There is also often the additional work that comes with professionalization that has nothing to do with actual game play itself but is tied to obligations to a team or sponsors. Having to create website content, use sponsor gear that you don't like, or participate in promotional activities rubs some pros the wrong way and feels like a burden, a distraction from what they really want to be doing.

For others there are larger biographic stories they are developing for themselves and situating their professional play fits uneasily into that. One top player I interviewed, who is under contract and has played for a number of years, surprised me by framing his play as a hobby despite, as he noted, "CS has paid for everything, all the money I've got since '04. I make decent money but it's still like a hobby so whenever I quit I'm just going to go to school." Calling it a hobby was surprising given that within the world of e-sports he is one of the most successful professional players. For me this tag at the end, about going to school, was telling. For some pro e-sports players being under contract and on a team is actually just something they are doing until they crack some other "real" profession. In the case of this guy, he spoke of wanting to go to law school and how e-sports was something he was doing until then. He was also one of the most skeptical people I'd spoken with about the potential for e-sports to reach a wide audience and be taken as a real sport. Perhaps one of the ambivalences around serious leisure and the transformation of hobby is in the area of vocational identity. There can be ambivalence about the activity you've managed to convert into a profession and trying to resituate it as leisure can be an important part of an identity story someone is constructing, especially when the activity is so marginal as e-sports.

When we talk about the blurred boundary between work and play, or the transformation of a play activity into sport and occupation, we are talking about a complex set of experiences, not easily boxed into pure fun or pure misery. There are a couple areas of research that can provide us some useful conceptual footholds in understanding what is happening for pro players who are transforming their play: leisure studies and the sociology of work.

Serious Leisure

There is a body of work in leisure studies that is helpful in broadening the conversation typically occuring within our consideration of computer games. A number of authors in that field have, through detailed ethnographies and case studies, shown how a form of seriousness can infuse dedicated leisure communities. While top-level professional gamers are certainly operating beyond the scope of just leisure, this literature nonetheless gives us some ways of understanding serious orientations to activities we typically identify as hobbies. In their review of recent work on serious leisure, Gillespie, Leffler, and Lerner write, "What these analyses all emphasize is that for amateur/volunteer participants in 'serious leisure,' an avocation is a central aspect of their lives. It is time, resource, and therefore identity intensive. As a created social world, it has its own ethos, norms, institutions and economic structures" (2002, 286). We certainly see this mirrored in professional gaming and there are two angles worth highlighting here: social organization and individual orientation.

Alan Tomlinson notes the sophisticated forms of social organization often involving "active and time-consuming work" that can take place in serious leisure communities (1993, 8). Gillespie, Leffler, and Lerner's (2002) work on "dog sports" discusses the amount of time and money that can be invested in the activity[11] and the highly structured forms of organization (be it clubs, training camps, competitions) that people (and their dogs) come to be involved with. They also note that people often develop "fictive kin" or "shadow families" whereby linkages between breeders, their dogs, and themselves form new bonds of relation.[12]

William Kelly's study of karaoke in Japan highlights what is perhaps quite surprising and counterintuitive for many Westerners, that "Although karaoke may be pursued for fun in Japan, it is also pursued seriously for fun" (2002, 153). This can involve everything from formal instruction to popular media programs on TV or radio and articles in magazines about good technique. Kelly gives us a fascinating picture of people who undergo intense personal development, complete with critical evaluation of their skills, in the service of a leisure activity. Improving oneself is a central pleasure of the fun.

This approach to understanding the complexity of what we often think of as nonwork activities was pioneered by Robert Stebbins and his work on "serious leisure" (Stebbins 1982, 2001, 2004). He clarifies that the term "serious" is particularly helpful because it "embodies such qualities as earnestness, sincerity, importance, and carefulness, rather than those of gravity, solemnity, joylessness, distress, and anxiety" (2004, 50). In his book *Between Work and Leisure* he provides a helpful definition, "Serious leisure is the systematic pursuit of an amateur, hobbyist, or volunteer activity that participants find so substantial and interesting that, in the typical case, they launch themselves on a career centered on acquiring and expressing its special skills, knowledge, and experience" (2004, 49).

Unlike Stebbins, I am using the term "play" alongside "leisure" because it holds a particular status in relation to computer games and is a language convention employed by both gamers and researchers. I should note, however, that some leisure scholars would constrain "play" a bit more along conventional lines of nonserious activity. Stebbins, for example, distinguishes between serious and casual leisure (2001) and puts play, along with things like relaxation and entertainment, there. He at times takes a somewhat retrograde view of traditional media (suggesting there is only minimal effort required in watching a movie, for example) but does leave open a space for "active entertainment" (which includes "riddles, puzzles, party games, children's games, and games of chance") to transition beyond casualness. As he puts it, "when participation in active entertainment requires a significant level of skill, knowledge, or experience, it ceases to be casual leisure" and may transition into "hobby or an amateur activity." (2001, 61). My argument here is to develop this approach even further given what we are empirically finding in the world of professional computer gaming.

Despite some of the road bumps encountered in laying Stebbins's notion of serious leisure onto the computer gaming domain, we can still find some useful hooks to use in analyzing professional play. Based on his work over several decades (looking at a variety of groups including jazz musicians and arts hobbyists) he identifies six "distinctive qualities" that characterize serious leisure and an individual's orientation to it:

1. The "need to persevere" and a sense that "sticking with it through thick and thin" and "conquering adversity" are core components of the activity.
2. The desire to, and sometime actualization of, making a career out of the activity.
3. The "significant personal effort based on specially acquired knowledge, training, or skill, and, indeed at times, all three."
4. The existence of "durable benefits, or outcomes" such as "self-actualization, self-enrichment, self-expression, regeneration or renewal of self, feelings of accom-

plishment, enhancement of self-image, social interaction and belongingness, and lasting physical products of the activity (e.g., a painting, scientific paper, piece of furniture)."

5. The development of an identity around the activity and deep identification with it.

6. The development of a "unique ethos that grows up around the expression of it"—that is, the "special social world that develops when enthusiasts in a particular field pursue over many years their interests in it" (2004, 52–53).

I find this list particularly helpful in illuminating much of what we find in e-sports and the pro scene.[13] We certainly see the real commitment in all sectors of the domain, from players to administrators, and as I've discussed, the desire to make a career out of e-sports is one of the strongest threads I've found. Players, broadcasters, even refs and admins require a great deal of skilling up and hold significant insider knowledge that facilitates competition. For the most committed there is a deep sense of what it means to be an e-sports player, broadcaster, or team owner and there is a rich social milieu in which it all exists.

Perhaps the one piece of Stebbins's list that is tricky for e-sports is the creation of "durable benefits, or outcomes." While participants regularly talk about how gratifying e-sports is for them, there is often still some searching, some caution, about its longevity and what it all means in a big picture view. The desire to "grow e-sports" seems to be linked to wanting to make sure it lasts long after any individual participant has gone, that it becomes a legitimate endeavor. The time and energy given to it is not simply just about players' own achievements, but is often tied to something bigger. Given that e-sports is faced with the challenge of its core site being virtual, the risk of all this activity being ephemeral is a consistent theme among those seriously considering the state of e-sports. What durability and longevity is for computer gaming is complex, and participants are often aware of this.

Given the still-developing nature of the professionalization opportunities in computer gaming, "serious leisure" gives us a way of talking about the intense dedication we see among the practitioners I'm discussing here, as well as the ways the activity intersects social processes and community.

Lifestyle Sports

A second conceptual component worth tossing into the discussion comes from work in an area called "lifestyle sports," which typically includes things like skateboarding, windsurfing, parkour, and other alternative sports. One of the things that can be tricky when trying to understand the activity of committed e-sports players is the seemingly betwixt and between nature of their activity; straddling something like sport (though it is so far from traditional forms that it confounds) and what often appears to be an almost lifestyle commitment to gaming. The long hours they put in on game play are often framed in relation to a broader subject position, that of "gamer."

Though sports and athleticism are frequently invoked, the identity of "computer gamer" is the foundation upon which e-sports and professionalization get built. This formulation of passionate engagement with gaming writ large speaks to a broader culture of commitment e-sports players have with computer games. As I will discuss in later chapters, even nonplayers in the scene (team owners, commentators, and such) regularly speak about their devotion to e-sports and gaming by pointing out that when their own skills didn't hold the promise of professionalization, they shifted to another career still within the e-sports world.

Belinda Wheaton has helpfully summarized the state of lifestyle sports research and provides several key components in identifying them. She suggests nine defining features:

1. Historically recent.
2. Emphasis on "grass roots" participation (versus spectating).
3. New objects, often new technologies, are a focal point ("boards, bikes, discs, etc.").
4. "Commitment in time, and/or money and a style of life and forms of collective expression, attitudes and social identity that develops in and around the activity."
5. "A participatory ideology that promotes fun, hedonism, involvement, self actualization, 'flow,' living for the moment, 'adrenalin rushes' and other intrinsic rewards." The focus is on "creative, aesthetic and performative expressions." There is often an accompanying resistance to "institutionalization, regulation and commercialization" and a possibly ambivalent relationship with spectatorship.
6. Frequently made up of "middle class, white, Western" participants, though may be more gender diverse than traditional sports.
7. "Predominantly, but not exclusively, individualistic in form and/or attitude."
8. Involves "non-aggressive activities [...] that do not involve bodily contact" though notions of risk and danger remain.
9. "The spaces of consumption are new or appropriated outdoor 'liminal' zones [...] mostly without fixed or created boundaries" (2004b, 11–12).

So how does e-sports line-up against this catalog? Some aspects, such as the newness of the endeavor and reliance on new technologies, provide a clear link. Other areas like the focus on grass-roots participation certainly speak to the way e-sports continues to be deeply rooted in close communities of practice and valuing actually being a player yourself, even if you aren't a pro. Indeed a notion of fun, pursuit of flow, and adrenalin rushes would resonate for nearly any gamer. The commitment factor also matches up and echoes some of the conceptual frames in serious leisure. The issue of demographic homogeneity is something I'll address a bit more later in this chapter, but we can certainly locate some truth to this observation within the e-sports scene (with a handful of notable exceptions).

The remaining three qualities: resistance to commercialization, individualism, and "liminal" zones of consumption are quite interesting in relation to e-sports. On the one hand despite pros (and other stakeholders) in the scene supporting the institutionalization and formalization of e-sports as an activity, you do find voices in the community that express ambivalence about the commercialization of play. Individualism is tricky since within e-sports there are a number of genres played, some of which facilitate solo play and some which are focused on teams. We can certainly say, though, that even on teams there is a strong sense of the individual player profile. The liminal spaces Wheaton identifies don't quite match up with computer gaming (she speaks of blendings between participant and nature, or redefinition of urban spaces for sport) and yet we can easily talk about the liminality of computer game play, with its complex distribution of embodiment and action between corporality and technology. Run alongside her list, I would argue e-sports seem to make a compelling entry into the category, albeit with some caveats.

What is particularly helpful about weaving in the discussion of lifestyle sports is it gives us not only another hook by which to reformulate our notion of sports in light of e-sports, but also opens up a discussion about the ways avid practitioners inhabit a much broader sphere of cultural values and practices that are also outside some of the frames of traditional sports. Lifestyle sports give us a way to think about sports values, and identities, beyond conventional models.

Unconventional Work

A final domain of research that can help situate the work of professional gamers is in the realm of occupations that do not produce a feeling of a 9-to-5 grind but offer their workers a sense of enjoyment, fulfillment, pleasure, and personal development. Stebbins, for example, has a notion of the "occupational devotee" that seeks to conceptualize those who are able to pursue jobs that allow for meaningful "self-enhancement" and "sense of achievement" such that the "line between this work and leisure is virtually erased" (2004, 2).

Ben Fincham's work (2007, 2008) picks up on a similar theme through his ethnography of bike couriers. He paints a picture of people who have constructed a rich life around bicycle couriering where their nonwork and personal lives are woven through with connections and activities drawn from their daily labor. Indeed the very distinction between "work" and "life" (where the term "life" is regularly a substitute for notions of leisure, fun, and self-fulfillment) becomes unsustainable analytically. In Fincham's research he finds that people taking up the job of courier find pleasure in the form of their labor but also develop meaning and significance that bleed out of occupational boundaries. He argues, for example,

> In the case of bicycle messengers, the identification with a particular way of being as a messenger was strong for many of the men and women that I came across in the course of the study. The job seemed to dominate what Goffman would describe as the "presentation of self" (Goffman 1959), with ideas of community and culture formulated around the job being of particular significance, and requiring particular attention (Fincham 2007). As an ex-messenger in Washington wrote, "being a courier, one quickly realizes, is much more than earning a living—it's a way of life, an attitude" (Fincham 2008, 621).

This resonates in my discussions with not only the gamers themselves, but others who make up the pro scene. Because pro gaming operates not only at the level of elite sport but also is infused with significance for one's identity and community, bracketing off its work qualities versus its "fun" qualities is untenable. Participants experience gaming, and their identity as a gamer, as much as a lifestyle as anything. Gaming is something that weaves its way through their leisure, their work, their notions of self, their communities. As Fincham argues, "distinctions between being at work and not being at work, implying a dichotomy in adult life, are overstated and that the discourse of a work/life balance is unhelpful" (2008, 619).[14] Pro players co-construct their professional identity, their vocation, alongside their leisure identity as gamer.

Socialization and Professionalism

Part of this negotiation between conceptualizations of work and play happens through a socialization process as players move from configuring their gameplay as hobby and leisure to, instead, serious endeavor and sport. As I previously suggested, a fairly common trajectory you hear when talking to pro players is the way they come to outpace their local friendship networks in terms of skill and start expanding their contacts to provide them additional challenges.

Yet even before they go to their first live tournament, players are already learning what it means to be a pro. As they hang out on IRC channels talking to other fans or visit websites, they encounter narratives about other players who are engaged in computer gameplay as e-sport. They read stories about their favorite players, watch matches, and begin to learn that the very identity of pro gamer is a possibility. Unlike traditional sports where becoming a pro football or baseball player is a known (albeit rare) career path, within e-sports there remains a powerful moment of discovery where people suddenly learn that you could play games for a living.

For the player who wants to continue on to a professional level, often they find themselves having to educate, and indeed convince, those around them (especially parents and family members) that this path is a viable option. Stories, near mythical, abound of pro players who staked everything on a single tournament, declaring to parents that if they didn't win they'd give up the entire dream, only to come back with prize check in hand and skeptical family members turning into supporters.[15] Of course the reality for many is much messier with their pro career beginning with lower-level ad hoc competitions interspersed with continued schoolwork. While a prize check is one early signal that a person is starting to transition into professionalism, it is often being signed to an established team that marks a pivotal career turn.

Players coming up through the ranks learn everything from how to communicate to other players during and after games to strategies and tactics. As I suggested in an earlier chapter, communities build powerful norms and learning all of these forms an important part in the development of a pro gamer's career. Much of this comes through online communities players participate in. Yet there are some things that seem to only be learned once players hit the regular circuit and find themselves in contact with people like tournament organizers, team owners, sponsors, and others who have a stake in players acting and presenting themselves as "professionals." In a conversation with a major tournament organizer, he spoke about how one of his jobs was simply trying to get players to adopt a professional attitude at broadcast matches—getting them to be aware of the camera, handle press conferences, meet VIPs, and generally present an image of good sportsmanship. One team owner I interviewed talked about the work of socializing players into a professional identity,

> As a coach and manager I've been dealing with that for years. My kids are drilled and trained and professional [...] respect and politeness and camera skills and interview skills and every other skill you can imagine. But a lot of kids come off the street. But I think you see that in every sport. When you get these young NBA stars, they're arrested for this, they're punching their girlfriend. Football stars are always in the news, getting arrested. Whenever you get young, raw talent that's 18, 20, 21, they're not polished and that goes across the board in every sport.

What is particularly interesting in e-sports, though, is the way it is still deeply tied to a larger gamer subculture, one that may not yet be ready for primetime and one in which that ambition is sometimes regarded with ambivalence and perhaps even scorn. One top player put it this way, "Right now the culture is very underground and the word we use is grimy. You know, like 10,000 person BYOC [bring your own computer, ala LAN parties]. You've got kids with stacks of fifteen Coke cans and eight empty boxes of gold fish [snack crackers] and that's what people love about it." For many a notion of authentic game culture rests uneasily alongside the requirements of professionalism.

Unlike traditional sports where, if a kid gets a glimpse of professional athleticism early on (an unavoidable occupational image in our culture) they not only start imagining that path but encounter coaches and supportive adults along the way to foster it, gamer activity is located somewhat differently. For someone who aspires to professionalism their activity still resides somewhere betwixt and between subculture and occupation. The values that shape how one behaves are thus similarly located, and get worked over as people move from being a casual player, to an amateur, to a professional (complete with contracts, cash, and obligations). Part of the work professionalization does is restructuring how what was once a hobby is reconfigured and reinterpreted.

Athletic Identification and Expression

Perhaps one of the earliest things I noticed about e-sports players was their frequent invocation of sports to help locate their activity and passion. In one of my first conversations with a top *Starcraft* player he made the somewhat joking comment that "*Starcraft* players are like chess players and *Counter-Strike* guys are like footballers." Catchy enough with its riff on stereotypes of the quiet analytic solo players contrasted to the loud trash-talking teams, yet he actually went on to describe his own prior history as a committed soccer player and talk about the ways he approached his computer game play similarly, with dedication, intense focus, and a love of competition.

This love of competition pervades the e-sports scene and players regularly mention their prior athletic histories as one way of situating their dedication to computer games and their adoption of a pro player career and identity. One top player told me, "I was really into baseball so I guess that's where I got my competitive spirit from." Another compared what he understood as his "natural talent" in ice hockey with a kind of "natural skill" for the FPS he competed in.

It is important to not overstate the way this athletic identification functions in the scene. Though frequently invoked—it certainly helps situate and legitimize intense computer game play—for some players there is still indeterminacy about how to think about pro gaming in terms of its sportiness. One team owner put it this way,

> Whether they think of themselves as gamers or as athletes is kind of divided. They think and know a lot of the same skill sets that are successful in traditional sports translate over to gaming whether it's hand-eye coordination, work ethic, discipline, teamwork, communication, you know, or just putting in the time every day. When everybody else doesn't want to do it you're still practicing and that translates across any sport but if you ask them, is this a sport? Some will say sure, some will say no.

In my own conversations with pro players I've found that for many linking to their prior athletic histories is an important framing move and way to tell their story. It is often a starting point in the narrative. The work it does is, at least in part, to try and legitimize what is often otherwise seen in our culture as not only a marginalized leisure activity but, combined with intensity and dedication, a potentially dangerous or deviant hobby. Hooking into athleticism helps situate a love of competition, a love of the fraternal nature of long-term play within a community. It also helps explain things like repetition and practice, embodied action, focused dedication, and the more analytical aspects of perfecting one's play. Athleticism and notions of sportsmanship become productive when ported over to computer games, even if at times the transfer of language also carries ambivalence.

One of the fascinating questions that can be raised when we import ideas of athleticism into competitive computer gaming is around issues of style and expression. Can you tell who someone is by how they play a computer game? Is there distinctive style that can be exhibited within a digital environment? For outsiders to the e-sports scene I suspect a common answer would be no. The notion that a computer gaming environment allows for personalized style can seem to some at odds with what is imagined as a fairly narrow band of action permitted by a computational system. Yet when you start talking to top players, or those who spend lots of time with them (or watching their matches), you hear a different story.

Not only do people talk about being able to identify players and teams by their style of play, you not infrequently hear talk about national styles of play. In these conversations you are hearing echoes of the argument Henry Lowood (2005a) makes when he talks about "high performance play" and the deeply creative action competitors can bring to in-game action (see also Newman 2008 on play as public performance). While I've not conducted any blind tests (showing players footage and asking them to name the gamer), what you typically hear is players talk about so-and-so's fast play style or the way they use elements of the world (box jumping, ultra-precise pixel alignment). You will also often hear them talk about the way a player innovated a technique in a game, using a piece of equipment for a purpose no one had thought of before, and often changing the way the game is played. Players and teams come to be known by their preferences (for example, a particular race in a strategy game or a gun in a shooter), identified for the way they specifically work over the game, and by extension their competitors.

Gender and Pro Gaming

We can't talk about the identity of professional computer gamers without weaving in a conversation about gender and its performance within the scene. As with traditional sports the issue is complex and can't be simply reduced to "no women play professionally." While the numbers of women playing at the high end are few, it is crucial that a discussion of gender not simply be conflated with a discussion of women. The construction of masculinity is central to understanding the nature of gender and professional computer gaming.

Masculinity and Game Culture

The status of masculinity within game culture is difficult to pigeonhole. On the one hand pockets of gaming can be utterly misogynistic, not to mention homophobic. Perhaps some of the roughest terrain in this regard can be found in corners of the FPS XBox Live scene where stories abound of people listening in horror as teenage boys shout slurs to their fellow players and force people to run a participation gauntlet. At the same time we can find spots where women, queerness, and playful reappropriations of conventional gender identities form a part of the gaming subculture (Jakobsson 2007; Sundén 2009). Game culture is actually quite diverse, made up of a number of conventions, values, and practices that are specific to various gamer communities. To talk about gender in computer gaming writ large is, while at times strategically important, analytically tricky to pull off. But just as research has now spent some time telling a more complex story about women, girls, and games—one that has moved away from "pink games"—we should turn our attention to understanding the complexities of masculinity in game culture not only to better understand the diversity at work amongst boys and men, but for the ways those gender identities relationally construct those of women, girls, and femininity writ large.

Geek Masculinity

Our starting point for thinking about masculinity and game culture has to be a consideration of geek masculinity. For some who take up both a strong interest in technology and playing computer games, a certain alternative identity is often formed: the geek or nerd.

In geek culture, the valorization of highly refined skill and mastery operates through technology, science, and gaming. Intensive commitment and passion for a domain is a consistent feature of geekdom, where extensive knowledge of specialized areas is not only a source of personal pride and enjoyment, but operates socially. Talking over minutia with your friends, or perhaps even the competitive jostling of knowing some arcane trivia, is highly valued. These performances of expertise, skill, and knowledge are not only sources of social connection and pleasure, but also work as important markers for inclusion and exclusion (Kendall 2002). Social capital is produced by, and circulates through, the mastery of domain knowledge.

This formulation is not just about gender identity, but often gets constructed around a much broader rebuttal of mainstream culture. Geek masculinity often provides a means for opting out of sports and athletic culture. This refusal is just as often about not wishing to participate in the entire set of social activities that *surround* a sport (and athletic subcultures) as it is about the physical activity of the sport itself. Facilitating an interest in competition or fraternal relationships but via activities like playing computer games thus becomes a powerful alternative modality for geek masculinity.

Some formulations of geek masculinity also dovetail with less heteronormative constructions of sexuality and identity. This can range from simple disruptions of the objectification of women to making room for queer identities or alternate sexual and intimacy practices like polyamory or BDSM. The subculture's ties to science fiction and fantasy certainly assist in creating imagined alternate worlds and possibilities for being. As Mary Bucholtz found in her research on nerd subculture in high school, because it often resists "hegemonic social expectations" and the "heterosexual matrix" that so predominate young people's lives (see also Pascoe 2007), lesbian and gay teenagers, as well as others who "have little interest in heterosexual preoccupations, align themselves with nerd identities and practices" (1998, 122). She importantly clarifies that "Heterosexual nerds are not necessarily less homophobic than their trendy counterparts, but because sexuality is not an organizing principle of nerds' daily lives as it is for cool students, lesbian and gay students may find that friendship with heterosexual nerds provides a relatively safe space in the homophobic environment of the high school" (123). Like other groups that adopt once-hurtful names, the very term "geek" has been reabsorbed back into the community for self-description as "a fond, self-aware form of teasing and playfulness" (Dunbar-Hester 2008, 206). It can even at times act as a badge of honor and embraced oppositional identity (Bucholtz 1998; Kendall 2002).

Though geek culture is certainly not exempt from its own forms of sexism (Dunbar-Hester 2008), its historical marginal status has lent itself more readily to alternative lifestyles. We would want to nuance the use of the term "marginal" a bit here since it is perhaps more accurate to suggest that geek masculinity cycles through several stances in relation to hegemonic masculinity. At times it is truly marginalized a la Connell's schema (1995) (though she would perhaps disagree), while at other moments geeks may actually occupy a more complicit mode. And depending on additional intersectionalities at work (race, class, sexual orientation), geekness, in any given person's embodiment of it, may inflect itself differently.

Technology and Hegemonic Masculinity

There is a more complex relationship we need to unpack further though and that is geek masculinity's relationship with hegemonic masculinity. Connell's work on hegemonic masculinity (1995, 2001; Connell and Messerschmidt 2005) is helpful in this discussion because it not only gives us a way to think about a more dynamic process of gender construction, but perhaps also helps us understand the double-sided nature of masculinity within game culture. Simply put, hegemonic masculinity is "the configuration of gender practice which embodies the currently accepted answer to the problem of the legitimacy of patriarchy, which guarantees (or is taken to guarantee) the dominant position of men and the subordination of women" (2001, 38). What is powerful about the formulation is that hegemonic masculinity exists in relation to not only femininity but, for the purposes of our discussion here, in relation to varying forms of masculinity that are contextually and historically situated, stratified, and often in contest. Rather than relying on essentialist notions of gender, Connell and Messerschmidt suggest that "Masculinities are configurations of practice that are accomplished in social action and, therefore, can differ according to the gender relations in a particular social setting" (2005, 836). Connell's dynamic model of masculinity (1995) ties with work by feminist scholars who have also proposed a more nuanced model of situated gender creation and performance (see, for example, Butler 1990). As people move through their lives the understanding and performance of gender morphs in relation to new social situations and artifacts, relationships, institutions, and cultural practices. And at the same time, the culture tweaks and shifts its own formulations of gender categories, with hegemonic masculinity still always keeping its eye on the support of patriarchy.

While we often find a valorization of nerds in popular movies, such representations do not, however, trump the preponderance of the "ideal man" in our culture. R. W. Connell, while noting the centrality of the subordination of gay men to heterosexual men within the hierarchy, adds that some heterosexual men are also oppressed through markers like "nerd," "dweeb," and "geek." For many gay men and some heterosexual men their identities become linked to femininity, the ultimate target of patriarchy. They come to reside "at the bottom of a gender hierarchy among men" (2001, 40).

The issue of the ways technology works over masculinity has been given some helpful consideration we can turn to.[16] Christina Dunbar-Hester notes that "technical mastery itself is a well-documented means of displaying masculinity" (2008, 214). Though hegemonic masculinity traffics in particular notions of the ideal male form, physical domination, and strength, technological mastery and the "heroic" creation of imagined futures has historically intervened in authorizing other forms of masculinity (Wajcman 1991).[17] In Lori Kendall's ethnographic work exploring masculinity online, she pointed out that the mainstreaming of computer technology has shifted the understanding of "nerd" somewhat, arguing that, "Since the 1980s, the previously liminal masculine identity of the nerd has been rehabilitated and partly incorporated into hegemonic masculinity" (2002, 81). This complex gendering of technology, and technological skill, is a crucial component in understanding geek masculinity (Douglas 1999). Though there is a flexibility around which any particular formulation of gendering works with a given technology (see, for example, Jennifer Light's 1999 consideration of women and computing), that technology is worked over by notions of who should, and shouldn't, be engaged with it—and what it means to do so. Because gaming has long been linked with technological savvy, it has benefited from particular forms of legitimacy (Dovey and Kennedy 2006).[18]

Athletic Masculinity

So far I've focused on geek masculinity owing to the powerful connection it has with game culture, but when talking about gender identity in e-sports we have to bring in a second trope, that of the sportsperson (typically a man) and athleticism. Betsy Wearing addresses the ideological power hegemonic *sporting* masculinity has, arguing, for example, that athleticism comes to stand in for an overall valuation of self, "To be better at sport is translatable into being better or more capable in other areas of life" (1998, 76). Inhabiting athleticism can form a powerful stance, offering access to a privileged form of masculinity that not only underpins notions of male dominance, but traffics in the valorization of strength, physical skill, and a kind of "survival of the fittest" model of hierarchy. Athleticism has also long been tied to rubrics about its "civilizing" powers, drawing it into complex relationships with race and ethnicity. Though sporting masculinity can be quite tricky to easily place when we fold in things like class, we can nonetheless see the ways athleticism has long been seen as an important component to building overall masculinity (and the stigma that can come from the image of the "wimp" or frail man). Unlike geek masculinity, which can be inflected up or down the power hierarchy, athletic masculinity holds a fairly congenial relationship to hegemonic masculinity.

While computer gamers have been historically conflated with the technically savvy (something that I'd argue is shifting significantly), their identity (as with geeks writ large) is also typically framed in opposition to traditional athletic masculinity. Though we have an entire genre of movies that traffic in the juxtaposition of the nerd versus the jock, with the nerd usually reigning victorious, in much the same way many women can feel the burden of stereotypical forms of femininity, there is a kindred form of masculinity that, "revenge of the nerds" aside, still weighs in its own way on some boys and men. Garry Whannel has argued that "Dominant masculinity is experienced by many men as a straightjacket, a set of conventions of behavior, style, ritual and practice that limit and confine, and are subject to surveillance, informal policing and regulation" (2010, 6). For some men, geek identity is one way of negotiating this.

It is, of course, important to note that while men may struggle with their own set of burdensome stereotypes this does not mean that all things are equal. My intent is not to obscure the ways male geeks still regularly benefit from systems of privilege. There remain significant structural forms of sexism that enact themselves on women in powerful ways. Nonetheless, we need better accounts of the diversity of masculinity within game culture, rooted in an acknowledgement of intersectionality where things like class, race, ethnicity, and sexuality also play crucial roles. We also need to find ways to talk about how hegemonic forms of masculinity are working in game culture, against both men and women.

Geek or Athlete?

So how do male professional computer gamers fit within this discussion? Quite complexly. On the one hand some of the players I've spoken with clearly locate themselves in a tradition of geeky passion for games, situating themselves always slightly outside mainstream culture. For these players being a geek, or specifically a gaming geek, is a core component of their identity, in which pro gaming is simply a natural result of that passion. The professionalization of their play remains deeply tied to its home within game and geek culture. They are typically not invested in porting into e-sports the hegemonic masculinity of traditional athleticism and sports. They can feel ill at ease with more traditional performances of sports masculinity they are asked to undertake ("posing" for television productions, having to look "polished," or maintaining a "tough guise" a la Katz 1999. See also Segal 1990). For some, their referent point will be to something *other than* sports (as in the *Starcraft* player who likened himself to a chess master).

On the other hand, one can hear a cohort of players talk about their prior traditional athletic achievements and participation in team sports. Pro gaming for them is not fundamentally tied to any deeply held geek identity but is instead part of the trajectory of being a competitive and athletic person. The public performance of e-sports player as traditional sports star—complete with money, women, and fame—causes no pause. Nicholas T. Taylor's study (2009b) of the MLG circuit paints a fairly devastating portrait of the ways hegemonic sports masculinity is performed, particularly within the corporate imagery and press materials for the league. We can turn to the work of scholars such as Michael Messner (1989, 1990) and, again, R. W. Connell (1995), who link organized sports to the reinforcement of hegemonic masculinity and a form of gender identity that often brings with it "separate (and unequal)" spheres between men and women. Within this formulation the e-sports player echoes the values of traditional athletic masculinity, simply minus the emphasis on physical qualities.

Each of these stances reflects an orientation to hegemonic masculinity in slightly different ways. And depending on *which* athletic tradition participants tie their own e-sports practice to, we may find slight variations on its relationship with traditional masculinity. There is no single type of masculinity within the e-sports scene (and indeed within computer gaming more broadly) and the forms present are constantly undergoing change as the larger culture integrates computer gaming into its list of acceptable leisure activities, not only for men but also for women. Within pro gaming you will find those who embrace more geeky forms of masculinity and those who align themselves more closely with traditional athletic masculinity.

On the ground, the look and feel of masculinity as it is constructed at tournaments has always struck me as too complex to easily categorize. When you go to a tournament you don't see rooms filled with geeks as in the *The Big Bang Theory* television show. You see young guys typically dressed in the fashion of the day, with haircuts like any other (for several years it seemed all you saw was the ubiquitous faux-hawk). While there may be what we'd call "geek" t-shirts here and there, overall the look is far more mainstream than not. Indeed, the fact that "geek" has become a kind of hip mainstream identity these days doesn't make the segregation and stratification of these things any clearer. And yet I do want to make note of the fact that the guys at these tournaments definitely aren't, for the most part, conforming to the mainstream athlete/sports star masculine identity. For one thing they are often still quite young and still very much in the process of figuring out who they are as men. There is awkwardness, and the ongoing construction of personal narratives as they skill up as a pro and try to integrate that new identity into their life. You also still find a real diversity of body types at tournaments. Unlike traditional athletics, which weeds through physicality and segregates (and excludes), within pro gaming you will find short and tall, skinny and chubby, fit and not. There is no classic male physique dominating the scene.

Perhaps what has often been the most perplexing—though of course this is exactly how the system works—is the way in which hegemonic masculinity both at times infuses itself into the scene while the very embodied presence of the participants would undermine it. Pro player talk can certainly be smattered with misogynistic or, at the least, retrograde notions about women. The notion that women are just inherently not going to ever be as good at computer games as men is all too common. Homophobic language, where calling someone "gay" is considered a slur and "fag jokes" are considered funny, remains a persistent component in parts of game culture.[19] C. J. Pascoe notes in her ethnography of a high school that "achieving a masculine identity entails the repeated repudiation of the specter of failed masculinity. Boys lay claim to masculine identities by lobbing homophobic epithets at one another. They also assert masculine selves by engaging in heterosexist discussions of girls' bodies and their own sexual experiences" (2007, 5). These components are certainly found within e-sports and are a pernicious aspect of it.

And yet very often the boys and men enacting these performances are themselves sidelined from hegemonic masculinity as we'd identify it in the mainstream by their own passions (for technology, for gaming), their own bodies (either ill-suited to traditional athletics or not conforming to mainstream ideal forms), or their own desires around intimacy and community. Their talk is deeply tied up in the specificities of computer gaming and that kind of intense focus and detail we think of as the hallmarks of geekdom. Measured against hegemonic masculinity, some of these guys would be found wanting. That men and boys who are themselves marginalized and othered by mainstream culture would enact the same kinds of discriminatory moves is, however common, still painful to watch.

Part of what is happening in the pro scene, and game culture more generally, is a struggle over the status of masculinity within it. Understanding gender as a dynamic process constantly under work, flexible and shifting, allows us to situate what is happening within geek masculinity and game culture into a broader conversation involving not only traditional forms of masculinity, but femininity as well (Butler 1990). As Wheaton (2004b) notes in her discussion of windsurfing culture, there may be competing masculinities at work within a sporting scene. The status of geeks in our culture, and what it means to be a gamer, is under hot debate in many circles.

The defense of "geekness," if you will, can play out in a couple ways. For some participants, gaming and e-sports offer a potential for disrupting traditional norms, lines of stratification (around physicality), or social isolation (where gaming forms possibilities for community and support).

We may hear echoes of "ambivalent masculinity" identified in other emerging lifestyle sports (Wheaton 2004b). In this slice there is less investment in reifying hegemonic masculinity.

There is a second branch of defense, though, that is slightly different. Listen to gamer podcasts and you'll hear a lot of tumult about the state of games and, by extension, game culture. Fears of casualness and, I think, a kind of implied feminization pervade. For many e-sports players and gamers in general, retaining "geek" in game culture is crucial for maintaining some sense of seriousness, focus, and intensity.

For others the quest to valorize e-sports links it strongly to athletics. It is woven into a battle to normalize a new twist on hegemonic masculinity to show that "real men" can play computer games (actually an invocation of the idealized "real man"). The fag jokes, athletic/star posturing, sexist language and objectification of women (often, devastatingly, of female pro players), and trash talk are part of performing a masculinity that seeks to simultaneously inhabit traditional forms of privilege while shedding the outsider status and marginalization geek identity has long held.[20]

Femininity and Pro Gaming

This struggle around masculinity has real and powerful consequences for how girls and women have access to and operate within not only pro gaming but game culture more broadly. Discussions of masculinity and femininity are tricky because it is easy to slide into conflating the terms with men and women and to unthinkingly embed the discussion within a heteronormative frame in a way that doesn't allow for recognition of both more feminine men and more masculine women (Halberstam 1998; Landström 2007). That is not my intent here. While I want to situate this discussion in a way that allows for the critical and analytical space for such categories—and indeed my own politics align more with these formulations—I also want to acknowledge that many people still closely tie their construction of "men" and "women" to these categories and that for them, shifts in understanding gender come primarily from broadening what is permitted *within* traditional masculinity or femininity (and by extension, to men and women) (see also Taylor 2008). It's a difficult issue and I'm hesitant to overstate either formulation. I do, however, want to signal my own interest in more nuanced theoretical frameworks.

Both Nicholas T. Taylor (2009b) and Todd Harper (2010) observe that women, when they are visible in the scene, are often there largely as supporters, observers, and fans. Taylor in particular suggests that their inclusion is often actually "*in the service of* [emphasis his] masculinized technoculture" (2009b, 159). This is at times certainly the case. But, as with some of my previous work, I'm drawn to the ones who *are there* for themselves, who are playing not just watching. Those who do engage in high-end competition sit squarely within the battlelines not simply around gender and gaming, but in the core debates about both technology and sports. In much the same way we could read e-sports masculinity through the lens of geek culture and sports, we might do the same in relation to femininity.

Geek Girls

We might begin, for example, with thinking about the status of geek girls and women who play computer games. While we now have a solid body of literature showing women's active engagement in computer gaming (Bryce and Rutter 2002, Cassell and Jenkins 1998, Kafai et al. 2008, Kennedy 2005, Kerr 2003, Lin 2008, Schott and Horrell 2000, Taylor 2006a), women remain all too frequently marginalized. Though it's not unusual to now see young girls out in public playing with their Nintendo DSs or shopping at the local game store, there is still an all-too-common notion that women who play games seriously are anomalies.[21] When stories are presented about women gamers the focus is increasingly on "casual" or Facebook games. That each of these genres is simultaneously decried as a scourge on the form should alert us to the stakes, and battles, currently going on in game culture around gender.

This turn toward linking women gamers with a specific type of game dovetails with the historical arguments that women play differently, that they want to engage mostly with identity or sociality in games or are not interested in direct competition. Though rebutted by evidence again and again, an imagined difference between men and women as gamers remains a persistent myth.[22] This fundamental segregation, typically rooted in a story of naturalized sexual difference, has been structuring traditional sports via notions of athleticism and gender for centuries (Bolin and Granskog 2003, Cahn 1994, Hargreaves 1994, McDonagh and Pappano 2008).

This model of difference intersects a notion of expertise and mastery that often underlies many of our stories about how men and women are. It goes to larger issues about how we conceptualize women who don't occupy traditional forms of femininity. Think for a moment about the figure of the geek girl. Perhaps your mind turns to one of the several variations of this figure in popular culture. One form traffics in the sexualization of the smart girl (the librarian who lets her hair down for the right man) while another riffs on the girl who plays with "boy's toys" (the "hot" girl gamer you sometimes see in ads). A third is that of the geek women rendered asexual or sometimes varied as "dyke."

I want to focus on the actual geek girls though, the ones whose images aren't created in the service of upholding traditional femininity but are instead real identities of actual women navigating a culture that regularly makes no place for them. Starting with Sherry Turkle's work on technologists (1984) and moving to more contemporary research on women who are deeply engaged with technology, we can get a sense of the lives of actual women who are involved with computers and gaming, who may self-identify as geeks or nerds, and who navigate our culture's ambivalence around gender and technology. What we find are stories of women for whom technology (and often science) form a core interest and passion. They may be one of a handful of women in their college class who are doing computer science or the girl who will regularly sit down to play an FPS. Her interest in technology rivals that of the men around her and as such, she can be perplexing.

I want to linger for a moment on this notion of passionate engagement because it goes to the heart of geek identity. Intensity of focus on something, comprehensive knowledge of the domain, and the public demonstration of such are all geek pleasures. In our culture, though, it is rare to find girls or women afforded the space or opportunity for this kind of intense focus. Consider the image of the boy pouring over his comic collection or baseball cards or the adult music nerd (perhaps most evocatively envisioned by Nick Hornby (1995) in *High Fidelity* through the character of Rob, with his ongoing rearrangement of his record collection). We have no shortage of images of men who set aside all other parts of life in a single-minded quest to solve difficult problems or achieve an ambitious goal (the wiz-kid technologist or genius scientist). The linking of highly focused, dedicated attention to a very narrow slice of the world is something men and boys are readily authorized to undertake in our culture. That this kind of focus typically leads to expert status highlights the political nature of what is at stake. Being in the public (versus domestic) sphere and able to intensely engage with a domain is deeply woven with power.

This kind of single-mindedness is then more problematically rendered when it is a young girl or a woman fixated on a domain not traditionally authorized for her (such as home or children). The woman who exhibits the kind of single-minded focus and passion we regularly see permitted in boys and men, when not wholly invisible, is either rendered as neglectful (playful mothers typically get this brush) or pathological (often the very gender identity of the woman comes into question). The insistence on moderation for women and girls goes to the heart of why geek identity can be such a profoundly oppositional identity for them. Assertions of knowledge, competency, and technical and scientific skill are core parts of geekdom for men and women alike. The geek girl is fundamentally upending systems of mastery and exclusion.

Like their male geek compatriots, geek girls also often eschew traditional performances of gender identity. Bucholtz's work (1998) on nerd girls discusses, for example, how they use clothing, voice pitch, even wordplay as methods for moving outside of hegemonic forms of femininity. This nonnormative performance of female identity is not without costs, however. Sexism (even within geek communities) is a constant struggle and it can come from both men and women (Bucholtz 2002). Women's sexuality, which is so often closely coupled with traditional femininity, can leave geek girls positioned (within the larger culture) in the strange spot of being thought of as asexual (much like geek men) or not heterosexual at all unless exceptional measures are taken to signal otherwise.

Sporting Women

As with the discussion of masculinity, we should weave in a consideration of sports and athleticism when trying to situate pro women gamers. Tess Kay has suggested three common rationales we've seen operate historically to regulate women's access to traditional athletics: medical (which is about being "physiologically unsuited to sporting activity" and potentially "damaged by it"), aesthetic (where playing the sport is deemed an "unattractive spectacle"), and social (where the "qualities and behaviors associated with sport are contrary to 'real' femininity") (2003, 90). These ideologies have doggedly reinforced women's exclusion from sports. Kay (2003) pointed out, for example, International Olympic Committee founder Pierre De Coubertin's long efforts to get women out of the Olympics even after they had been allowed to participate. And as the skirmishes over the 2010 Winter Olympics' exclusion of women from ski jumping shows, the issue is, stunningly, far from settled (Laurendeau and Adams 2010).

Underlying these formulations are foundational beliefs in the difference between men and women (and indeed that we can speak in such broad universal categories). They come to support arguments that would propose sports for women be more "naturally" tied to notions of aesthetics and grace versus strength and speed or a desire for indirect (versus direct) competition, if they are thought to enjoy competition at all. Such a position would typically argue that women do not enjoy contact sports or aggressive action.[23] While the specter of the physically frail woman doesn't hold much traction anymore, there nonetheless remain persistent models that suggest different inherent abilities, or lack of them, around cognition, spatial reasoning, or hand-eye coordination between men and women. These rhetorics are not unique to computer gaming but indeed are regularly found in traditional sports as well (Bolin and Granskog 2003, Cahn 1994).

Women and Pro Gaming

This collision of ideologies surrounding gender, technology, and sports puts pro women gamers in an incredibly precarious position. Though they often share similar pleasures alongside their male counterparts—Kennedy (2005) notes the recurring themes of enjoying "athleticism, balance, coordination, and risk taking" among female *Quake* players, for example—they face additional challenges. Their love of gaming and dedication to it—to the degree that they would construct highly specialized skill sets and identities within particular titles or genres—regularly marks them as unfeminine, "other," or simply curious in our culture until compensatory signals are given otherwise. Interestingly the majority of the women I've seen in the pro scene are also engaged with the FPS genre so their involvement with gaming takes place within a domain that is typically seen as the most violent and rough.[24] As Kennedy (2005) quotes one female *Quake* player, "People say it's not ladylike to sit in front of a computer or want to play a game where you run around with a shotgun, but why not? I get insulted a lot and told I'm like a boy, but I'm not, I'm just a different kind of girl" (185). That they would additionally frame their activities within a model of sporting or athletic identity implicates them in the baggage it also still carries about competitive women.

The on-the-ground lives of women in pro gaming reflect a complex navigation, and negotiation, with not only the practical issues of being a top e-sports player, but the additional challenges being a woman in the scene presents. There is certainly a slice of game culture that runs newbies through a gauntlet (typically denigrating them for their lack of knowledge and expertise via taunting and harsh verbal exchanges) and the sexism found during these moments can be particularly grating to some. As a response (and indeed survival strategy) many women will either completely hide their gender when possible (turning off voice communication, picking gender-neutral names online, not linking their "real" life with their gamer identity) or preemptively address the issue (adding a kind of "yeah, get over it" style statement to their forum sig or making a joke of the situation when they first "out" themselves as a woman to fellow gamers).

For women who choose to let their gender be known, ultimately unavoidable if they go pro, they can find themselves mediating an expectation of otherness or "female masculinity" (Halberstam 1998). Compensatory signals to reassure others of their gender identity, such as pictures (or avatars) meant to convey sexual attractiveness, mentions of other "girlie" interests, or notations of hobbies or other activities that perform a more traditional femininity are not uncommon.[25] I am not suggesting that when we see these among girl gamers we are witnessing either intentional performances or inauthentic representations of self. Signs of traditional femininity can coincide with geekdom and girl gaming. Kennedy (2005) argues, for example, that "by foregrounding both their 'femaleness' and their skill in the game they offer a different set of meanings to computers, computer games, and technological competence" (199). It is also at times strategically deployed as a way of engaging with sexism and stereotypes that would otherwise sideline the woman gamer.

Some women choose to adopt the more dominant stance by acculturating—adopting forceful player names, engaging in trash talk, having an in-your-face attitude, and even making sexist remarks. As Kennedy (2005) notes, this is not simply "aping masculinity" but invokes something more akin to a mythical "monstrous feminine" which is woven through with often playful invocations of dominating yet oppositional identity. Some try to simultaneously enact both ends of the spectrum—a dazzling display of performative agility where they come to represent *both* a hyper masculinity and femininity (kick ass and take names while dolled up).

Ultimately many pro women players experience their commitment to e-sports as constantly challenged. Their dedication, knowledge of the domain, and overall "gamerness" gets pushed in ways men in their position might not face. The idea that there are women who hang out in the scene to be "star-fuckers" or simply meet men is perhaps one of the most pernicious variations that serious pro women run up against. All of these twists and turns represent the performative work women gamers do when occupying slices of game (and indeed, sports) culture.

While these all represent an important burden on women players, there are other structural factors that additionally shape their access to, and success in, the pro gaming scene. There is a common refrain you hear when you start talking to people in e-sports that suggests the reason we don't currently find more top women playing is that they simply aren't good enough. This can get spun a couple ways. Occasionally you hear a retrograde notion of biological differences between men and women. These theories suggest inherent limited abilities of women to excel in computer games. This is sometimes formulated around a notion that in the past men were hunters and women were gatherers and thus, it makes sense that women would not be as good at computer games, which often require hand-eye coordination or shooting skills. Other times they are based on vaguer biological notions, tying into stories about varying forms of cognition rooted in sexual difference. Sometimes they are framed as a kind of pop-psychology take on women as not interested in fighting or competition.

Another theory, much more commonly heard, about why we don't see more women in the pro scene is framed as a kind of perplexed question. The formulation typically goes: "Anyone can play computer games and anyone can enter tournaments so if women aren't there it's just because they aren't good enough, aren't trying hard enough, right?" (see also Harper 2010). This model imagines both computer gaming and e-sports as a fundamentally individualistic and meritocratic venture. What it obviously misses is the deeply sociological nature of play and professionalization and the way structures shape access and opportunity.

As I have argued elsewhere, participation in computer gaming is fundamentally constructed through social and cultural formulations of identity and leisure, as well as institutions and structures we inhabit (Taylor 2008). Our even considering certain activities acceptable for ourselves is tied to larger cultural stories about what women and men are allowed to do (not to mention how our class, race, or sexuality shapes what is deemed legitimate). Top female players face the double-identity challenge of not only pursuing an e-sports career (something men in the scene regularly identify as an often fraught path, at least until they start winning significant money) but doing so *as women* in a culture that generally speaking has no good model for (1) highly competitive women, (2) participation in an activity typically seen as violent and aggressive (particularly in the case of FPSs), and (3) understanding their being geeky, passionate about gaming, and having focused engagement with a specialized domain unrelated to areas linked to traditional femininity. The identity challenges—both personally and in how one's location is understood and legitimated by one's family and peers—are no small matter for pro women gamers.

Beyond the issues of leisure, work, and identity are larger structural factors that shape participation. We are introduced to games, taught how to play, and skilled up by our engagement with others. Not only do girls and women often face an uphill battle when it comes to choosing computer games as a leisure (not to mention professional) identity, they are often marginalized in their access to communities through which they could develop their gaming expertise. Sometimes this is simply that they don't have a strong network of friends to play with. At the more extreme end, stories abound of women who can't get practice matches if they are known to be a woman because "boys don't like losing to girls." Those who do get regular play opportunities still face additional challenges in being a regular member of the high-end competitive community. Whereas a slightly less talented male player will sometimes be brought onto a team and skilled up (often based on their friendship and other network connections), women are very rarely (indeed I cannot think of any cases of this currently) given similar opportunities. As any athlete can tell you, being able to play with and against people slightly above your level is key to improving. If women are locked out of meaningful challenges that allow them to hone their skill they will not be able to compete at the same level as the men in the scene who, via their access to more robust networks and the easier occupation of gamer identity, are able to develop professional skills.

Separate and Unequal

Despite the meritocratic myth that infuses pro gaming, contemporary e-sports is deeply segregated, with women and men generally playing on different teams and in separate tournaments.[26] As such there has been a reification of the gendered division we find in traditional gaming. This sits uneasily alongside a common feeling that, unlike traditional sports, where an ideology of physical difference predominates, there is no real reason men and women can't play together. While tournaments typically make no formal claim about the competition being only for men, because of the way expertise is built and access to teams is structured, in practice competitors tend to be only men unless there is an explicit women's category.

When there are women-only divisions within tournaments the response alternates between grudging acceptance and outright vilification. Those who accept women-only competitions can present a range of reasons for their support. Some believe there are real underlying inherent differences between men and women in relation to gaming skill such that segregating women into their own competitions is the fairest thing to do. Their model is typically aligned with traditional athletics and splitting up men and women in competition simply fits a classic binary akin to the traditional organization of sports. As one person framed it, "You study all traditional sports down through the ages, from the Olympics from basketball, soccer, football, baseball, women participate in their own leagues because of a skill gap."

Others, indeed often women competitors themselves, are more pragmatic in their support of the gendered division. They often recognize the structural factors that are holding women back from reaching the highest end of competitive play and argue that until women are able to perform at the same level as the men, it is important for the development of the sport and the players themselves to foster a space that still supports the best of women's play. One team owner who both recognized the economic uses of pro women (meaning sponsors liked them for their visibility) and also saw the structural factors at work put it this way:

> Some people are like, yeah, well, they should be separated and I feel like it makes sense from a certain perspective because I believe that they are, that in the e-sports culture a girl has a disadvantage as she tries to make her way up the ranks. Not because of any innate physical differences but rather because she just has sociological disadvantages, institutional disadvantages, from being a girl in a boy's world.

The gendered division of competition is often seen as simply a stopgap measure until women are structurally supported and skilled up enough to be able to compete against men—though how that big leap will happen is typically little thought-out.[27]

Many men in the scene, though, find the existence of women's tournaments an outrage, an injustice. Of all the hot-button subjects you can hit in e-sports, this is one of the most loaded. The frustration typically comes not from any deep-seated concern for the collective costs of gender segregation on both women *and* men, but instead from a feeling that women are getting unfair and undeserved attention and benefit. The line generally goes that women-only competitions valorize weaker play and that the women competing against each other, while admittedly better than average players, are simply not as skilled as the men in the scene. The argument is typically that if they were they would either be on men's teams or competing in matches against men. As one male team captain simply stated to me, "Women just aren't good enough at *Counter-Strike* to play against men, so that's why they have the tournaments for them."

Underlying this line is very often an economic argument, though it is rarely framed that transparently. The concern is that there is a scarcity of resources (sponsorships, prize money, team and tournament slots) and that it is being wasted on players who are not the best but who receive them simply by virtue of their gender. There is also often a feeling that women-only tournaments are not meritocratic events but publicity stunts meant to garner attention. In addition to tournaments being critiqued along these lines, some women's teams themselves are also taken to task. The support they get from sponsors is seen as a gimmick tied not to their skill but to their gender.

I want to spend a moment unpacking this because it is a complex issue. It is certainly true that very often women's gaming, including women's pro gaming, is constructed as a marketing ploy. The supposed novelty of women gamers—and indeed it is only an *imagined* novelty given the actual large number of real women playing computer games—has been used to sell everything from soda to computer equipment. It is also the case that some pro women's teams have strategically deployed more traditional gender performances to trade on this (through the use of sexy poses juxtaposed against weaponry or tech, for example). That tournaments, advertisers, and even sometimes the women themselves have been complicit in "playing" gender in this way in the pro gaming scene is undisputable. But unfortunately this is typically where this critique stops, and this is a fatal analytic move.

The ability to use women's gender and sexuality in this way is *only* possible because of the deeply sexist ground upon which gaming and e-sports is built. It is the *assumed difference* (decidedly rooted in inequality) that drives these moves. And it is also this framework that sets up differential systems of access and exclusion. Those who are frustrated by women-only competitions or the way hybridized geek femininity is used for advertising and hype purposes within gaming need to take a step back and turn their critical attention to the underlying systems of misogyny that make these things possible. Far too often they are targeting the wrong culprits, the women themselves.

We need to think about slightly varying forms of accountability. By this I mean simply that pro women players themselves who participate in more conservative gender moves so that they may stay in the scene perhaps be granted some leeway. They are playing the meta-game according to rules that have been established well beyond e-sports culture. We see this in traditional sports all the time, where elite female athletes are constantly called upon to symbolically demonstrate their femininity (as both a cultural and at times, personal, reassurance).

As a feminist of a certain type, I don't want to entirely let these performances off the hook. We all bear responsibility for oppressive systems and need to be accountable for our complicity in them. But I don't place the young women who are simply trying to snag a sponsor to fund their trip to a match in the same category as advertisers, tournament organizers, and team owners who, having real power to formulate more progressive models of equitable gender relations, choose to stick with tired old ones. The male pro players on the circuit, including captains who help build rosters, are accountable for the small everyday ways they perpetuate sexist systems.

We should remember too that women's teams are often pressured by their sponsors or tournament organizers to construct highly traditionally gendered representations of themselves (a discrepancy often so clearly, and painfully, seen when you look at photos they produce themselves for their fansites) or participate in their own segregation if they want to remain in the professional domain. I would very much like to see the people who rail against women-only tournaments or teams turn their critical attention to the *institutional and systemic roots* within the scene that are really at the heart of the matter. Practically, this means real reflection and change in e-sports involving everything from dismantling the newbie gauntlet to more progressive systems of training and recruiting new talent.

Mainstreaming Geeks

For those who follow how gender plays out in sports, especially women's sports, most of what I'm describing is terribly, painfully familiar. Rather than turning traditional formulations of sports and gender on their heads with the advent of e-sports, when it comes to women and girls we see more of the same as we always have. Geek masculinity has had some impact on pro e-sports, but geek femininity has had much less. This is perhaps not surprising when we take into account the complex relationship geekdom has with hegemonic masculinity.

More broadly though, the meaning of "geek" is, however, shifting and we've yet to see the impact on e-sports. Geeks seem to suddenly have become all the rage, with everyone saying they were, or are, a nerd. Whether or not hegemonic masculinity is simply undergoing a tweak in order to absorb whatever oppositional possibilities geekdom held is yet to be seen (though history probably makes me less optimistic than I'd like to be).

At the same time, computer gaming's ties to geek identity are being significantly loosened. While historically computer games have been a domain for a very particular demographic (white, middle-class boys and men who have had access either to personal computers or university labs), this has shifted in important ways over the last several decades. In addition to the growth of women gamers, console games (especially via used and one-generation-old machines) have increasingly been picked up by the working class and communities of color, broadening the demographics of who is playing. Mobile phone and more casual gaming have also worked to breach the age gap we often associate with gaming. One of the biggest implications of these shifts is that in reality most computer game players do not actually self-identify as geeks or nerds but instead locate their time with games as simply one more activity among many. Increasingly, computer gaming is integrated into the leisure identity of a broader range of men and boys (not to mention women and girls). Playing computer games need not tie you to a geek identity and, as it becomes a mainstream leisure activity, it need not automatically assume any oppositional stance to hegemonic masculinity.

Just for (White) Boys?

The conversation around performances of gender and the structure of the scene must also take into account the ways race and ethnicity intersect pro gamer identity. In my previous discussion of geeks, while I tried to nod to how sexuality intersects the issue, I sidestepped how race, for example, complicates it. Ron Eglash (2002) notes how the imagined "compulsory cool of black culture" has been historically situated against geek identity. Though black nerds act as a "pioneering" category, the overall trope is one in which black racial identity becomes oppositional to technoscience and notions of "acting white" can take their toll on some.

While there is relatively little research specifically devoted to understanding computer game play among, for example, African Americans, there are a couple notable exceptions that help us situate the issue in relation to pro gaming.[28] It appears that any stigma or reticence typically associated with technology can be muted when it comes to digital games. DiSalvo, Crowley, and Norwood write, for example, that "African and Hispanic American youth are more likely to play digital games than are Caucasian American youth" and cite a 2001 study which found that young African American boys "spend more than one hour per day playing video games" (2008). Their work highlights the ways gaming is located within console culture for African Americans and around preferences for fighting games as well as "sports games or games that featured characters from other aspects of their lives—sports figures, rappers, and comic book characters" (2008, 134). They also note the important social and competitive components of playing for these gamers and, citing work by Kolko, Strohm, and Lonian (2003a), suggest that it is much more common within these communities to be playing with someone in the same room versus alone. DiSalvo et al. argue that some of the practices and norms found in computer gaming actually run against the ways African American players understand what constitutes fair play.

> It seemed that the extension of games as a part of their sports practices included an element of good sportsmanship, which in turn limited the amount of modifications, hacking, and cheats that the player used. This practice of good sportsmanship in video game play did not encourage agency with technology. By accepting the default game setting, the rules and expected play, young men were not modifying aspects of the game to "game the system," they were not looking at the computation behind the games as something they could manipulate. (2009, 2)

This research raises some interesting angles for thinking about diversity in the scene. The historical focus in e-sports around personal computers as the primary gaming device has a profound effect on who gets to skill up and compete. As DiSalvo et al.'s work highlights, for some communities consoles are the primary means of engaging with digital games (see also Kolko, Strohm, and Lonian 2003b). We could also link this to a conversation about how women and the economically disadvantaged have historically been sidelined by the focus on PCs (women often getting hand-me-down computers and the working class having none). In those countries where there is a robust gaming café scene—a place you go and pay an hourly fee to play popular games and get online—this effect is somewhat less pronounced. Players who cannot afford their own equipment can still play and train via these spaces. But in places without game cafés, not owning your own machine and having net access are crucial barriers to becoming a top player. While sharing a machine with a roommate or a family member can be a partial solution, it can prove tricky. A "machine of one's own" can be invaluable. Access to personal computers and the Internet has, of course, changed dramatically over the last several years and more and more people have access previously unimaginable. The historical impact of PC-centric gaming in e-sports has to be accounted for nonetheless.

There are also the ways notions of fair play complicate how one might experience or have meaningful engagement with e-sports community practices. In pro gaming it is common for players to tweak their settings and be comfortable with modding their technology or software to produce better results and gameplay experience (a form of technicity a la Dovey and Kennedy). If these kinds of activities are seen as running counter to legitimate play, as DiSalvo et al.'s research suggests for African American console players, then the practices of the pro scene may in fact be at odds with how a player constructs their own sense of fair play and competition.[29]

These structural barriers and varying notions of fair play also intersect forms of racism that continue to be all too common within game culture (Nakamura forthcoming). Though we typically hear most often about homophobia or sexism in gamer communities, racial epithets are not unheard of and continue to inscribe forms of exclusion. Once players hit online play communities they immediately expose themselves to taunts and recriminations they are shielded from when playing with just their friends and family. In much the same way women can be daunted by this experience, people of color sometimes confront real hassles and frustrations in the broader game culture. We would be remiss to overlook the ways these practices hinder full participation in competitive gaming and the detrimental effect they have on creating a truly diverse e-sports scene.

The most notable, and growing, exception to the general homogeneity within e-sports seems to reside within the fighting game scene. While the FPS and RTS genres seem to largely uphold the stereotype of the white male gamer within Europe and North America, the fighting game community has supported a more racially and ethnically diverse set of players (albeit still mostly male) (see also Harper 2010). Some of the top players in the scene are Asian and Asian American and you can find other players of color in highly ranked positions. That the fighting game scene originates in the arcades, and is not centered around the home PC, is crucial. It also transitioned into a console scene, a second key factor in situating its more heterogeneous configuration of player opportunities and identities. Consoles, especially those that are a generation old or purchased used, have been an important point of entry for people who can't otherwise afford computational technology. And while console games certainly have settings that can, and are, configured especially for competitive play, they are not quite as malleable as PC games where a variety of hacks and tweaks can be applied to the game itself and the very hardware everything is running on is diverse and endlessly configurable.

I must note one important caveat about a discussion of race and diversity in e-sports. This is not an easy question because, as a global sport, competitive computer gaming exists in a number of national and regional contexts that dramatically shape the issue. Each have their own ways of formulating notions of diversity in specific cultural contexts. Teams also regularly build their rosters internationally such that while the majority of a team's profile may be built around white North American players, there may be one major discipline within a franchise's roster made up of gamers from another part of the world. For example, a successful North American franchise might be made up entirely of Brazilian players, or there may be a mix of Asian and European players on a team roster. Situated globally, it is certainly the case that there is ethnic diversity within the scene, especially in venues like the WCG that use national affiliation as a core structuring mechanism. That said, there is nonetheless a relative homogeneity in terms of race and ethnicity within the North American and European scene where a majority of players still seem to be white men. Players of color are typically the exception and in much the same way sexism operates as a gauntlet for new players, we could similarly speak about the racism (typically covert but sometimes overt) that also acts as an access filter for both high-end and everyday play.

Becoming Pro

One of the most important things looking closely at the practices of high-end competitive computer gamers reveals is that playing can be a complex form of expressive human action. Rather than gamers being simply "button mashers," professional players illuminate the skill, strategic thinking, embodied knowledge, and complex human-technological hybridity at work in producing sophisticated computer game play.

Ultimately, though, their ability to shift their gaming from casual activity to professional occupation is complex. It is never just an issue of individual skill but the ways an entire system of practices, institutions, values, and forms of identity work on, and through, that player. A career trajectory from amateur to professional involves the transformation of what was once simply a leisure activity into a new serious endeavor. Structural factors, networks of opportunity and training, formulations of personal identity, and cultural legitimacy all form core components upon which the ability to become a pro gamer is built. As with all computer gaming, professional play doesn't exist in a bubble where individual skill is the only factor that matters but is instead constituted via a complex process.

Unlike traditional sports where there are institutionalized paths into professionalization, e-sports players are typically piecing together their careers as best they can. They often have to negotiate tricky domestic situations, where family and friends may not entirely understand what they are trying to do. They undergo socialization into professional identities via amateur and pro player communities. As they get signed to teams they break through to some layer of formal support but it often holds its own set of new challenges, from contracts to sponsorship to being on the road.

For women, the path to professionalization is fraught with additional challenges. Too often they are seen as anomalies within highly committed play communities and retrograde notions about gender present hurdles for the women trying to create e-sports careers. This ongoing struggle is linked to a larger conversation about the nature of both "gamer" and "athlete" within e-sports. Professional computer gaming is torn between these two models of high-intensity play, each of which constructs an idealized form of subjectivity in a slightly different way.

4 Growing an Industry

Contemporary sports are inextricably enmeshed with a much broader construction of athletics as industry. While amateur activities can be found, a good portion of our everyday experience of sports is now funneled through a complex circuit that includes transnational media products, stars, sponsors, and commercialized ownership.[1] Similarly, though hobbyist and indie computer game development are seeing a resurgence, that field is also squarely located as a global media product within a much larger industry of computation and digital leisure products. The rise of professional computer gaming has thus, unsurprisingly, itself undergone a transformation over the last decade where small, grassroots play intermingles with large-scale coordinated commercial efforts. Though the space is still very much under development and is by no means a well-oiled machine like the NFL or FIFA, it is important to take note of the structural developments happening in the service of pro gaming.

While pro players continue to be the lead story when e-sports is covered by mainstream media, there is an enormous amount of work taking place at other levels that is key to understanding the industry's development. From the very first tournaments I attended I was struck by the presence of older men who were there running the event, signing and managing the players, keeping the network up and running, providing sponsorship money, and paying out (or sometimes withholding) prize money. These were typically guys who, when you inquired about their own story, had once played at an amateur (or occasionally) pro level who were still passionate about a particular game or about computer games in general, and often had a dream of making what would otherwise be a hobby a real job. While often well known inside the scene, they would not be the ones showcased on television if e-sports ever broke into the mainstream. Yet they were key to e-sports development.

When we start looking at the business side of e-sports we find a number of other new professionals emerge. Team owners, referees, administrators, and sponsors now mix in among the up-and-coming young players. While they often fund these initiatives out of their own pocket in the hopes of future payoff, a number have managed to make a day job out of pro gaming. A variety of infrastructures—from teams and leagues to new economic conditions—have been developed over the years to support pro e-sports play.[2] We do not get the famous stars like Fatal1ty or Grubby without the behind-the-scenes work of organizers and business people. In this chapter I will explore several business models that have arisen in (and sometimes disappeared from) the e-sports scene. I'll discuss how pro gaming is interwoven with sponsorship and often fragile economic models. Turning attention to larger considerations and battles around intellectual property and governance, I'll also take a look at how the regulation of pro play has become one of the most interesting, and contested, areas of development.

Managing Play

As I signaled in chapter one, while e-sports has its roots in grassroots gaming communities, the formal organization of competitions and tournaments has been an important part of the history of professionalization from the beginning. Whether it was organized matches at early venues like Quakecon or dedicated tournaments organized by the CPL, the management of professional play forms an important part of the story of e-sports. Over the years many organizations have emerged and dissolved. When I started this research project I began making post-it notes for each new tournament or league that sprung up, sticking them to my wall to help me keep track. Over the years I've had to notate the majority of them with "closed" as organizations dedicated to e-sports fell by the wayside. The successes, and failures, are instructive.

Two Leagues, Two Models: CGS and ESL

At the Game Developer's Conference (GDC) in 2008 I ran into a fellow researcher who mentioned that he had heard a talk earlier from a company running pro e-sports events. Given the paucity of attention to e-sports over the years at GDC, this caught my attention and I was curious to track down who it was. After some program skimming I spotted that it was the CGS, the Championship Gaming Series. Since launching in 2006 (via a premiere tournament named the Championship Gaming Invitational) the organization had developed a reputation as a well-funded operation and for many represented a hopeful future for e-sports. Several people I've followed over the years had now found themselves on the CGS staff. Since its full-fledged launch the CGS had gobbled up many of the major teams and players and consolidated them into one all-encompassing league. The promise of regular salaries, high tournament payouts, and mainstream media coverage via DirectTV and other partners proved enticing to many people. I kicked myself that I'd somehow missed them on the program but when I spotted them listed in the exhibitor section I went off in search. When I finally found their area it was not a traditional booth showing off new games or business ideas but instead a kind of mini-meeting room cubicle, bare of pretty much anything but table and chairs. I knocked on the door, peeked my head in, and found one of their business development guys sitting at an empty desk prepping for his next meeting. We chatted briefly, swapping business cards, and I mentioned I'd be in California for a bit and would love to come down to see their offices and do some interviews if possible. He was fairly encouraging and when we got back in touch after the conference he made a point of putting me in contact with their press officer to set things up. Within a month I found myself in Southern California heading to their offices.

As I made my way in my rental car from downtown Los Angeles to Marina Del Ray, a somewhat upscale beach and boating community south of Venice, I was curious to see what the offices and on-site operation for the CGS looked like. Winding my way through packed Southern California roads, I located the nondescript building on a side street. The address was all I had to go on, there was no large sign out front, but as I pulled around to the back lot I spotted the company logo outside a door. While waiting in the lobby for my press contact, I watched ESPN on a flat-screen TV and scanned the covers of a variety of sports magazines. When I was ushered into the main office area I found a fairly large open space built out into that familiar new media shop look. Cubicles held people working, while a dedicated enclosed studio area for TV and audio productions. Various executives' offices were along the outer walls. Some game posters decorated the walls here and there, but the very slick visuals for the CGS—logos I was familiar with from their online site—were also present. The overall feel was of a pretty nice, yet rough, loft-style space well outfitted. This was not the fold-up chairs and table operation I'd grown familiar with from e-sports but instead looked like a start-up with some money behind it.

As the press officer led me into a conference room for a phone interview with the main producer he made sure to give me their official press packet, complete with well-produced DVDs showcasing their players and competitions. One entitled "Myths of Gaming" contained mini-stories meant to refute assumptions like "It's not a sport," "Gamers are boring," "Gaming's not a team thing," and "It's not exciting, there's no emotion." Geared to people (most likely potential sponsors and network stakeholders) who know nothing about gaming aside stereotypes and need to be shown that this is not a niche geeky thing but a new "All-American" sport, it offered high production value footage and staged vignettes of pro players and competitions.

All this well-produced exterior—from office space to marketing materials—was no accident. The CGS was not done on the cheap but funded (to the rumored tune of fifty million dollars for five years) by Liberty Media's satellite service DirectTV in association with Rupert Murdoch's News Corp (BSkyB and STAR).[3] From the outset, even with the initial Championship Gaming Invitational tournaments that were run before the launch of the actual league as a kind of test-bed, high production values and a polished appearance were present. Though the initiative was launched with advice from long-time experts in the scene including Craig Levine (founder of Team 3D and E-sports Entertainment), rather than being directed and managed by hardcore gamers and e-sports aficionados, the core executive team was made up of men who had spent time in the entertainment or sports industry and were often lawyers or business school grads. The CGS made no bones about wanting to bring together the sports elements of pro gaming with the entertainment value you could find in a well-produced poker show. Andy Reif, the organization's CEO, was quoted in an ESPN article on the launch of the league as saying, "Mike [Burks, executive producer] and his team are going to place the viewer inside the action with sports-style coverage, unmatched production values, and sixteen different HD cameras. By providing the right production values and storytelling, we will raise the sport to a new level" (Gaudiosi 2007).

As I describe in more detail in the next chapter, the CGS did some innovative things when it came to transforming competitive play for the televised format. It is also notable, however, for the ways it experimented with other core organizational structures. Though even at the first e-sports event I attended I met a team owner who signed players to contracts, the CGS set itself apart both for the number of contracted players it held (topping 180 by the final season), the amount of their salaries (the highest I have seen unofficially sourced was $30,000 USD/year), and various bonuses. In addition to players, the CGS also salaried team managers, commentators, website content producers, administrators, and a variety of other people to manage and run the league. It is not the introduction of these roles that is notable but that in the vast majority of e-sports they are carried out either by hardcore fan-voluntary labor or ad hoc contract work, not by people who are able to make e-sports their regular day job. For everyone laboring in the e-sports field (often underpaid) for years, the fact that the CGS was giving lots of people steady paid work was significant. For many it felt as if e-sports were finally standing on solid ground, getting the attention and legitimacy they always deserved.

The CGS also made some interesting choices in how it structured competition. As a league it was made up of a number of teams (eighteen total by 2008, the year it folded). Originally launched with an eye on the North American market it was quickly—some say too quickly—transformed into an international league with European and "Pan-Asian" regions. As one executive said to me about the global ambitions, "Eventually, I think we want to look very much like European football. So in the long term, you know, there's a league in every country. And there's teams in every country and then the winning team from each country will move on to the regional championship and then they'll move on to a world championship." This was a hugely ambitious plan, especially for an organization that had in essence only been up and running for a couple of years.

While two CGS teams were pre-existing outfits (Jason Lake's Complexity Gaming and Craig Levine's Team 3D), essentially the CGS created an additional sixteen new brands—new teams with new general managers and rosters pieced together from existing teams worldwide. They were constructed around regional affiliations ("San Francisco Optx," "London Mint," "Singapore Sword") and with an eye toward capturing fans who would identify with the team. This focus mirrored a general attitude at the CGS that the scene's personalities were crucial to pulling people in, be it via player profiles or by showing the personalities of general managers. If you look at the CGS press materials from this period you certainly get info about the games. But it's accompanied by in-depth player and team profiles and stories, complete with high-gloss photos. The focus on personalities was no accident. Tying into this human factor was seen as key for e-sports to grow. As an executive put it (and indeed echoing Hyong Jun Hwang of South Korea's OnGameNet), "You know, you want to build up stars, right? Because I think if you look at every sport it grows more...you have a better chance of being a more popular sport and growing fans if you have consistent stars." In a sport with young players and fairly high turnover, this was no small feat.

This orientation is strongly informed by bringing together not only traditional sports media approaches but also a desire to translate e-sports out to a general public via traditional outlets like satellite and cable TV. One of the top executives explained how to get fans, saying, "You get them through television, you get them through live events, and you get them more and more through online and mobile." Given this understanding of building a fanbase gamers certainly seem like a demographic ripe for the picking. This formulation coincided with an optimism born from two other trends: the rise of poker and the X Games.

During my visit to the CGS I heard several people reference poker as a great example of taking a game lots of people have experience with, combining it with aspirational qualities, and mixing in a good dose of technical innovation (the "lipstick camera" that shows the player's hand) to bring to a mainstream television audience an entirely new entertainment experience. A second common referent point I heard was the mainstreaming of "lifestyle" or "action" sports and their distribution via venues like the X Games, an ESPN initiative that focuses on competitive skateboarding, snowboarding, motocross, and other sports typically excluded from traditional athletic competitions. That the sporting subcultures described by Wheaton (2004a) were being identified as prime conceptual anchors for e-sports is especially poignant given the ambivalence toward commercialization identified by lifestyle sports scholars.[4]

Closely tracking along these inspirational waypoints with poker and the X Games was the desire and ability of the organization to go after sponsors not typically seen in most e-sports. Though some technology and game companies sponsored the CGS, it also actively sought to push beyond the traditional ranks. In addition to backing by News Corp and Direct TV, Mountain Dew was a key sponsor, which only strengthened the association they sought to build between themselves and outfits like the X Games.[5]

As I will discuss more in the next chapter, this focus on capturing a broad audience for e-sports not only affected game choices for the competitions but speaks to how the CGS constructed its core audience and its relationship with the community. The organization was very smart in bringing in several well-respected and established e-sports personalities. The executives recognized some value in maintaining contact with the scene's roots and the gamers who had long supported high-end competitive play. As was explained to me about this transition moment, "Well, I think its crossing over from a hardcore participant-driven activity to mainstream sport. And that's the hardest and without losing the hardcore face because they kind of give you the legitimacy of what you do."

In my conversations with these high-profile people over the years they often talked about the balancing act they recognized in the endeavor—building new audiences and making certain necessary trade-offs yet retaining "authenticity" to the core e-sports constituents. They regularly spoke about being the voice of the community in meetings or proposals put forward to grow the league. They tried to advocate for approaches that made sense for e-sports as a sport, not just a media product. This was a difficult role given the institutional imperatives but for those inside the organization who were committed to e-sports more broadly, they often saw it as one of their core tasks. They were also in the position of having to translate out to the fanbase the rationale and import of CGS choices. For example, game selections were not always what the most hardcore fans or players would have picked, yet they were never so far off-base (for example, something like *Tetris*) as to be completely alienating. Ultimately game choices were very much driven by the need to produce a compelling televised product and this underlying fundamental consideration always shaped the way the CGS negotiated between the grassroots and the mainstream, and the kind of mediation work some in the organization had to undertake with the community.

CGS decisions, and in general the overall structure of the league, cannot be understood without taking into account the core executive team structure and their orientation to North American sports and media products.[6] Though the CGS was certainly engaged with the native e-sports scene through bringing in knowledgeable people with experience in competitive pro gaming at the middle and lower tiers, it is clear when looking at the executive team, and many of the decisions that were made along the way, that the initiative was built from a very different place than most e-sports ventures. It was, as one executive put it to me, "sports entertainment."

What is instructive about this case is that it provides one model for how competitive computer gaming might be situated in a larger media or athletic landscape. Where people put their main reference point matters in how e-sports then get formulated and what kinds of institutional supports are built. The actualization of computer game play gets carried out via specific models, some of which will play up particular angles and downplay others. Situating e-sports as a form of sports entertainment will not only call forward a particular relationship with athletic identity, but a general orientation toward spectatorship and, likely, broadcast models.

Given so much is still unformed in e-sports we can find diverse approaches and different models still vying for ascendance. Several years after my visit to the CGS I was in Cologne for a conference and had the good fortune to visit the offices of Turtle Entertainment, an organization that has been around since 2000 despite the ups and downs of e-sports. They run the successful Electronic Sports League (ESL), one of the more robust amateur-to-pro operations. I was jokingly cautioned by one of the staff that their offices were on the "bad side of town" but I didn't take them too seriously. They were located near my hotel, just across the Rhine, and Google Maps made it look walkable. As I headed over, the area indeed transitioned from the very tourist friendly to the increasingly industrial. I double-checked my phone a few times and assured myself I was going in the right direction but the plain office buildings and derelict railroad tracks on the opposite side of the street didn't inspire much confidence. Looking at the clock I saw I had arrived fairly early, which gave me time to get lunch. What I hadn't counted on was there not really being any restaurants along the road. I spotted a kind of hot dog stand outside an office building and saw a grocery store pretty far down the street but ended up just grabbing a quick sandwich and drink from the nearby gas station and sitting in a grassy area along the road to eat. It was a far cry from the Starbucks I stopped at around the block from the CGS offices.

I found the building and entered what appeared to be a makeshift reception area. A few ESL banners hung on the walls and I could see various packages waiting to either be picked up or distributed. The guy working in the space called up to my contact who then came down to get me, leading me into the locked part of the building where the main offices were. My main contact, a PR manager with the organization, was someone I had met earlier at a game research conference I attended. He, and several of his colleagues, were periodically in attendance at that event and during my visit that day I became very aware of the organization's supportive stance to academic work on the subject of e-sports. As I was given a tour around the building (a confusing maze of generic white corridors with very quirkily decorated offices of the sort you often see in tech companies or universities), the scale of the organization became more and more apparent. At the time of my visit they had 170 employees (compared to around 40 at the CGS not counting the seasonal TV production crew) and had recently expanded their office space.

Much like the CGS, I was given a press packet though it was remarkably different in overall tone and appearance. While the CGS had offered multicolored booklets (documenting their World Finals) and several DVDs of prior events, the ESL packet was a simple folder (albeit in color) filled with basic text pages in black and white detailing various facts and figures about the company. The included CD did have some images and small trailer movies, but the focus was more on conveying the scope of the larger e-sports gaming community and various tournaments than on slick images of particular players.[7] Interestingly they had their own version of the "Myths of Gaming" DVD the CGS had given me, but the ESL's take on this genre took the form of a PDF called "13 Theses" (a playful nod to Luther's 95 and thus perhaps not entirely surprising given it is a German company, but still a bit odd in the context of e-sports). Much like the CGS DVD this document was about highlighting the sporting and social aspects of computer game play, listing things like "eSports is the expression of a cross-linked community" and "eSports boosts fitness and teamplay." It was apparent that no matter where the company is located, e-sports organizations feel the need to do some basic advocacy work on behalf of gaming.

As an organization the ESL, run by Turtle Entertainment, differed from the CGS both in its founding and in how it structured its overall approach to e-sports. The organization from its inception was built by and around both former e-sports players and tech-savvy guys. The founders, all in their mid- to late thirties, came with strong roots in computer gaming and technology, and the Internet more generally.[8] In particular, Ralf Reichert (the COO) was one of the cofounders of the still-influential Schroet Kommando (SK) team, which had proven to be one of the most resilient e-sports properties around, having been launched in Germany in 1997 around the game *Quake*. This early rooting in computer gaming, e-sports, and technology stands in notable contrast to an organization like the CGS, which attempted to leverage a different set of executive profiles, using media and new lifestyle sports as anchor points.

It was also interesting to see how the ESL was made up not simply of a top-tier competitive layer but actually built around a majority of beginner and amateur players. With a total member number around 2.4 million and running a wide range of tournaments in a variety of games (not simply the standard titles you see at most e-sports tournaments), the ESL was much more broadly constructed around computer games and e-sports writ large than simply a pro outlet. During my conversations with people at Turtle, I was struck by how much emphasis was placed on supporting a very broad community of gamers, of which the most elite slice was only just that, a slice. While the titles played at the professional matches mirrored what you'd typically find in many other tournaments (*Counter-Strike*, *Starcraft*, *Quake*), as a whole the organization supports competitive play among any number of diverse titles that vary by region worldwide (including *Trackmania*, *GTA*, and even poker). Though in the final season before the CGS closed there was some talk about the launch of an amateur series and ways to harness broader community involvement (especially off-season), the ESL stood in notable contrast for supporting a range of skill levels, across a variety of titles, and formalizing competition all the way down to the amateur level (complete with administrative and technical systems for handling cheating and accusations of such).

The economics of the ESL—both in terms of the funding of the organization and the players—intersect with what we often see in other e-sports outlets. The majority of the funding supporting Turtle Entertainment and its various outlets (of which the ESL pro events are just one branch) comes via several different paths: membership fees players pay for having additional services via the website and sponsorship/advertising.[9] Unlike the CGS, which used significant seed money from DirectTV, the ESL (though obtaining a small amount of start-up "angel investor" money) is funded through cooperation with sponsors and member relations. While sponsors and advertising are common funding mechanisms in e-sports, the ESL's development of player-member funding is notable. Unlike some other leagues it does not contract players directly but supports them via tournament prize winnings. Pro players within the ESL pro league are thus either independent or typically under contract with autonomous teams.

Perhaps the other biggest comparison point with the CGS is the approach to spectatorship, something I'll talk about in detail in the next chapter. While television was the CGS's holy grail, the ESL has grown a significant ongoing set of on-site spectator events for e-sports, especially with its frequent local competitions in Germany. While these are not focused on the professional side of gaming, they nonetheless show an interesting commitment to harnessing the local enthusiasm of the gamer community. They have also taken a very different approach to distributing video from matches, hosting ESLTV, an online video service. The focus is on providing online coverage of events including both live streaming and video on demand. The Cologne offices are home to a studio set, with several different small stage areas dedicated to interviewing, as well as a news anchor desk set. Yet these productions, while polished, all go out via the Internet. Rather than seeing the audience as one sitting on the sofa watching TV, the ESL imagines their demographic will primarily be accessing the content via their computers. Indeed the sofa-based audience does not seem to be one they are chasing after. The ESL model is one much more deeply linked to a larger player community, ranging from amateur players all the way to experts. The fact that it is also not contracting out teams and players, but instead building on the already existing independent team structure, signals another important difference from the CGS.

While I have so far focused here on just two models in particular, it is enormously important to note that there are a variety of tournament and league management models in operation around the world. Comparing the CGS and ESL is convenient for the way it highlights some recurrent fundamental tension points in the development of the scene: traditional versus online media, broad community-based versus exclusively elite play, and traditional media entertainment and (American) sports industry as jumping-off point versus computer game and Internet industry driven. I would be remiss however if I didn't mention several other prominent organizations and the ways they are structuring competitive e-sports play.

Perhaps one of the most successful initiatives in pro gaming has turned out to be based in the console scene via Major League Gaming (MLG). Though officially launched in 2002, it is only in the last several years that consoles have really gotten a strong foothold and gained serious notice in the broader e-sports community. This is perhaps not surprising given the transformations that have occurred in console gaming in just the last few years. We've witnessed the launch of the Xbox 360, the PS3, and so centrally important for e-sports, the widespread ease of networked play with consoles. As computer gaming has shifted from being a primarily PC-driven activity to one in which consoles (and indeed a myriad of other devices) play a significant role, the space for e-sports to grow has also shifted.

The MLG is primarily rooted in the United States (though there has been some recent expansion into Canada) and supports not only pro play through a special circuit, but fosters a broader player community via matching up people through the GameBattles website and a variety of amateur competitions. In this regard it is similar to the ESL for focusing on a community beyond the most elite players. Like the CGS, though, they do contract top players. The signing of Tom "Tsquared" Taylor for $250,000 in 2006 garnered a fair amount of press and attention in the community. They have also signed two four-person Halo teams, Final Boss and Carbon, for $1,000,000 over three years.[10] Mike Sepso, MLG chairman and cofounder, clarified in a 2008 article how these players make their money, saying, "The very top earning MLG Pros make over six figures annually when you count prize money, endorsements, sponsors, and appearance fees. MLG does not pay a salary. In some cases, we act as manager to top Pros and guarantee them a base amount of money from sponsors over time and we sometimes pay the pros promotional fees for the time they spend blogging, doing appearances, etc. for the league" (Sepso 2008).

The MLG has also been one of the few e-sports organizations to consistently break through to various lifestyle sponsors (like Old Spice and Dr Pepper). Though it has a content-sharing agreement with ESPN (who seem to regularly dabble into the e-sports scene but have not yet fully committed to it), it appears mostly through its online and "broadband Network" outlets (like ESPN360.com). While it had a series run on the USA Network in 2006, its broadcasts still primarily reside online in the form of streaming events and video-on-demand. The MLG does not rely on sponsorship or partner funding alone, however. Along with a few other e-sports organizations (Meet Your Makers in Denmark being the other notable example), they have also experimented with acquiring investment capital over the years. The 2006 season saw the injection of $25 million from U.S.-based Oak Investment Partners (MLG Admin 2006b; Sepso 2008) and $10 million from Ritchie Capital (MLG Admin 2009). In 2009 they picked up an additional $7.5 million from Oak again, bringing their total outside investment to $42.5 million (Caoili 2009).

Perhaps one of the trickiest components of the MLG in terms of their broader acceptance into the hardcore e-sports community has been around the games that get played at the top level. The 2010 circuit offered *Halo 3*, *Tekken 6*, *Super Smash Bros. Brawl*, and *World of Warcraft* (though it was eventually dropped from their roster). While these are some of the most popular computer games out there, debate can always be found among aficionados about whether particular titles warrant the "sports" moniker. For some hardcore e-sports fans the game choices have head-scratching inclusions. The serious regional limitations of the league (encompassing the United States and only recently Canada) have also left it fairly disconnected from global e-sports and the regular roster of players and teams you find within major tournaments. The organization's inclusion, starting in August 2010 at their Raleigh tournament, of *Starcraft 2* has ended up providing both a place where the PC has been brought back into the league and where the most internationalization occurs. As a national league it has proven one of the most notable for its longevity and growth in terms of sponsorship, visibility, and cross-media branding. With the demise of several larger initiatives the more PC-based e-sports community has been paying a bit more attention to the MLG's success and the role of console leagues in the future.

Another historically strong model has been tournaments with regional qualifiers culminating in a "world" finals competition.[11] As I discussed previously, the World Cyber Games are perhaps most famous for this formulation, though the Electronic Sports World Cup (ESWC) (expanded in 2003 from a nationally based ongoing French LAN party) has also been influential. Regional qualifiers under these type of structures are typically licensed or contracted out to local partners who then handle the on-the-ground details of producing a regional qualifier. The main organization also typically develops sponsorships, often pulling in several major companies to support the circuit or final. In the case of the WCG they have had a close alliance with Samsung as a major event sponsor since its launch. Though large competitions like the WCG Grand Finals get aired on South Korean television, generally speaking even these bigger tournaments have not made much headway in breaking through to traditional media. Coverage is instead typically provided via online streaming and VoD (often via third-party sites), and a phalanx of on-site journalists for various gaming and specialist e-sports websites typically handle the reporting. Occasionally networks such as MTV will be present for some special short-format program filming (as was the case in Seattle for the 2007 Grand Finals) or the local TV channels and newspapers will turn up for a kind of novelty story coverage, but for the most part outside of South Korea the event is largely invisible to a broader public.

Teams and Their Owners

Though league organizations form a crucial part of the industry, teams are still heavily structured through individual ownership. It is time to look a bit more at how independent teams, and their owners, form a core part of pro gaming.[12] In the same way tournaments have sparked a whole new professional identity for a group of people wanting to organize official events, often with ambitions of creating the next NFL or FIFA, perhaps some of the most entrepreneurial business people in the scene are team owners and managers.

When I look back at my own entrée into the e-sports world, one of the first people I encountered was a prominent owner and manager of a top team based in Europe. Dressed in a button-down shirt and nice pants, it was clear he wasn't another teenage player but I didn't know where he fit into the picture. As we spoke he talked about owning one of the largest global teams and how his players were under formal contracts, complete with benefits (and how he sometimes had to engage in serious competition with other teams to land them). He talked about scouting and recruiting, eventually letting players go as their skills dropped. He chatted about the way his organization functioned "like any other normal company" though he also was clear about his own roots in the scene as a former player and someone still passionate about gaming. He encouraged me to visit the team's website to see the fanbase, as well as the branded logo merchandise available for sale. It was a serious pitch, intended to legitimize e-sports, his team, and his own professional identity as a team owner. He took it seriously and clearly was invested in it being represented as an important part of the future of sports—and a viable business opportunity.

Over the years I was fortunate to have other conversations with him and watch his team grow, get investment funding, fold, and then be revived as a brand (albeit without him at the helm). During those years I spoke with a number of other team owners and while their own personalities and unique approaches certainly differentiated them, I always heard waypoints back to this first conversation with its focus on a passion for gaming, the nitty-gritty details of team ownership, the complexities of managing a fairly young set of athletes, and the challenges of making an e-sports team a viable business and sports franchise.

In an early article on sports teams, Brower (1977) identified several characteristics of owners worth considering further in an e-sports context: fandom, civic philanthropy, paternalism, boundary lines mitigated via coaches, cooperation and affiliation among owners, owner power, a fraught relationship with unionization, and financial reward. Brower notes that owners are typically, at least initially, drawn to owning a team out of a love of the game and some hopes of having fun. He argues that, "Almost without exception, owners are superfans rather than merely prudent financial investors" (1977, 17). I have also, with very few exceptions, found this mirrored in my conversations with team owners. They regularly talk about their own prior gaming experience, often having played at an amateur level or perhaps even in some pro matches, but realized the limits of their own skill set and decided to shift into another aspect of the scene. One man described to me his own transition from being a player (first of football and then CS) to an owner:

> I was an all-state football player when I was in high school and I really missed that feeling of competitiveness and I've always kind of been the coach type person and I wanted to be a sports agent like Jerry Maguire, the movie, and so it just really filled a lot of roles for me to where, you know, I was just playing one day and I was really angry. I was trying to build this team but I didn't know, on the team was just a bunch of friends and they weren't practicing and everything else, so my wife looks at me, more out of irritation with me than anything, and she goes, "Why don't you just start your own team?"

Their commitment to e-sports can at times sound almost like a form of community service, especially given how many of them fund otherwise precarious ventures out of their own pocket. They regularly speak not only of "growing e-sports" but of the power of computer gaming and their enthusiasm for it.

In many ways this can be seen as dovetailing with a kind of civic philanthropy Brower and others have noted in relation to traditional sports ownership, whereby the team is seen as (or at least rhetorically positioned as) providing benefits to a region and a city. The owner, by extension, becomes a moral actor engaged in good for the community. While e-sports owners don't frame the issue in terms of regional benefits, one regularly hears a commitment to bringing the good side of gaming to a wider public and promoting the sporting aspect (with the various ideological values that come with that). The community being supported in this model is the gaming community writ large, a group of people who are often seen as delegitimized, even vilified, by a broader society. E-sports, and the work team owners do to support them, are in this narrative an important helpful intervention for all gamers.

One difference from the account Brower provides for this motive for ownership, however, is that in traditional sports this "super fandom" and civic virtue are generally only able to be realized because the team owner is independently wealthy and has no real need to worry about the money side of a sports business. He writes, "The 'millionaire sportsman,' the great majority of owners, have no apparent pressure to make money from their team operation" (1977, 22). I have not found this to be the case in e-sports. While team owners often have enough liquidity to front costs, and perhaps even support a team that does not break even over several years, the scale of wealth does not match traditional sports. Aside from only an example or two I have encountered, e-sports owners are not independently wealthy. Indeed many of the people with ownership stakes in the scene are quite young and may even count the position as their first "real" job since graduating college. While some have prior professional experience or training (law or business school, for example), they just as often have only resided in technology-based sectors (versus sports or entertainment) or are graduating from college and transitioning into a professional life.

Brower's handling of fandom and civic philanthropy seems to coalesce into a kind of paternalism on the part of owners, who often "look upon their players as does a father upon his children" (1977, 26). Given the gender make-up of e-sports historically (owned and run by men and populated mostly by male players), that this relationship does appear is not surprising. Some owners (as well as other managers, league operators, etc.), particularly the slightly older ones who have had a career outside of e-sports, regularly situate themselves in mentor/father/guardian roles in relation to the young men who play on their teams. For younger team owners I've not found paternalism but instead a kind of grudging caretaking. The guys on their teams may not be much younger (if at all) than them and player hijinks, disorganization, or laziness are more likely to be met with frustration rather than seeing them as young and in need of mentoring. Because the financial entry to e-sports team ownership is significantly lower than in traditional sports the dynamic—produced by virtue of age, money, and experience—between owner and player can be quite different than what is found in traditional professional sports.

Another area that is altered in e-sports, in part from financial factors but also due to its overall immaturity as a field, is the boundary line between owner and player. While Brower identified paternalism at work in many traditional sports owners, he also noted that this was mitigated through a complex relationship owners had with team coaches and managers. As a developed organization there were often several layers of expertise and management between the owner and the players. While some traditional sports team owners maintain very direct control of their teams, at mundane levels there will still be other actors intervening in day-to-day situations.

On this count e-sports probably veers most significantly from traditional sports. For example, in general there is no robust model of coaching in e-sports.[13] As I've queried people about this over the years I've rarely heard any strong case for it. While a *Counter-Strike* crew typically will have someone who is either formally or informally the captain (sometimes it is the same person who acts as the "strat," or strategy caller) there is rarely a consistent coach who acts, and mediates, between the owner and the players. Sometimes you find teams taking on coaches during boot camps or intensive practice sessions but they are rarely kept over the course of running an international circuit of events. Though many owners travel to matches with their players and may stand alongside at matches, offering encouragement or perhaps some general thoughts on play, they tend to not see themselves as traditional sports coaches and in practice operate well outside what we would consider coaching tasks (strategizing tactics, prepping practice sessions, troubleshooting performance, and motivating). What this means organizationally is that there is often very little buffer between e-sports team owners and their players. The actual content of play still remains fairly set apart from the day-to-day concerns or work focus of the owner, who is likely preoccupied with securing sponsorships, managing a website, interfacing with tournament organizers, and handling mundane travel and bureaucratic details.

The level of detail e-sports team owners are typically engaged in means they tend to lead a fairly administration-heavy life (aside from a handful of teams who have scaled up operations enough to divide the labor). This also means that they are very involved in a range of aspects of the scene, from contracting new players to handling travel details. One owner, when discussing with me the types of things he does, compared it to the early days of baseball.

> Back in the old days of American baseball, coach didn't have talent scouts.[14] He didn't have base runner coaches, pitching coaches, batting coaches, outfield coaches—he was a coach. He had to judge the talent, work with the outfielders, work with the base runners, work with the pitchers, work with the hitters. He had to do everything, he was just the coach. It's all the evolution of sport. Right now I'm the baseball coach in 1820. It sucks [laughs]. No I'm just kidding, I love it.

While fandom often draws people to team ownership, the day-to-day reality of managing a team, including heavy doses of administration, certainly shifts the "fun" balance. As with players, the labor of owners is sometimes hard for outsiders to recognize. Taking care of finances or other bureaucratic matters is easily interpretable as traditional work, but what about other aspects? For example, traveling with the team to a competition, or scouting new talent? One owner described the difficulties of the job, especially as it is often done in a home office where family and friends may have trouble parsing the work/home/labor/play lines. For example, I was asking him how he preps for picking new players (and letting old ones go) when he spoke about how much time was involved, saying, "Three, four, thousand hours of research trying to figure out who's the best at what game and who can do it on stage." When I followed up by inquiring about what research consists of he said,

> Websites and interviews and matches and you know...a Xbox over here and we have computer over there. My wife's going nuts. I'm like, "I've got to watch this." She's like, "You're just watching, playing video games." I'm like "No, I'm really working, I swear to God." I've got to study these kids, you know. Because if I don't study these kids, who else is going to do it for me? I have advisers and suggestions and everything else but when I'm sitting up there, live on TV, I've got to make those calls. I've got to drop these kids.

Given the overall smallness of the most elite layer you also typically find that people who have been in it more than a year or two know each other, especially at the team owner level where they may have come up through the ranks themselves (starting as a player or perhaps admin). Brower suggests a certain degree of familiarity team owners have with each other, often knowing details about their competitors' financial standing or personal lives. This is without a doubt mirrored in the e-sports scene. It is far too small a community competing over a fairly finite set of resources for people with some longevity in it to not be very aware of what is happening with other teams. Given that the players who make a real professional mark in the field may also switch teams a number of times over the course of their career, knowledge (including rumors) travels well in e-sports. Brower quotes John Mecom, who was at the time "majority owner of the New Orleans Saints" as saying, "It's a very close fraternity. And you've got your rivalries; you've got differences of opinion. But we're all partners in the sport of professional football. We've got to all stick together" (1977, 34).

The fact that the pro world is small and most owners know each other fairly well and have a shared love of gaming and building e-sports, even having drinks together after matches, does not mean that there is not cutthroat competition. As one team owner put it to me, "people are, like I said, Spy Versus Spy. They're always looking over their shoulders." Vying for players and sponsorships is a constant in an e-sports team owner's life. The scene does not regulate via a mechanism like a formal draft, so despite the use of contracts, there remains a fairly competitive, often ugly, side to player retention and recruitment. Players hop teams, sometimes taking tales of bad management with them. There can also be higher stakes issues that arise around salaries. For example, one owner described to me the frustration, and destabilization, competitive bidding provoked:

> And, you know, they [another franchise] always had a really good *Warcraft* team and they had like solid sponsorship money and then one year they just exploded with this venture capital. And he [the owner] just started muscling people out of the way and he drove like the price of the players for *Warcraft 3*. He was very heavily criticized for his driving up the price like crazy because he was paying everyone like, I don't know, 80 grand a year or something.

As in any commercial venture, scarce resources and financial competition certainly animate these disputes. And while e-sports has broadened a smidge as to where it is able to pull in sponsorship from, there is still a small number of major corporations that any ambitious team tries to pull in funding from. The pot of top players and top sponsorship dollars is still limited enough to produce serious, sometimes acrimonious, wrangling.

Interestingly Brower speaks to the way team owners hold collective force, in part because of some degree of cohesion. He highlights the power of NFL team owners in shaping league decisions, pointing out they pay the commissioner's salary. They often act for the good of the larger collective (as they conceive it), though such action is generally based on a shared set of social values among the owners. Part of what he suggests is that the homogeneity of the owners in terms of race and class produces a kind of easy consensus. Within e-sports we could pretty easily do a similar mapping but it would be problematized by the international nature of things. Americans and Scandinavians, for example, do not approach all issues the same way and nationality can certainly trump other demographic categories.

The status of e-sports team owner power is perhaps one of the most oblique issues for me after years of research. On the one hand, a number of pro teams have joined together to create the G7, an organization dedicated to cross team advocacy (something I'll talk about in more detail later in the chapter). And various tournaments and leagues certainly consult with team owners about matches. But we have also seen, via the CGS case, that when enough money enters the scene the power of the team owners—to negotiate, to maintain their organization—falters. It is also very unclear how many teams have actually sought legal remedy for unpaid prize winnings or broken contracts, a huge tool in the traditional sports organization arsenal.

Despite this somewhat weakened version of owner power, we have not seen the skirmishes around player unionization that traditional sports have faced. Outlets like the G7 attempt to formalize (and perhaps thus preemptively manage) player relations to some degree but there has yet been no significant move among e-sports players to collectively organize and mitigate owner power. It is tricky to say why this has not happened. Part of it is likely owing to the relative age and inexperience of e-sports players, many of whom approach their new career with simple gratitude at being able to play computer games for a (modest) living or even just to get funding to cover their basic costs to attend tournaments. Dovetailing into this is the high churn rate for pro players.[15] Many simply do not stay in the scene long enough for the costs of professionalization (extended out to health concerns, an "adult" salary that could help support a family, and eventual retirement) to factor in. Finally, given many people do not yet see e-sports sustained or large-scale economic viability (aside a poster boy or two, there is no one yet really growing rich off e-sports) it may simply feel not worth it—there is no financial incentive to push for player rights. As Brower argues, team owners prefer a more paternalistic model in relation to their players, one which also keeps those players fairly powerless. Whether or not e-sports players can be seen as powerless is tricky, but at the minimum there appears to be a status quo at work when it comes to owner/player relations.

Finally, I would be remiss to not include the fact that team owners, e-sports and traditional alike, are certainly motivated by financial reward.

While passion for the game may bring them into the sport, the focus changes over time. Brower quoted a basketball team owner as saying, "Owners go into sports for fun but want to make a profit once they become committed to ownership" (1977, 2). E-sports team owners are, I've found, particularly entrepreneurial and indeed optimistic (perhaps sometimes to a fault) that they are getting on the ground floor of something big. Most of the ones I've talked to suggest that e-sports are, indeed, the future of sports. They tend to frame them as the culmination of Internet and computational technology meeting leisure, and place their bets on inevitable success. They frequently, indeed understandably, paint themselves as pioneers—risk-takers who are investing in the future. Though they are generally honest about the financial costs of investment (and the tolls it can take on their family lives), for the most part they are disarmingly optimistic (at least in public). Perhaps it is hard to be otherwise when you've staked a professional identity and livelihood on a venture most average people don't even know exists.

Funding Play

Though you typically encounter headlines about tournament winnings when you read popular press articles about e-sports, very little attention is given to the underlying funding mechanisms at work in supporting the scene. While there has been some investment funding supporting e-sports, sponsorships remain at the heart of the economic model. For most organizations they provide the core source of funding and are crucial in making all of this high-end play a viable business endeavor. Sponsorship can range in forms, from manufacturers providing a team peripherals (headphones, mice) to financial support for salaries or travel costs. There are also instances of a game company itself giving funding to a tournament with the proviso that their own game be slated as one of the supported, and featured, titles. Lucrative sponsorships are the real prize, often making or breaking a team or player's chance to stay active and compete. Sponsorships also typically support tournaments, including not just prizes but various operational costs. Given how important securing sponsorships is, team owners, leagues, and tournament organizers can spend significant amounts of their time cultivating these affiliations. This ranges from cold-calling companies to solicit support to fostering longer-term relationships with key people in a sponsoring organization.

While there are a number of companies with experience in e-sports and thus they know what is involved (and what they are getting into), very often the person soliciting sponsorship must do a lot of groundwork. If a company is not one of the traditional e-sports sponsors (SteelSeries, MSI, Intel) they may need to first be told that pro gaming exists (think back to the general "evangelizing" DVDs I described), be given some sense of what happens at tournaments, and be reassured that the endeavor is real and the people competing not oddballs but viable public faces for their product. They have to be persuaded that sponsorship equates with a valuable marketing opportunity.

Other than perhaps a few instances of tournaments or teams being supported out of pure appreciation for the sport, sponsorship boils down to a marketing decision. Traditional sports athletes, teams, and events are carriers for corporate messages and e-sports mirrors this, or at least attempts to. The most professionalized teams have their jerseys emblazoned with sponsor logos and the gear they use at tournaments will be from the company supporting them. Team and tournament websites will carry product logos, often with links to purchase sponsor products. Events will have sponsor banners and sometimes demo booths set up if it is a combined expo/tournament. Ultimately team owners and tournament organizers work hard to find sponsors and convince them that supporting e-sports provides concrete return on investment.

The more professionalized the organization the more formalized this process will generally be. Reporting back to a sponsor can consist of documenting website views, click-through rates, the number of tournament spectators or streaming media/TV watchers for matches, and team and player standings. There can also be a significant amount of relationship management that takes place. Very often the representative on the corporate sponsor side may be the only person in their organization who sees the value in linking with e-sports. Or they may be a marketing person who believes gaming and technology is a good path to reach a young demographic but they don't know a whole lot about computer gaming. In these situations the team owner or tournament organizer may need to do a lot of ongoing education, often making sure that the point person has a good handle on how to pitch team sponsorship within their own organization. In the case of the handful of consistent e-sports sponsors there is ongoing management of the relationship, often over years. One team owner explained the range of interaction:

Owner: [One company] is super about getting to the hard core of its community that is watching the matches and they want to be by far the number one company for that. And I think they are.

Me: So they care about team performance?

Owner: Yeah, he [the company's point person] and I, we're really good friends. We talk about my line up anyway. He's like, "How's your new fifth working out? I saw the match the other day. That was good, good result." He cares. Most of the others don't really care. They care about like the custom video content I do for them. Most of my conversations with my [other sponsor] rep only have to do with status of custom videos, the blogging that we're doing.

Whereas traditional sports have a firmly established value to many corporate sponsors, and the relationship between marketing and athletic organizations is at this point clearly formalized and structured, within e-sports it is still very much an emergent phenomenon. For many organizations sponsoring e-sports is a marketing experiment, which means that the fates can shift quickly. Because so much of the financial basis of e-sports still rests on sponsorships, this is not trivial. As one e-sports editorial noted regarding the fragility of this economic model, "While, for example, football clubs rely on sponsors, advertising, gates, TV rights, player sales and private investors, the majority of eSports' organizations can only count on the support from sponsors—which, in the grip of recession, always tend to engage on [sic] cost-cutting moves—to finance their operations" (Miraa 2009). During the recent global economic crisis this mechanism manifested itself quite clearly, with a number of organizations tightening their marketing budgets and focusing their money on known traditional outlets rather than e-sports.

Perhaps the biggest difference between traditional athletic sponsorship and pro computer gaming is that e-sports still struggles with breaking out of a "geek" reputation and snagging lifestyle brands (or even those associated with traditional athletics like Nike). Much of e-sports sponsorship still sits firmly within the scope of technology products such as Intel, SteelSeries, or MSI and not the ubiquitous brands you see in traditional sports like Budweiser, AT&T, Toyota, or Bank of America. As I previously discussed, while South Korea has made real headway in connecting with mobile phone services, North America and European e-sports have still not cracked, in any sustained large-scale way, the mainstream wall.

For many this is particularly frustrating, especially when you can see that other nontraditional sports receive sponsorships from beyond a niche pool. Extreme sports, BMX and mountain biking, skateboarding, wakeboarding, and a variety of other non-Olympic sports have managed to secure sponsorship from brands such as Redbull and Vans. These sports often have a clear subcultural or lifestyle link that helps tournaments, players, and team owners make connections to potential sponsors about the consumer identity that can be tapped into. These corporate sponsors see value in partnering with these emergent, often a bit more edgy, activities. E-sports, perhaps because they still carry baggage about the stereotypes of geek culture and computer games, are often not seen as providing readily apparent connections to lifestyle brands.

There are several notable exceptions of e-sports outfits managing to cross the technology-sponsor barrier. The ESL has landed Adidas, Volkswagen, and Suzuki for periods of time and Major League Gaming has scored some partnerships with sponsors like Old Spice, Bic, Doritos, and Hot Pockets. Of course, several of these (Doritos, Hot Pockets) fit well into a classic "game-nerd" identity stereotype. Several teams including Evil Geniuses, SK Gaming, and Meet Your Makers have made some headway over the years in partnering with nontechnology brands, making deals with Adidas, Kimikuro (the energy drink), and Puma. There is still little evidence of multiyear sustained lifestyle partnerships among teams, however. More often than not these instances seem to be fairly experimental and quite contingent on persuading a key person in the sponsoring organization rather than a systemic valuation of e-sports by the company.

Often such sponsorships are still fairly one-directional whereby the sponsor's logo will appear on the e-sports website or t-shirts but you will not see the team identity cross back over onto the product space. A notable exception does come to mind. In 2008 MLG secured a deal with Dr Pepper whereby one of their premier players, Tom "Tsquared" Taylor, appeared on bottles, thus publicizing MLG well beyond the traditional e-sports scene and also linking Dr Pepper's identity with high-end console play.

Figure 4.1
MLG player featured on Dr Pepper bottle ad, 2008.
Image from Major League Gaming.

A second example of a product using e-sports as a way of branding itself (versus simply providing one-way support) comes from how the technology company SteelSeries (a brand carried in major stores like Best Buy and other international outlets) has deeply linked their profile to competitive computer game play. There is a much more reciprocal relationship between the e-sports scene and the company than you usually see. As makers of headphones, mice, and a variety of other peripherals they not only actively sponsor e-sports but also solicit feedback on upcoming products from top players. When you visit their website you immediately see their involvement with e-sports. This connection is also meant to signal authenticity. As their webpage notes, "From day one, SteelSeries has been focused on making high performance gaming gear used by the most demanding, top professional gamers worldwide and peripherals that provide superior quality and a competitive edge to gamers of all skill levels. We believe, as most gamers do, in winning, not trying!" (SteelSeries 2011).[16]

While there are some examples of lifestyle brands making their way into e-sports and at the same time e-sports making their way back out *onto* a brand, such initiatives pale in comparison to what we've seen in South Korea. There is, however, hope that this invisible wall is eroding to

Figure 4.2
Internationally known pro player Manuel "Grubby" Schenkhuizen featured on the SteelSeries website's front page.

some degree with the rise of gaming as a mainstream leisure activity. The influence of *World of Warcraft* in particular is worth considering in the game marketing equation. Despite many in the pro scene being deeply ambivalent about *WoW* as a viable sport, the fact that it has drawn in so many people—twelve million subscribers worldwide at its highest point (Blizzard 2010b)—and from a more diverse demographic than previously associated with computer games, makes it an interesting case. Some companies appear to be starting to key into the number of untapped consumers and are thinking about marketing opportunities. The last couple of years have seen several ad campaigns directed at *WoW* players. In 2009, for example, Mountain Dew offered specially colored versions of their soft drink (blue for Alliance, red for Horde) with *WoW* imagery to appeal to the game's players. Coca-Cola has also done several entertaining and popular advertisements in China, which boasts a huge player base, using the game as a central storyline. Copies of the ads circulated on fan sites across the world. Though these campaigns have not been directed toward hardcore e-sports fans, they do signal some shift in how computer games are increasingly seen as viable products for companies to piggyback on fan brand enthusiasm.

Regulating Play

At the beginning of this book I introduced the notion that computer game rule sets are not simply handled via the software but often involve a constellation of negotiations and practices that either alter or "route around" the in-game system to support a given community's play norms and requirements. Part of that argument was that the actual play of computer games and construction of the pro e-sports scene is strongly managed via noncomputational methods that have emerged among not only players but tournament organizers and other stakeholders. I would here like to extend this consideration of how pro play is managed and regulated through a variety of other mechanisms that are not tied to rules but instead to larger organizational, political, and structural factors including legal arguments, contractual arrangements, and governmental and nongovernmental bodies.

IP Issues and Licenses

As I've discussed a bit so far, one of the main regulating mechanisms within e-sports is the sale and purchase of licenses for tournaments. This can range from organizations having formal agreements with game companies to use their games in an ongoing tournament series (and broadcast) all the way to ad hoc one-time agreements between an organizer and game company. Licensing takes place not just around games themselves but the tournament or organization brand. Very often larger companies will themselves subcontract out to regional affiliates for a tournament or qualifying match. In both cases there is a distribution of organizing and publication/broadcast rights through formal contracts, often involving financial remuneration.

In previous work I've done on MMOGs one issue that repeatedly came up was the status of games as objects of intellectual property (IP) and, by extension, the ways these spaces and their players were then managed and regulated in accordance (Taylor 2006a, 2006b, 2006c). Within MMOGs it is not uncommon for companies to assert their ownership of a game including its software, aesthetic contents, and mythos. MMOGs are often seen by game companies as having an "essence" that must be protected, and legal provisions for extensive brand policing are put into end user license agreements and terms of service or use that players must regularly accept to play the game. *World of Warcraft*, for example, includes in its terms of use wording that you regularly see associated with these kinds of games: "The following rules are not meant to be exhaustive, and Blizzard reserves the right to determine which conduct it considers to be outside the spirit of the Game and to take such disciplinary measures as it sees fit up to and including termination and deletion of the Account" (Blizzard 2010a). Fairly strict forms of regulation regularly happen despite the fact that players are simultaneously encouraged to make these game worlds real and "their own" in some sense, through their participation. The emergent practices and products of player communities, simultaneously fostered and curtailed by game companies, are one of the constants in the genre. Rather than static out-of-the-box software products, MMOGs are ecosystems in which co-creation—between a game company, technologies, and users—is the norm. Over the years I've tracked various struggles and disputes around these issues, from fan fiction to modding to player action in games. When I turned my attention to professional computer gaming I thought I had left the world of IP wrangling behind. I was mistaken.

Issues of intellectual property can be fruitfully analyzed when they crystallize in disputed situations. This was certainly the case in my research on MMOGs where, for example, players auctioning their characters (and attempts to prohibit it) provided a crucial glimpse into the thicket of games and intellectual property.[17] It was in these contentious scenarios that broader conversations about ownership, authorship, forms of action and agency, and the relationship between structure and culture were made clear. Within pro gaming a key case to help us explore the status of IP and competitive gaming spaces has appeared in what has been dubbed the "KeSPA versus Blizzard" situation.

KeSPA is the Korea E-Sports Association. While formally a nongovernmental body, it originated in 2000 after approval from the Ministry of Culture and Tourism,[18] the governmental agency that has long been interested in supporting gaming and, by extension, e-sports. As has always been the case with South Korean e-sports, commercial involvement is a driving influence both in terms of policy and staffing. KeSPA is no exception, having been originally chaired by Young-man Kim, CEO of HanbitSoft at that time (the company that brought *Starcraft* to Korea) and in 2010 being run by Jin woo Seo, copresident of SK Telecom. The board of the organization (twelve members) is made up of executives from major corporations. While there are annual membership dues that provide operational monies for the organization, the financial support for the maintenance of leagues comes through sponsorship deals (such as with Shinhan Bank, which has sponsored the Pro League for a number of years). When there are government initiatives related to the business of e-sport—such as the Korean e-Sports Games, an amateur competition meant to help build computer gaming as a leisure activity for all—additional funding is provided from the public coffers.

If any national organization has had a major impact on the development and growth of e-sports it is KeSPA. While with any large outfit like KeSPA there are both fans and (often severe) critics, the impact it has had during its existence is indisputable. The organization exists within a national culture where digital gaming is not only big business, but significantly supported through public policy and the government. KeSPA has held tremendous power in shaping the face of e-sports in South Korea and that country in turn has proved to be a powerful, at times nearly mythical, waypoint for e-sports internationally. The organization takes a fairly expansive view of what it can be involved in. On the one hand, it does things like promoting "teenage game culture" and supporting "game-related international interaction business" (KeSPA n.d.), which echo the kinds of things you see the Ministry of Culture, Sports, and Tourism express interest in.

KeSPA is, nonetheless, probably best known for its concrete work in pro e-sports. It has managed tournaments at a number of levels and venues, including involvement in the creation of dedicated e-sports stadiums. Unlike most of e-sports where players come and go leaving little historical trace, KeSPA oversees the official registration and tracking of professional players in South Korea. Not only do they handle rankings and statistics of these players and teams, they provide them formalized professionalization paths. They are also centrally involved in securing sponsorships and building ties with nongaming organizations, handling broadcasting rights for competitions, and dealing with game licensing. It is in this area of broadcast rights that the case at hand arises.

In late April 2010 news broke, first via the Korean site Yonhap News and then translated out into English (most notably via the influential Team Liquid website) that Blizzard was ending all negotiations with KeSPA pertaining to future partnerships. Mike Morhaime, one of Blizzard's cofounders and CEO was quoted as saying, "We've been negotiating with the association about intellectual property rights for the last three years, and we've made no progress at all... ...[sic] We're going to stop negotiating with them and look for a new partner" (Yonhap News 2010). Given the enormous popularity of Blizzard's games in South Korea and KeSPA's influence, this was huge news (though murmurs of problems had been circulating among insiders). The Team Liquid website posted an article offering additional details and quoted from "Mike Morhaime's letter to Korean e-Sports fans" (cited as originating at the Korean Fomos website).[19] In that article Morhaime is quoted as saying, "In 2007, we were shocked and disappointed to learn that KeSPA had illegally sold the broadcasting rights for *Starcraft* tournaments without our consent. With this clear violation of our intellectual property rights, we were forced to become more actively involved in the situation and make our voice be heard" (Supernovamaniac 2010). The announcement of this break in ties came with the much-anticipated launch of *Starcraft 2* just on the horizon, sending shockwaves through the e-sports community. Broad discussions about what this meant for not only South Korean e-sports, but the scene more generally, circulated.

While many games are played at the pro level in South Korea, it is *Starcraft* that has been the foundation upon which Korean e-sports have been built. The original *Starcraft* dates back to 1998 and despite its age has remained one of the strongest e-sports titles in South Korea. Blizzard had already set the community buzzing in June 2009 when they announced that the new version of the game would not include LAN functionality, something historically crucial to competitive tournament play. Without it matches would have to be coordinated through a centralized server system, Blizzard's Battle.net, rather than be set up ad hoc at tournaments around the world.[20] Such consolidated control can seem at odds not only with e-sports' LAN roots, but the overall diversity of setups and venues in which tournament play occurs.

Concern about this underlying technological change was mediated, however, by a recognition that Blizzard has long been supportive of developing e-sports. It has been one of the game companies most willing to think about their product in an e-sports context both in terms of running their own matches and also entering into partnerships with organizations wanting to bring tournament play to their titles.[21] Their long-time collaboration with KeSPA speaks to the ways the company recognized the potential of e-sports early on and has taken steps to foster its development. As Anderson Mccutcheon (2010) of the *SC2 Blog* detailed in a helpful overview article, Blizzard, as early as 2008, frequently included a consideration of how the yet-to-be-released *Starcraft 2* would fit into their overall support for e-sports. He notes Blizzard spokespeople regularly talked about supporting the game specifically as an e-sports title, of having their own in-house e-sports group to support organized competitive play, and wanting to see the game's competitions continue to be broadcast.

Over the course of two interviews I had with Paul Della Bitta, senior director of Global Community Development and eSports at Blizzard, I found this awareness about e-sports and attention to fostering it notable for the way it was positive about the future of pro gaming and offered definite support of the scene more generally. Part of Della Bitta's job is managing the global e-sports team, which involves everything from running Blizzard's own official e-sports tournaments worldwide to supporting third-party tournaments. He repeatedly emphasized Blizzard's support for the e-sports community and praised how much development there has been generally in competitive play. While the majority of game companies pay little to no attention to e-sports and tournament play, Blizzard stands out for their activities.

One of the interesting questions this raises is the extent of Blizzard's involvement in managing how their products are used within pro gaming. Della Bitta reiterated several times that "developing games is our core business" and pulled back from painting too strong a picture of Blizzard being very hands-on in relation to third-party e-sports events. As he put it, "We're not in the business of e-sports. You know, we make games, we make video games. We see e-sports as an extension of our community because this is a group of people in our community that not only enjoy playing our games competitively, but also enjoy following these games and the players that play them competitively" (Personal communication, 2010). Their preferred model appears to be finding strong partners to work with and license to.

Yet at the same time it is clear that they do see e-sports as a domain in which their active involvement is beneficial. They are constructing software that is going to get used in those spaces and, by extension, prove to be a powerful marketing tool. Della Bitta noted Blizzard's attention to the players in these tournaments, saying, "Our main focus in supporting our third parties is actually on the players. We want to make sure that the organizations are running quality events, the players are getting paid, that they're being treated well" (Personal communication, 2009). He expressed concern about things being handled unprofessionally (via tournament conditions or failure to pay out) and how "protect[ing] the players" was important for Blizzard. He said, "If a player competes, we expect them to get paid. And if someone signs a license with us, we expect there to be some level of quality and we expect that those things are taken care of" (Personal communication, 2010). While he would not directly address the KeSPA situation or their claims (nor did he link this issue of player treatment to KeSPA specifically), this concern for quality or the fair treatment of players certainly extends beyond any simple IP claim.

Given that Blizzard sometimes runs their own matches it is clear that they do at times make very specific decisions about how tournament play should unfold and certainly have opinions about how competitive play is best handled. If you attend any major Blizzard convention these days, be it Blizzcon or the World Wide Invitational, you can see the company's recognition of the power of large-scale spectator-based competitive play through the various matches they support. Exhibition or finals matches at these events typically take place on some main stage with a packed audience and have some commentator (also often acting as a host).

There is an attention to detail that goes to the heart of the conditions for competition. I asked, for example, about the use of mods since I've argued in the past that they can fundamentally alter gameplay (Taylor 2006b and 2009). Della Bitta said about their use at *World of Warcraft* competitions:

> As far as add-ons go, we're pretty clear that we frown upon having add-ons at events because in our minds add-ons allow players to, it kind of takes away from the skill level, to compete at a high level, if you're using an add-on that allows you to heal or retarget or, getting specific here, but say take out a shaman's totems with your pet and a one-button. That's not how the game was meant to be played. That's not the way that the arena system specifically is designed. We actually don't allow add-ons in our own official tournaments. And most of our partners, if you've looked into it, will not allow them at live events as well. (Personal communication, 2009)[22]

Figure 4.3
Arena tournament match at Blizzard's World Wide Invitational, Paris 2008.

This sentiment, that there is a preferred model of play that designers and game companies have, is not unusual. Indeed it often poses one of the most rich, if vexing, areas of MMOG play. At the same time, Della Bitta pulled back from any suggestion that Blizzard would take a heavy-handed approach to shaping how e-sports play should be carried out. When I queried whether Blizzard would, for example, want a role in how future leagues were developed he replied,

> I think that we would like the opportunity to at least give advice based on what we know and what works for our products and what the players and the communities surrounding our products enjoy. We have been observing this globally. We're very familiar with our players and our communities. And again, more of a, if you will, a consultant role. We want everybody to succeed and we want e-sports to succeed, but again, it's not our core business so to become involved in that regard it's almost like you're talking about creating its own organization, like a FIFA or something like that, to oversee the sport. Because e-sports is not based on a single sport. There's games that come and go, you can base it on genres of games but it's just a different environment than traditional sports. (Personal communication, 2009)

It is in this complex mix of Blizzard engaging in building the e-sports scene but also wanting to signal some limit to their activity that the KeSPA issue sits. On the one hand Blizzard is clearly invested in the growth of e-sports (in as much as it speaks to their player base), whether it be via their own tournaments or in their recognition of the popularity of the scene and its impact on their titles. On the other hand there is reluctance to simply take over the professionalization of their games entirely, recognizing that e-sports actually encompasses more than just Blizzard titles and is an entire area unto itself. Games like *Starcraft* are a direct product of a game company, but also exist in a broader ecosystem of games and e-sports structures. Direct intervention on that can be tricky.

This is a not unfamiliar dilemma for game companies as they watch their products go out into the world and develop a life all their own. There is a constant dance between wanting to assert property rights around these products—managing and often containing their actual use—and recognizing the limits of doing so. While a game company may support what e-sports brings to the overall promotion and culture of their game, they typically still see themselves first and foremost as a game *producer*—not sports provider.

The emphasis on production folds itself into IP debates in powerful ways. Morhaime clearly noted in the Yonhap interview that, "Blizzard obviously has the IP rights to the *Starcraft* series, but those rights aren't being respected, and we can't keep having these fruitless negotiations with the release of *Starcraft II* at hand" (Yonhap News 2010). In the case of KeSPA versus Blizzard there are underlying thorny issues about the boundaries of these IP rights.

Della Bitta clarified the issue in my conversation with him, noting that the dispute was prompted by KeSPA's sale of the right to broadcast *StarCraft* in South Korea to IEF (International eSports/Entertainment Festival), who in turn licensed the rights to MBC Games and OnGameNet. Interestingly, when I asked if this was just a money issue he said no, that "it's not about the payment itself. It's more of we really just want acknowledgement of our IP." He continued,

> You know, this is one way that we described it in the past: it's, you know, as if someone in Korea painted this amazing painting and then someone in the United States, say, took an image, you know, a digital version of that painting, made postcards and sold it without acknowledging the rights of the painter or giving them any kind of consideration whatsoever. You know, we wouldn't think that that was fair. (Personal communication, 2010)

In public statements KeSPA continues to declare at least some recognition of Blizzard's rights. In the English version of their response to these allegations, which was distributed via e-mail to select outlets, they agree (in fairly awkward wording) that Blizzard has a right to a "rational level of usage fee and appeal its support of marketing and promotion for product line-up of Blizzard with continuous investment such as sharing all contents which belong to KeSPA like pro gamers, broadcasting and sponsorship" (KeSPA 2010). When run against the authorship model Della Bitta's and Morhaime's comments suggest, we can see that such a statement might sound far too lukewarm and even quite provocative.

KeSPA also seems to be balking at what they assert is a general overextension of Blizzard's right to manage other aspects *beyond* broadcast licensing, including:

1. Set the contract term for using its games to one year
2. Prior approvals about all league operations such as contracting sponsorship, marketing materials, broadcasting plan
3. License fee for running of league and all license fee of sponsorship inducement
4. Ownership of all broadcasted programs, program videos
5. Right to audit KeSPA. (KeSPA 2010)

While I was unable to get Della Bitta to confirm or refute this part of KeSPA's claim, it is worth noting nonetheless that part of the larger public argument KeSPA appears to be making is that e-sports, and the play of particular games within that domain, while certainly intersecting a game developer's commercial interests, extends beyond it. Though I could not get KeSPA to comment directly on the matter, we can piece together an instructive picture of their position from a handful of public statements. For them, the fact that e-sports (and any particular title) exist in a much broader context means they cannot be regulated simply as a single-authorship property over which the game company holds sole discretionary power. For example, in a translation of their May 3 post to the Korean Fomos forum they are quoted as saying:

E-sports is a newly emerging sports industry based around video games, and is a gaming business as well as a sports-entertainment business that provides game developers an opportunity to increase revenue and customer satisfaction, and provides sponsors the opportunity to promote and market their products. Taking these features into consideration, if a game is to become a popular E-sports competition, the game developer and the E-sports organization must have a flexible relationship. If a game achieves success as an iconic E-sports competition (*note: KeSPA does not name Starcraft specifically*) [sic, translator's added note], and the developer pursues profits by declaring that their copyright is valid in the sports industry as well, then

> that is a large obstacle for E-sports' growth and establishment as a future sports-entertainment industry. (KeSPA 2010)

A small, but significant, idea embedded in this statement is the suggestion that something may shift once a game reaches "iconic" status. Here, and in other places, KeSPA seems to be suggesting that there is a new sport with a growing public presence that is not captured by simple licensing transactions. The moment a game becomes a part of the culture, and in this case part of a future sports *industry*, one that has stakeholders well beyond any single game development company, appears to be a crucial conceptual moment in KeSPA's argument.

The argument also leads us to consider the ways other stakeholders situate themselves. As an important national organization in the South Korean scene, KeSPA plays a much broader and powerful role in constructing, and legitimizing, e-sports. In an e-mail interview I had with Jay Shin, who is in charge of international business at KeSPA, he noted the wide range of activities the organization does in structuring and supporting pro gaming. I was struck by an additional description he offered of the work the organization does in relation to developers:

> • To host e-Sports leagues or tournaments, it is inevitable for KeSPA to cooperate with developers.
> • KeSPA makes examinations of games when the developers want to make them "official e-Sports title."
> • If KeSPA approves the games as "official e-Sports title," the developers can host "Official leagues."
> • KeSPA dispatches official referees to the leagues. Referees take charge of all matches and save all records of the leagues.
> • KeSPA qualifies the winner of the official leagues as a Pro gamer.
> • Through KeSPA, the game developers promotes their games and gains more and more users. (Personal communication, 2010)

This is an interesting scenario because it signals a more complex two-way relationship between a governing e-sports association and game developers than simple licensing transactions capture. KeSPA does not see itself as merely asking permission from developers for use of their games but argues that it actually provides value back out to developers through authorizing and legitimizing particular titles, a kind of KeSPA stamp of approval. These titles then get promoted in formal activities. Part of what is at work here is an argument that e-sports is not simply taking from developers (by using their games), but is authorizing games to circulate within an e-sports domain and in turn providing valuable marketing for game companies. One former major tournament organizer (not associated with KeSPA) said about his own handling of this issue, "There is no way that I was going to pay a developer or publisher to use a game because I saw my role as marketing their game. We're putting up a million or half a million dollars for people to play your game and you want to charge us? No, I don't see that."

What we are witnessing in this case then is the commercial interests of Blizzard colliding with the commercial interests of not only KeSPA, but perhaps even more strongly its own partners and members, who include various sponsors and corporate affiliates. E-sports promoters often see what they do as producing value for a gaming franchise while developers not infrequently see event organizers as simply using their product to build new revenue generators. Unlike much of the previous academic work on MMOGs, which identified a key tension point as residing between players and game companies, in this case we can analyze the collision of a new viable commercial enterprise arising from another.[23] These are entirely new sets of commercial relationships being negotiated within computer gaming, albeit quite bumpily.

On one side Blizzard, though citing straight IP considerations, does appear to feel it has some stake in the ways its games are played on the pro circuit and how players are treated within the e-sports scene. It not only constructs pro play within venues like Blizzcon, but as Della Bitta's comments show, it is concerned with pro players' experience and the conditions of third-party operators around their game. This is a concern that extends well beyond simple licensing or straightforward IP issues. While on the one hand their primary interest is formulated as a game producer, that they care about the ways their game operates in a broader context should be no surprise. I would argue the split in their rhetoric shows that you cannot untangle production from play. They are interwoven.

At the same time KeSPA appears to be arguing that there are many aspects related to e-sports writ large that are outside the purview of Blizzard's direct intervention, regardless of the fact that one of their titles is being used in tournaments. KeSPA's position seems to be that while it wants to give Blizzard some due (and, we can expect, money) for providing a game that is widely played, it wants to limit its power to intervene in the running of South Korean e-sports. It also wants any straightforward IP argument to be mediated through a consideration of the broader cultural relevance of the property at issue. They are making a provocative argument about what happens when an IP takes on significant public identity. Their claims read as a formulation of some autonomy even though the underlying field of play rests on a decidedly commercial product that is not their own.

What makes this case particularly important is the fact that South Korean e-sports has certainly developed—both economically and culturally—well beyond the contribution any single company has made. Indeed even Della Bitta noted the "ecosystem" in which e-sports exists. This applies to both KeSPA as an organizing body and Blizzard as a game development company. The constitution of pro e-sports is not simply a result of each of their sole initiatives, but comes from a diverse and motley mix of actions, policies, and practices from a range of actors (including other game companies, tournament organizers, and broadcasters). While Blizzard has provided a key foundation via the game software, the realization of pro play (within the game, but also the meaning it is given well beyond it) is constituted through much more than the technology.[24] Though KeSPA certainly has their own (commercial) horse in the race,[25] the larger point they are making about the overall sense of ownership of a pro gaming space is on target—it should not be construed as residing in the hands of a single company. Just as we can talk about MMOGs as co-created products (between a game company and its players), e-sports are as well.

It is easy to see how Blizzard might find this a slippery argument and one that elides the core IP issues. But it is worth lingering over because it does ask us to reckon with the broader question of what happens when commercially authored properties become powerful cultural actors in which the public may actually have a considered stake (Coombe 1998). Lea Shaver and Caterina Sganga (2009) draw out, for example, how the International Covenant on Economic, Social, and Cultural Rights addresses itself to the public's right to participate in a range of aspects of cultural life, including sports and games. They note that as such spheres increasingly tap into networks and online life, critical implications emerge. That this conversation would now intersect a new form of sport and the governance of a digital playing field is perhaps unsurprising. And while the advent of e-sports poses interesting legal questions, they are not entirely unique. Traditional sports and athletics are rife with similar battles.

There are numerous patents, for example, whose scope involves the regulation of physical action, from a "method for putting a golf ball" to forms of physical training (Bambauer 2005, Clement 2000, Kieff, Kramer, and Kunstadt 2008, Kukkonen III 1998, Weber 2000). While these are often set up to try and differentially benefit specific players or teams, they speak to the much broader notion that human action can be adequately scoped so as to be patentable or protectable. Griffith (1997) discusses the application of copyright to athletic performances that are more than "routine" action but encompass performance and artistic qualities. Expressive human action (be it sporting and/or artistic) has long been the subject of legal debate. Moberg (2003) addresses the issue of the copyrightability of "play scripts" (in American football) and choreographed action more generally.[26] Though much of e-sports play falls into routinized action, considering its expressive, artistic, and performative potential (both as individual and team action) certainly provokes deeper consideration of the boundaries of ownership between game companies, teams, leagues, and players.

This is a thorny area and the ownership of athletic performance has regularly come up in traditional sports (Griffith 1997) where the rights of publicity on the part of the players and the rights of broadcast on the part of league operators are at stake (Choi 2002, Cianfrone and Baker III 2010, Matzkin 2000, Quinn and Warren 1983). E-sports introduces yet another stakeholder into the already fraught mix—developers who assert IP rights as formal owners of the game and, in turn, the digital playing field.

A number of new border cases, beyond the Blizzard/KeSPA dispute, are right on our horizon. Though games themselves aren't deemed copyrightable, as Bruce Boyden (2010) notes, their "constituent elements" are, which includes game pieces, graphics, and even a particular expression of the rules (Malkan 2009, Prettyman 1976). One can thus imagine scenarios in which a game company, exerting IP rights, precludes a tournament from using particular rule sets or mods that may override their software because they fear it corrupts the intended spirit of the game (and brand). Depending on how mods or alternate rule sets are considered, interesting challenges may arise. And an entire refusal to allow a tournament to use a game at all, modded or not, also comes into question. When a game company can, in essence, take the ball and go home we've entered some new territory.

We can also certainly imagine legal battles surrounding the ownership of match videos and their distribution or streaming via third-party websites. Beyond issues of who owns a recorded game session (the game developer, the tournament licensee, the team or player, the spectator who recorded a match playback file), forms of distribution may also pose legal challenges. As online real-time streaming of video continues to grow (via sites like Ustream, Justin.tv, Stickam, or even cloud computing game services like OnLive), containing broadcasting to formally licensed enterprises will prove difficult. Traditional sports are themselves already confronting the ways such technologies allow fans to circumvent constraints arising from complex licensing deals (MacDonald 2004). If you visit any of those sites now you will find quite a few players (including pros) transmitting their play sessions out to a global audience.

The computational nature of digital games, in which the software is constituted through databases and bits of code, seems to lend itself particularly well to tangled formulations about what actually the "thing" is. Disputes around player performance statistics have already played a role in the legal scholarship around forms like fantasy leagues (Shane 2006) and the fact that computer game action in part exists as discrete bytes of code, easily captured, recompiled, and redistributed, means this issue all too easily falls into that domain.

It is thus perhaps not too far-fetched to envision a debate about who owns the creative gaming action of a top e-sports player. Are they, for example, legally allowed to capture and distribute their own in-game performances? Can and should e-sports players claim a similar right of publicity as traditional sports athletes do or will game companies, organizations such as KeSPA, or tournament operators themselves assert ownership? How might notions of publicity rights be complicated when part of the embodied performance of the athlete is enacted via avatars or within coded systems? Who, in fact, owns an e-sports athlete's performance? Or visual representation (avatar and non)?

As we have seen, in the era of the Digital Millennium Copyright Act the vigorous assertion of a broad construction of IP rights has been the norm among large media companies and game culture has been right in the thick of it. E-sports, perhaps as much as any endeavor for the way it intersects serious commercial and economic interests across a range of actors, is well positioned for some vexed battles. Aline Lotter, in 1978, suggested that more needed to be done to centralize the public interest stake within ongoing law and sports skirmishes. This reminder remains important as we enter an age in which the commercialization of leisure reaches ever-growing heights. In the realm of games and the law, not to mention digital culture more broadly, the encroachment of overly narrow definitions of ownership is the hallmark of our era (be it remixing or player auctions). But we need careful critical reflection on how to sustain a vibrant culture—including the domains of sports and leisure—amid the powerful alignment of technology and retrograde intellectual property formulations. That a new prong of our culture, e-sports, is being entangled in this trend, while not surprising, should cause us pause.

Ultimately, in the case of Blizzard versus KeSPA, Blizzard decided to end negotiations and instead cut a licensing deal with Gretech-GomTV (who already cooperated with Blizzard for e-sports events and coverage) allowing them broadcast and tournament rights for Blizzard's products.[27] As with many computer game cases, no legal move seems to be pending to push the issue to the courts. This is no small incident, though, both for what it means for the future of South Korean e-sports and broader conversations about the status of ownership in e-sports.

Governmental Initiatives and NGOs

As we've seen in South Korea, governments and other interested parties are regularly solicited for, and offer, support for computer gaming and its professionalization. As contemporary leisure and play increasingly includes serious time (and money) spent on computer gaming, government officials, public policy stakeholders, health advocates, sports organizers, and avid gamers themselves have sought to situate the activity into broader conversations about leisure, sportsmanship, and health. Often infused with an interest in enfranchising teens into structured activity, a variety of initiatives have been launched to try and formalize—and legitimize—the play of computer gamers within various structures. This is regularly combined with broader national governmental interests in supporting a technological or creative industries sector of the economy. For many, computer games offer a hope of bringing teens into healthy structured sportsmanlike activities, as well as provide a boost to envisioned high-tech economic growth.

It is fairly striking to see the variety of national initiatives that have arisen over the years that attempt to promote an e-sports plan for South Korea. As should be clear by now, South Korea has been extremely active in national play initiatives, where the government has identified technology and computer games as an important part of its economic growth profile, and this attitude has extended into organizing e-sports much more formally than any other country. This pattern can be found—albeit to a much lesser degree—in Europe and, increasingly, other Asian countries.

There has been a lot of activity within various European countries to establish computer games under the moniker of e-sports, albeit with no major success. These initiatives are regularly tied to professional gaming, though they often try and include a public service component as well. In Denmark and Sweden public funding is available for special interest clubs. Movie clubs, football clubs, scooter clubs, and a range of others are all fairly well supported within the system. Perhaps unsurprisingly e-sports clubs have appeared on the scene as well. Often initiated and sponsored by slightly older men who see themselves as past their own gaming peak but still avidly interested in fostering and supporting the gamer community, these e-sports initiatives sometimes link up to larger social concerns about health and activity, seeking to provide a clear structure for computer gamers to play within.

Quite often I have met people managing pro tournaments who are also actively involved in fostering initiatives to build coherent national scenes integrating business and government interests in e-sports. In the United Kingdom several prominent members of the community launched an initiative, the United Kingdom eSports Association, to formalize e-sports play and provide an outlet for advocacy and organizing activities. Similarly in Denmark there have been several attempts to launch various e-sports associations as a way of both solidifying the community and building a platform for seeking support from the government. An International e-Sports Federation was launched in 2008, positioning itself as a coordinating organization between member nations (including KeSPA and a number of other organizations in Asia and Europe). One of its main goals is the standardization of e-sports.

While South Korea, Europe, and North America have so far held the lead in formalizing e-sports, China is emerging as a new and powerful force.[28] Chengdu, China, for example, was chosen as the host city for the WCG Grand Final in 2009. The scale of events there can be quite large, often even moreso than in established e-sports markets. Initiatives like Wuhan's International E-sports/Entertainment Festival in 2008 drew 10,000 in-person spectators and players and 100,000 participating online (International E-Sports/Entertainment Festival 2008).

As governments turn their attention to the issue, it is generally not without some ambivalence. Many are unsure of where exactly to locate their e-sports initiatives—should they be situated within the realm of entertainment and leisure or within athletics? Given the often ambiguous status of computer gaming as a leisure activity, let alone a serious endeavor, gaining traction within governments for some kind of formal recognition of the value of their play can prove challenging to nongovernmental association organizers.

One thing that is very clear when looking at any e-sports organization, be it team, tournament organizer, or national e-sports initiative, is that they are regularly engaged in symbolic and political work on the behalf of game culture more generally. Whether it is advocating national legislation or simply trying to pitch the idea of sponsorship to a potential partner, e-sports companies regularly work hard to try and legitimize (and indeed unstigmatize) computer game play, and the hard-core fandom you see in e-sports. Part of the work undertaken in this realm is trying to recalibrate public and governmental perceptions of computer gaming and gamers themselves. This involves situating digital play alongside things like athletics, "healthy" social activities, and, especially in the case of children, morals and values development. Given the residual stigma playing computer games still has in many countries, this is no easy task and indeed the uneven success of many national initiatives speaks in part to the real challenges the promotion of computer game play at a serious and focused level presents.

Advocacy can also take place vis-à-vis governmental regulation of game content via ratings systems or legislation. Germany is a particularly good example of this dynamic. Due to a fairly severe ratings and content censorship system, some titles commonly played by teenagers in North America are heavily regulated in Germany. There has been a significant amount of concern (not to mention bad "science") about links between computer game violence and real violence. This means that for organizations putting on e-sports tournaments in Germany, there is a fair amount of necessary education and advocacy work. As one German tournament organizer put it, a form of "evangelizing, educating people that [playing computer games] is a good thing and not a bad thing." Indeed is it a constant part of doing business. This involves everything from meeting with politicians and policy makers to holding open house-type events where those who have influence on the public conversation, and policy, get a chance to try games and talk through their concerns.

Industry Cooperation: The G7

While there are a number of examples of national initiatives to support the development of e-sports, there is one notable organization working within pro gaming to coordinate efforts across several teams, the G7. Founded in April 2006 by seven professional teams,[29] the G7 is an attempt to provide some cross-organizational collaboration and a formalized collective voice between top teams. The G7 is a notable development in the North American and European arenas given e-sports' otherwise fluctuating and somewhat volatile nature. The organization notes in its mission statement that it seeks to:

- Improve and represent e-sports in all its aspects, as well as provide a platform for stability for member teams
- Provide a communication channel for the community to improve e-sports, through the unification of teams
- Strive to achieve the following; cooperate with leagues and tournament. (G7 2010a)

To this end it has drafted a standardized contract for the member teams (much like you see in leagues like the NFL or MBA), consulted with tournament organizers, provided team and player advocacy, and provided a set of rankings between teams.

Assessing the G7 is a tricky matter and for most e-sports fans the organization's role and impact can be unclear. Unlike KeSPA, many e-sports fans don't really know about the G7. As various member representatives often note in public interviews, however, any lack of visibility and publicity around the organization simply speaks to its effectiveness—they are working so hard behind the scenes nipping problems in the bud that they tend to stay off the radar. They have, however, made several very public pronouncements over the years that have drawn attention.

Perhaps one of the biggest issues e-sports players face is tournaments not paying out prize winnings. This is one of the biggest dirty little secrets of the industry. Though there are notable examples people regularly cite of failed payouts, the extent of the problem is likely unknown to most fans. The G7 has made a number of concerted attempts to advocate on the behalf of players who have not received prize money. In September 2009, for example, they launched an initiative requesting players or teams who had not received earned prize money contact them with full details, which the organization would then use to attempt to arbitrate the matter (G7 2009a). Information collected from this survey was to then be used to "assign and publish past and current e-sports organizers with a prize payout status rating. Gamers and sponsors can then consider these ratings before attending or sponsoring future events. Subsequent collection submissions and ratings will be regularly conducted to help hold e-sports organizers honest and accountable" (G7 2009a).

They noted in November 2009 that "In just two weeks we received over 150 e-mails from community members with claims totaling $355,208" (G7 2009b). In December 2009 they then launched an additional initiative—three online petitions against the CPL, ESWC, and Global Gaming League. These petitions were meant to garner community support for G7 action against these tournament organizers' alleged failures to pay out prize winnings (including, they note in the press release, possibly contacting relevant attorney generals for legal follow-up) (G7 2009c).

Though the comprehensive database of failed payouts has not yet appeared publicly as of the time of this writing, the organization made several statements regarding specific tournaments and organizations. In particular they focused on discussions with two organizations, the CPL and the ESWC. These are perhaps the most well known of the alleged payout failure cases. Though some conversations appeared to develop between the G7 and these organizers, no real progress seemed to be made in money actually changing hands. Accountability has been particularly tricky in both cases given both the CPL and ESWC changed ownership (with the ESWC undergoing bankruptcy). The new owners have, while sometimes making statements suggesting they wanted to settle accounts and do right by players, apparently done little in the way of actually paying out.[30]

In a fascinating twist to the ESWC case the G7 announced in June 2010 that *it* would actually step in on the financial side of the failed payouts. Noting its support for the ESWC attempting a "successful resurgence" postbankruptcy, the G7 announced that, "Since the ESWC is yet to address prize money owed to past winners, including those from 2008, the G7 Teams will allocate 10% of prize money won at ESWC 2010 to the ESWC 2008 winners" (G7 2010b). Though the press release additionally noted it was requiring the ESWC to make sure future winnings were paid and the prior lapses were publicly addressed or risk future boycott by the member teams, what is striking is the way this action illuminates the complex tension between various stakeholders in the scene. The financial stability of teams requires tournaments to stay up and running, not only for payout purposes but to have stable venues the sponsors recognize and trust. It is thus in the G7's direct interest for a formerly strong organization like the ESWC to reemerge and provide venues for play. At the same time failed payouts put these two organizations, not to mention the players caught in the middle, into a much more adversarial relationship. It is tricky to think what an equivalent of this situation might be with regard to traditional sports but perhaps if we imagine a television broadcaster stepping in to pay NFL salaries we begin to sense the oddity, and complexity, of the situation.

This example is the most unusual I have found when looking at the G7's relationships with various tournaments. In general their actions have been much more traditionally organized around things like advocacy and boycotting. For example, they successfully pushed back on policies by a tournament (WSVG) to enforce wearing certain headphones, which could have jeopardized their teams' own sponsor relationships. They have initiated tournament boycotts, citing failure to pay prizes (CPL). They have additionally issued public warnings about events they have found questionable ("Project eSports"). Though their actions sometimes lack public follow-through (the press archive at their website is even itself incomplete), it is clear that within North American and European e-sports they have been an important organization and provide a glimpse of the power concerted cross-team advocacy can bring.

Contracts and Unionization

The regulation of e-sports remains fairly ad hoc though the most long-standing teams and organizations have tried to formalize things such as player relations via contracts. As I briefly mentioned, the G7 has drafted a standard player contract for member teams to use as a starting point. The contract, which can be amended by any member team, details everything from loyalty expectations and what are traditionally thought of as "morality clauses" to number of practice and match hours per week and sponsor relations (see the appendix for a copy of the standard contract, including insurance coverage). Details about salaries, prize winnings (some teams keep 10 to 20 percent to subsidize tournament travel), bonuses, and other financial arrangements will typically be formulated in relation to specific player negotiations. Like traditional sports contracts, individual players will sometimes warrant special clauses and conditions. Other non-G7 teams often rely on contracts that have been passed around and shared from various owners over the years, getting slightly modified along the way to fit current needs. They also may draw up their own fairly informal document, even detailing conditions via e-mail.

Despite these attempts at formalizing labor relations there have, perhaps unsurprisingly, been serious problems over the years on a number of fronts. While the failure of tournaments to pay out prize winnings is perhaps the most publicized financial ethical violation, one regularly hears players talk about, for example, not being properly paid or reimbursed travel costs by their teams.[31] Though most players operating at the top level hold some kind of contract with their team, legal remedies—although often threatened—are generally not sought by e-sports players. The number of professional outfits players can work for is still quite small by comparison with other sports (or professions) and thus the labor conditions for most players are still deeply entwined with informal and interpersonal processes. A player may leave a team because they haven't been paid a salary for several months and while they won't file a lawsuit, they will generally spread the word to fellow players and the owner of their new team.[32]

Given this situation, there is continual speculation about the possible development of a player union. While there have been some attempts to float the idea, it never really gets off the ground. It is hard to know exactly why but a few possible explanations come to mind. In general the players involved in pro gaming are still quite young and as such, often do not have the tools and experience to tackle the larger systemic issues, and organization, unionization would require. Given e-sports are also not really known broadly outside the niche of game culture, its athletes are not seen as possible members to any larger player union that may assist traditional athletes. There is also the issue that many (especially young) players are often simply grateful to get any help or legitimacy in supporting their game play and so longer-term organization may feel out of step with their own thankfulness for any support at all. This point ties into a final issue, which is that it often takes an e-sports player a number of years to come to feel a sense of full professional identity as a gamer-athlete, one which may warrant true representation and advocacy. Given the scene often makes it difficult for people to stay in it over the long haul, however, there is thus a contravening tendency to churn through players before they reach professional maturity. Unlike traditional sports where there is a known path to professionalization (albeit a highly competitive one) with eventual clear payoffs and legitimacy—all supported by a range of organizations and auxiliary professionals—the indeterminacy of e-sports as a space for professional identity works against building, through institutions like unions, long-term systems of representation and advocacy. As long as there is not a more robust system of socialization into a professional athletic identity I suspect unionization will not come to e-sports players.

Globalizing the Industry

Perhaps one of the most notable aspects of pro e-sports is its transnational nature. Aside from leagues such as the MLG, which tend to remain focused on North America, historically e-sports have been produced via a complex mix of regional and global activities. As players come up through the scene they often modulate between tight local roots and larger international connections. While regional qualifiers or national tournaments continue to form a part of the pro circuit, big-ticket tournaments in e-sports, such as the Intel Extreme Masters or the World Cyber Games, are distinctively international in orientation. Large stable teams regularly draw their players from a range of countries who generally do not have any physical connection with a national home office but instead mediate their engagement with the team online, at tournament venues, and in occasional co-located boot camps.

At a very practical level this means that e-sports organizations—be they tournament organizers or teams—are often negotiating complex waters with regards to contracts, national policies, and local laws. In the case of tournament organizations they very often license out their brand to a local organizer who is better equipped to deal with regional specificity. This strategy is not without risk as the global brand is handled by a local partner over whom real enforcement may be difficult.

The global context of e-sports also means that organizers and teams are having to navigate varying political and cultural climates with regards to not just e-sports but computer gaming more generally. Games that may be the norm and perfectly acceptable in one country may be heavily regulated (or banned outright) in another. Various countries, or even regions, may situate computer game play within the culture in slightly different ways. And norms around play (including who plays) and appropriate behavior may vary slightly. While computer gaming exists as a decidedly global product, it simultaneously inhabits local contexts that situate it accordingly. As a business venture the people who come to e-sports and build organizations and institutions around it must operate in a fairly nimble way to accommodate and address the dual global-local status of gaming. Given it is such a young industry and so many of the people involved are improvising and making it up as they go along, this is no small challenge.

Ultimately the organizational issues facing e-sports traverse a complex terrain that ranges from the simple day-to-day management of teams and emerging professionals to thorny legal matters. That this all simultaneously takes place on both a local and a global stage only compounds matters. As this chapter shows, the growth of professional computer gaming is tied to the development of both ancillary actors and serious commercial interests. Its rise is not simply a story about the transformation of digital play into sport, but the production of that activity as a new form of industry.

5 Spectatorship and Fandom

Probably one of the most perplexing ideas surrounding pro gaming is the notion that watching a computer game match as a spectator would be interesting. Even among players, who themselves have the everyday experience of looking over a friend's shoulder while they play or watching others while awaiting a controller for their turn, there can be skepticism. The power of computer games is seen first and foremost as located in the way they ask us to interact with them, to be engaged. The classic formulation of engagement within game studies says it is direct action upon the game that signifies the heart of the play experience. Perhaps the most frequently quoted passage in this regard is Aarseth's statement that, "In ergodic literature, nontrivial effort is required to allow the reader to traverse the text" (1997, 1). Games are thus typically contrasted to reading or watching TV by virtue of their requiring our concerted action upon them. Much core theoretical work in the field has rightly noted the ways computer games call us to be active participants, including their reliance on our actions for scenarios and characters to come alive.

In this frame, the very notion of spectating computer games seems at odds with their nature. While we are used to fans watching traditional sports, picking out their favorite players, and avidly following their careers, imagining young computer game aficionados as an object of admiration can seem a stretch. Yet computer games are objects of spectatorship, increasingly replete with fans who follow the every move of their favorite teams and players. If that combination wasn't enough to turn on its head long-standing notions about what computer games are, and what they can be, we are confronted with another crucial actor in this story of spectatorship and fandom—the professional computer game commentator. Sitting at their microphone, broadcasting to a room raptly watching in-game action or speaking to a network or television feed, they provide

Figure 5.1
World Cyber Games 2007 Grand Final in Seattle *Warcraft* match.

information about the game and players, racing to keep up with the action occurring on screen.

This chapter will explore how the evolving world of professional e-sports rests on a construction of these games as objects that can be watched and appreciated by viewers, many of whom are not only players themselves but will become fans. It will discuss, from a fan and spectator perspective, the tournaments that provide the competitive venues for the pro players. And it will look at how that activity is mediated and fostered by a nascent group of people who are themselves trying to build a profession out of commentating and reporting on these games.

Making Room for Spectatorship and Fandom in Game Studies

Much of our current formulation of agency and action in computer game studies rests on the distinctly foregrounded hands-on-the-keyboard player. This player-in-action, commanding the game and his or her forces, is a central figure in much theoretical work. This is understandable. Early computer game studies focused on distinguishing the medium from other forms, ones in which the primary actor—the movie watcher, the reader—was figured as fairly passive. The primacy and valorization of "interactive" —a central rubric through which game studies has theoretically defined itself—has nonetheless often overlooked the vast literature problematizing the notion of the passive traditional media consumer. My intent is not to negate the importance of the hands-on-actor as a key figure of agency in computer games, but to situate such formulations more broadly. Crawford and Gosling helpfully suggest we remember the paradigm shift, which "does not see audiences as passive, but rather active producers and performers who draw on the mass media and consumer goods in the construction and maintenance of their social identities and performances" (2009, 56. See also Crawford and Rutter 2007). Perhaps in the same way traditional media was given a fresh look through the intervention of scholars in the Birmingham school and later analyses of actual media engagement, we can do a productive flip in game studies and ask what role spectatorship and audience have in constructing the play experience and gamer action.[1] As Holin Lin and Chuen-Tsai Sun argue in their work on arcade spaces, "The presence of onlookers, their behaviours, and their skill-based rankings shape the interactional frames that surround game platforms. Onlookers assist in enhancing and expanding gameplay when they accept the roles of focused audience members or learning apprentices, thereby turning play into public performance and supporting the showroom frame" (2011, 134). It is thus worth pushing back on an overly simplistic model of engagement with computer games that places the hands-on-the-keyboard actor as the prime object of interest.

From the very earliest days of video game play, rooted in the arcade or computer lab, spectatorship had a central role. While multiplayer gaming has become the norm, thinking about the turn-taking inherent in most 1980s arcade games can remind us how standing alongside and watching others play formed a key part of the experience. The quarter or token placed on top of the machine that held your place in line while you stood slightly off to the side watching the current player was, for many of us, a big part of the arcade experience.

You watched moves, sometimes marveling at skill or smiling at your own better abilities in comparison. As you took your own turn at the machine, moving from spectator to player, you would often feel eyes on you and either up your game or falter. While the high score screen would temporally anchor these competitive moments they were powerfully enacted and embodied in the copresence of players.[2]

Figure 5.2
Wellington Ferry Terminal, 1988.
Image from the *More Than a Craze* online exhibition curated by M. Swalwell and J. Bayly (2010), photo courtesy of Dominion Post Collection, Alexander Turnbull Library, Wellington, New Zealand.

As consoles arrived and became domestic leisure objects, simultaneous multiplayer action was a more viable option. The earliest versions of Pong certainly come to mind, but legions of young children raised on Nintendo machines provide us a clear picture of (little) hands on controllers. And yet within the home, spectatorship around computer games is still hugely important. Younger siblings often watch older ones play through difficult passages, learning and then imitating moves. Sometimes players are introduced to a game, watching someone give an overview, or perhaps taking the controller to maneuver through a difficult section. Friends may come over to the house to play, and given there can be more people than controllers, take turns. And even when the game itself is not formally designed as multiplayer, participants round-robin through, cycling between taking in-game action and spectating.

If we factor in PC gaming, this reliance on spectatorship becomes even more apparent. While a handful of games offer multiplayer on a single keyboard (someone using AWSD keys and another using arrow keys) for the most part over-the-shoulder constructions of PC play dominate when people come together in physical space. Things like taking turns or division of labor (where one person "drives" the character and another helps with puzzles or directing action) are not unusual when friends or family gather around a PC game.

There has been some exploration of this space of spectatorship in games and James Newman's contribution (2002, 2004) is notable. He proposes that game players can be seen as moving through several phases or types of play, periods of being "fully interactive," "partially interactive," and "noninteractive." Though he is still working here with a notion of interactivity in a fairly instrumental sense, it nonetheless helps nuance the picture of player activity and opens space for spectatorship. He also notes a division of labor that can occur during gameplay and suggests that the map-making or puzzle-solving participant who does not actually have a controller is still involved in an important way. He writes, "While these players cannot be seen as having any interactive control because they possess no direct link to the interface of the game and cannot perform or execute commands, they nonetheless demonstrate a level of interest and experiential engagement with the game that, while mediated through the primary player, exceeds that of the bystander or observer" (2002, 409). As he astutely argues, we often sloppily reduce what counts as meaningful interaction with a video game based on a fairly narrow definition of activity.

As Emma Witkowski and I note in our work on LANs (2010), these initial pushes to widen the space of who we account for in the gaming moment can be productively expanded to deal with even the bystander or observer. There are certainly different types of bystanders and, as Lin and Sun (2011) point out, varying forms of spectatorship produce several interactional frames. If we are watching a game we are unfamiliar with and give it more than a passing glance, perhaps stopping to linger and watch a skilled player, we do a significant amount of work trying to interpret what we see, trying to connect it to a title within the genre we are familiar with (relying on known visual cues or conventions like health bars) to help us make sense of what we're seeing. Sometimes we have nothing to connect it to and yet can nonetheless be drawn to the action on screen and the visuals. If, however, we are experienced bystanders, we bring a whole host of complex cognitive action to bear on that moment. We may do sophisticated on-the-spot analysis of the player's actions, even going so far as to mentally troubleshoot a move or strategize ahead. If we are spectating a match we may shift our attention between the screens of competitors, piecing together an overall picture of the gaming field and synthesizing the distributed activities into a broader story of the game. For the professional player observing a match, often after the fact via a recording, this can involve a complex breakdown of actions and counteractions, as well as planning future tactics and strategies for when that competitor is directly faced in a live match.

Beyond the cognitive work the observer does, there are important affective and embodied aspects of spectatorship worth addressing. When I watch someone else play a computer game I am often activated internally as a player. I may feel excitement, tension, remembrances of my own similar play moments. Watching may inspire me to get back to my own machine and play. While we regularly notice the ways players hold their body in relation to play—leaning into the screen, muscles tensed—spectators can also become activated in their bodies, sitting forward in anticipation during a tense moment, intently focused on the screen, feeling the visceral reverberations of the digital action within their bodies, cheering with excitement or clapping when victory happens. Melanie Swalwell has written on how embodiment is interwoven within digital games for both player and spectator. She argues, for example, that we should consider the ways in which "one's senses can be *taken by* a game" (2008, 82, emphasis hers). She presents a complex rendering of the lines between digital and corporeal embodied experience, something that echoes what I've also found both in games and within nongame virtual worlds. While work on platforms like the Wii has certainly moved the conversation on embodiment and play forward (see, for example, Simon's 2009 piece on the Nintendo console), it is important we situate corporeality in digital gaming well beyond those moments in which the technology explicitly requires us to stand up and move our arms. Even when players are sitting on a sofa or at a table, they are always already engaged in embodied action (Bayliss 2007, Dovey and Kennedy 2006, Lahti 2003). Though new gaming interfaces may highlight and bring to the foreground the way physicality involves itself in digital play, there is no moment in which this is not the case.

If little is written in game studies about spectatorship, fandom is the companion ghost. Though media studies has excelled in tackling the nature of fandom within traditional media (see Jenkins 1992 and Hills 2002, to name only two influential works), amazingly little has been ported over to understanding computer game fandom. This is particularly surprising given how central, for example, the figure of the "fan boy" is within game culture. Perhaps it has not been dealt with adequately because game scholars themselves haven't fully reckoned with their own fandom when it comes to the study of games (the "aca-fan" arising from the hybrid of

Figure 5.3
A *Street Fighter* match, DreamHack 2009.

academic and fan). Our own love of particular titles or genres is frequently the unspoken methodological scaffold on which many studies have been built. To put a discussion of fandom in the terrain of game studies would bring to the foreground often unarticulated foundations. And yet fandom is such a significant part of game culture, and indeed research about it, we should not overlook it.

Within gaming there are a number of ways fandom can be sliced. Some players will follow a title for years and across multiple platforms, even when disappointed by particular installments. I am thinking here about the diehard *Final Fantasy* players who have played every version of the game (be it on PC or console), seen spin-off movies, and eagerly await its next installment. We can also talk about the ways players become fans of a genre. Not all computer game players play all kinds of games. In much the same way people develop taste preferences in film or literature, game players typically have genre preferences. This means they will prefer certain styles of games and play, for example first-person shooters, puzzle, or horror games. Genre fandom typically expresses itself through the demonstration of cross-title comparison, historical knowledge, and perhaps even specific tastes around famous developers or designers. We may certainly even identify "fan-scholars" (Hills 2002) within game culture who do important critical and interpretive work, drawing out and articulating personal and communal passions.

Understanding the complexity of computer game and e-sports fandom remains an underdeveloped aspect of game studies. Yet it is one of the most powerful affective sites within the domain and is tied to play experience. As many media studies scholars have argued for several decades now, fans do not simply consume but are crucial participants in the *production* of cultural products. In the case of e-sports, though they may not be the professionals on the field, they infuse energy into events, giving meaning and social importance to activities, and often provide important contributions through their participation in various media (online and off). Hills (2002) notes there is a powerful "affective play" at work in fandom, which signals something more than simply cognitive modes of engagement. Fandom can weave the passions people feel about a game, a genre, a character, a designer or developer together with their sense of identity. It can publically perform otherwise internalized values and commitments. Being a fan forms a powerful node through which social affiliations and connection with others are formed. It is also woven through with hierarchies and stratifications, offering powerful modes of social organization. Fandom is both expressive and constructive. It thus becomes an important area to look at if we want to better understand gamers and game culture.

The Nature of E-sports Fandom

People generally do not come into the scene expecting to be fans or spectators but typically first think of themselves as players and then, after some exposure to videos on demand, websites, or podcasts come to transform their own object of leisure into one that is simultaneously about fandom. This is potentially a distinctive feature of e-sports. Unlike traditional sports where fans may never have actually played the game themselves, in computer gaming the path to pro gaming fandom is often born directly out of their own experience with a title. One young fan who was an avid gamer himself described his own introduction to e-sports this way:

> Well it started off with that one of my friends came over with his USB stick to show me a video. He told me it was an awesome video about some clan playing a cup. The video he showed me was a review of ISC 2006 (Complexity won, go to Youtube.com—write "complexity" in the searchbar—take the first one). And this video actu-

ally gave me goosebumps, because I knew that this was it. This should be my Arsenal or FC Barcelona. After watching it I was curious and started to Google it and research it. After I found [their] homepage I have been fan since that (a year or so).

This is a great, and very typical, example of the way people can be brought into the scene by friends and the kind of powerful connection they can feel to teams. Sometimes friends are fans of the same team (as with this young guy and his friend) and sometimes there is playful rivalry. In both cases the fandom and shared moments of spectatorship build ties between players. As they continue to game themselves, their fandom around e-sports becomes another layer of engagement.

Because the border between amateurs and new rising pro talent is not as clear as in traditional sports, many regular players can also find themselves playing against emerging pros. This connection, between everyday leisure and fandom, between amateur and pro players, helps build strong affective attachments. It also helps make e-sports fandom a fairly tight and closed subculture. The insider/outsider distinction can feel strong to someone just starting to be interested in e-sports.

What is also striking is how much fandom extends throughout the scene. In my conversations with people involved in all aspects of e-sports the passion and love for it came through over and over. At events you could tell referees were often fans of the very people they were judging. Commentators were regularly supporters of particular games or players, though they worked hard to keep those comments to the "back stage" or more informal venues. Tournament organizers and journalists were often fans who had transformed their love of the games into a professional identity that allowed them to keep a foot in that world. Of course, even in traditional sports those involved are regularly there because of their commitment to the game. But I was always struck by how apparent and on the surface this love was in the e-sports scene. It felt as if it had not yet undergone the step of professionalization that seeks to mask that consuming engagement into objectivity. I often think of e-sports as very much in the teenager stage of development—full of emotion, passion, enthusiasm, not yet entirely jaded by experience but also often not as polished in its public face as it otherwise might be (though this often serves the dual purpose of signaling authenticity).

What is also interesting about fandom in e-sports is that loyalties can divide along a number of different vectors. There is no predictable segmentation like in traditional sports. E-sports fans can be fans of a particular game genre, a title, a player, a team, a national identification, and even in

Figure 5.4
Refs watching the main stage at WCG Grand Final 2007, Seattle.

rare instances, a particular tournament. As an early report on e-sports suggested, five factors structure the possibility of sport spectatorship for computer games: identification, personal interest, social value, focus and depth in activity, and clear conflict (Game Research 2002). Whereas traditional sports regularly build on regional affinities, you can never quite predict along what affective axis an e-sports fan resides. This trend of uncoupling regionality and fandom has certainly been on the rise in traditional sports for many years now. Whitson points out that though "professional sports operators routinely appeal to civic (and national) sentiments when it suits their commercial purposes, the languages of communal traditions and loyalties are increasingly supplanted by corporate images and by the discourse of consumer choice" (1998, 59). It is within this mode that you find the Liverpool football fan who resides in a small Swedish town or the European who has a favorite U.S. baseball team. Such transnational allegiances are common within e-sports.

I have talked to people who will follow a player no matter what title they cross over to because they are so impressed by their skill. People will sometimes follow a top-ranking team for years even as the roster changes.

And at international competitions spectators will cheer their national team. There are also those that are die-hard fans of a game (*Counter-Strike*, *Starcraft*, and *Warcraft* perhaps being the most notable in this regard) and will track it over the years. Players may come and go but they see the title as the core. Ultimately whichever vector an individual selects in relation to their e-sports fandom, there is typically a strong affective component to it. One well-regarded e-sports blogger noted that even the "bad boy" teams can pull people in, saying, "And I think that it's almost weird that it [fandom] might even start with the teams you actually hate."

Perhaps some of the most astute reflections on the complexities of e-sports fandom have come from those commentators involved in broadcasting games. In a discussion with one I inquired if he felt you could be a fan of and spectate a game you had never played yourself. He replied,

> You can but it'd depend on what kind of emotional attachment you'd built. I think for the first time it'd be just a normal team. For the second time why you would come back is the key question. It's got to be interesting, you've got to find a player you like in a very short space of time or you've got to have an affinity to a team. And I think the CGS hits those marks really well because they're providing a local team that might be from somewhere you were born or you were raised, went to university, went to college, or had a job at. Something, some link, some random link. Or it could be it's the right [team] color.

One of the striking things in this quote, and something you hear over and over again when talking to e-sports fans (including the ones who professionalize into working sectors of the scene) is this complex mix of happenstance, affect, your own play, and the more fact-based side of fandom that ultimately comes to produce forms of engagement with the scene. In the same way the professional players I discussed in chapter 3 consider and weigh their own passion for competitive gaming against identity markers such as geek or athlete, e-sports fan likewise move through complex constructions and negotiations, both internally and within their social networks, to situate their fandom. Sometimes the strongest tie is to feeling—almost unable to articulate—for a player or team, an admiration, an aspirational orientation. In other instances their fandom creates a productive oppositional space (a la the "geek"). Other times they express deep engagement with particular game titles and mechanics, most clearly situating and describing their own passion through facts or a pleasure in the structure of the thing. In all these ways we can see that the nature of e-sports fandom is varying, plucking different strings in different people. Yet a consistent word, a note, I heard again and again was that of passion.

Building a Fanbase, Online

This process of constructing fandom is complex and people are pulled into it in a range of ways. As previously discussed, the community around professional gaming is deeply tied to its larger location in the LAN scene and the ways pro players are often still tightly connected to amateur and casual players. But it is important to note the variety of ways (aside from actual play) that the community is not only fostered, but educated about and inducted into pro gaming. The Internet certainly makes developing a large pro game community feasible. Whereas prior initiatives to formalize the competitive player community had to rely on traditional media, the communication, distribution, and organizational possibilities the net brings radically change the landscape.[3] Crawford and Rutter (2007) describe the way gaming audiences and fandom are constructed through a "mediascape." Through the use of websites, blogs, podcasts, streaming media, and VoD playbacks, fans are able to follow matches occurring around the world featuring their favorite games and teams. Just as importantly, they post in forums, debating specific performances, player skills, and events that happened at a tournament or simply cheering on their favorite players or teams.

Forums and Chat

A large part of the ongoing construction of the e-sports community takes place in forums and venues such as IRC (Internet relay chat) channels. While much of the conversation on sites sticks to fairly straightforward sports talk (teams, players, tactics, and the like) at times broader themes arise. One of the most common threads is actually a fundamental debate about the viability of computer games as sport, and a professionalized one at that. Most fans understand that this object of their interest and passion is not really legitimated in our larger culture, and certainly not at the level of sport or professional activity. Part of the work the community regularly engages in is debating the very construction of computer games as a sport, a professional endeavor, and an object of their passion and spectatorship. Sometimes this takes the form of questions about the nature of a sport, and sometimes it boils down to discussions about whether the larger culture will ever really be able to get it the way these fans do. Often it revolves around questioning the strategies being used by broadcasters and teams to push e-sports into mainstream culture. For example, when the U.S. broadcaster CBS featured a WSVG competition on their Sunday afternoon *Sports Spectacular* show in 2007 and featured not only FPSs but also

Guitar Hero, many e-sports fans debated (and indeed bemoaned) not only the quality of the show, but the strategic decisions around the titles, the format, and the timing.

Very often fans themselves burrow down into a kind of microanalysis of the scene by questioning which titles are most viable for spectatorship and yet still hold to a high e-sports standard. Games that might provide bridges to draw in new viewers, such as *World of Warcraft* arena matches, are highly debated in regards to their ability to be a "real" sport and whether or not they are actually spectator friendly. As *WoW* has been picked up by tournaments, boards are regularly filled with arguments about whether or not the game is a good one for the pro scene. Posters question everything from whether or not it is intelligible and viewable for nonplayers to if it actually carries, at a fundamental level, a true test of skill warranting its inclusion as a professional title. [4] Attempts to tweak matches to fit either broadcast or spectator situations (via changing rules or adding components such as customized avatars or fancy staging) are also met with mixed reactions—from support of such changes as necessary to bring in new fans to worries about the dilution of the actual sporting components. The tension between an idealized model of e-sports as "pure" sport in contrast to commercial interests and audience building is still regularly discussed.

The degree to which fans are themselves debating the construction of computer gaming as professional sport is notable. Unlike baseball or soccer fans, these people find themselves inhabiting a fan culture that is still very much in the making and not deemed legitimate by the larger culture. Given the stereotypes computer games still can hold, it is not simply that e-sport fans occupy unknown territory, but that the object of their interest and commitment to it is at times seen as abnormal. While mainstream culture has come to terms with passionate football or basketball fans who avidly follow their teams, dress up in jerseys to match, and set aside prime weekend time to sit in front of the TV and watch multiple games, given the status of computer games in the culture, e-sports fandom is often regarded either quizzically or suspiciously. While we are coming to terms with this form of contemporary leisure, passionate engagement with it tends to remain under suspicion.

Yet e-sport fans are often deeply invested in the construction of these games as sport and as professionally viable, in having the players whom they respect seen by the outside world as skilled and talented. They can have strong opinions on what it needs to succeed and while many are convinced of its inevitable rise, there are moments of pessimism. They have also found themselves in the position of having to reckon with even more loaded subjects when the relationship between sports, politics, and the construction of pro gaming as an international activity arises.

One particularly powerful example was the way the fan community worked through a politically charged event at the 2007 World Cyber Games final in Seattle. During the closing ceremony Liu You-chen of the Taiwanese team went to the stage to receive his bronze medal for *Project Gotham Racing* but rather than holding up the People's Republic of China flag during the victory presentation, instead donned the banned Republic of China Taiwanese flag. The result was not only a number of angry shouts from some audience members but further reports that after the closing ceremonies the Taiwanese player was accosted back at the hotel by members of the Chinese team who were upset by what they considered an offense. The incident was covered on e-sports sites and also made its way out into traditional news venues (Shu-ling and Chuang 2007).

The use of the various flags is interwoven with disputes over independence and, as with the Olympics, the Taiwanese team was supposed to use the officially sanctioned PROC Chinese flag. Their choice triggered not only some volatile actions at the event, but a complex debate about nationhood and sovereignty on the fan boards afterward. In the comments section of various articles poster after poster chimed in and not only debated the actions of both teams, but invoked politics and history. For some there was an absurdity to a decidedly digital endeavor getting tied up in geopolitics. For others, especially players from Taiwan and China, this was no trivial matter. Given the WCG promotes a very clear rhetoric of national engagement, there was no way to separate the performance of national identity in e-sports from existing political struggles. Many posters wrote with conviction and passion about the importance of these symbolic performances at such events, often only to be confronted with replies that suggested they take their politics elsewhere, away from e-sports. As with traditional athletic events, national and group identity can easily find its way into the conversation and sports are never entirely set apart from the real world—indeed they often encapsulate core cultural and political struggles. E-sports fandom is not immune to this.

Team Sites

In addition to the third-party sites that make up a large portion of the online community for fans, most teams themselves host websites and forums. These sites provide not only information about the team itself, but general e-sports coverage. As a kind of hybrid news and team info site they

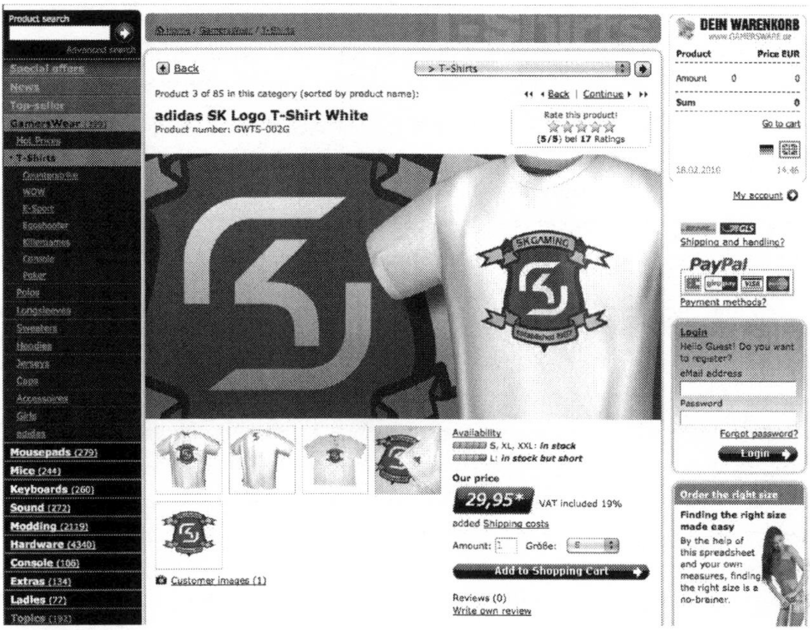

Figure 5.5
Merchandise available for purchase at the SK team website.

often aspire to be one of (if not the) main stop for pro fans. In addition to news and forums, some offer merchandise for sale.

Many team sites also engage in fostering a larger player community with forums that provide opportunities to talk about games generally. Part of the value of doing this is tied to financial considerations. Team sponsors validate their support of e-sports by reaching potential consumers, and one of the most important benefits of fostering a fan community around your team site is economic. With money coming to teams and players via corporate sponsors, being able to demonstrate you have a large fan base who will see products and logos is crucial in showing value. Team sites usually have large sponsor banner displays and if they host an online shop fans can buy endorsed products like mice, graphics cards, and keyboards.

At the same time they are building specialized fan communities, sites are often engaged more generally in validating this form of leisure. Unlike traditional sports where participation and knowledge is created and sustained at multiple areas—in the school, in the family, via community recreation centers, in the media, even in church—computer game play still exists apart from traditional forms of leisure in the minds of many. While it is gaining legitimacy, its status is nowhere near as solid as traditional sports. Team sites do work by building enthusiasm for playing computer games, and in doing so they construct potential fans (and valuable eyes for sponsors). It is certainly the case that if you play a game yourself it is much easier to slide into spectator mode, connecting to the action on screen and needing less interpretation by a commentator about the basics of what you are seeing. Team sites thus engage in the work of supporting game culture more generally, as well as in developing fans for their own players.

This can happen in a few ways. Player contracts can stipulate a certain amount of writing for the website that must be done. Those entries can range from reports and impressions of a tournament to tech reviews or sharing game configuration settings. There are also often general editorials written by someone on the staff about a latest game release or speculation about upcoming titles, as well as general coverage of the scene. Stories at team websites are ways to connect the fans to both players and teams, but also in supporting a broader gamer identity and pastime. Unlike traditional sports that do not regularly invest in connecting fans to the actual play of the sport they are enthusiastic about, e-sports sites constantly leverage broad participation among the fans themselves.

In addition to all of this official communication is the ubiquitous "community" section you will find at nearly all team sites. Forums devoted to topics beyond elite play, such as general talk about a title, upcoming releases, or conversations about platforms and systems also make up a large portion of the websites. Community areas are a part of many traditional sports franchise websites as well and their construction speaks to the way fandom is formulated in part as a collective identity and actually something continually reproduced, not only at the very moment of spectatorship of a tournament but during all the downtime. And not unlike traditional sports team websites, e-sports team forums also often provide nongame-related sections where people discuss movies, music, social life (threads on women, sex, and dating are not uncommon at e-sports sites), and occasionally politics.

Building a player community writ large is also key to fostering future talent as players transition from playing with friends to amateur and professional-amateur (pro-am) competitions. Given the lack of broader structural support for building new talent (as we have with traditional sports in the schools, for example), identifying and developing future players is much more unstructured. While there have been a few examples of farm team models, the community of pro-am competitive players around any given title is certainly still small enough that coming up through the ranks and being known is a crucial part of seeding future teams and sustaining tournaments. Given the somewhat rapid turnover of the playerbase, generating new talent is an ongoing challenge. Pro players often keep blogs at team sites to maintain contact with fans, providing concrete information about their machine and game configuration settings, which become important tools for future players as they refine their own gaming. The wide distribution of match videos is another way in which future talent is cultivated, whereby new tactics and moves are demonstrated, picked up, and refined to the next cohort of players. Match videos can act as aspirational devices, seeding new ranks of competitive players. In general the distance between pro and fan is more shallow than in traditional sports and this is reflected in the kinds of public communication done at team sites.

News Sites and E-sports Journalists

Computer game journalism is still in a nascent form and news coverage of e-sports is no different. In addition to the team hubs, there are a handful of sites players and fans can consult that also distribute news. Websites like Got Frag, Cadred, Team Liquid, Gosu Gamers, Game Riot, or ReadMore provide a range of information including tournament coverage, editorials, player and manager interviews, and general game reviews. While a fair amount of the content at sites falls into reprintings, press releases, or links to other sites, a number of outlets work to provide original material, including interviews with players or coverage of matches or disputes.

Like other sectors of the e-sports scene, the professionalization of the gaming journalists covering these athletes is still very much in the making. There are two fairly clear tiers at work. There are definitely a handful of people who have spent a lot of time covering players and tournaments, have built up reputations as reliable reporters, and manage to make a full-time living focused on pro gaming. On the other hand there are quite a few young people who contribute to its coverage in part-time or volunteer ways. In this group many seem to simultaneously occupy two positions, both fan and information distributor, whereby they may simply repost press releases or build news by linking to other source sites. Given e-sports is not flush with money, it should not be surprising that news coverage often either falls into the hands of the teams themselves, volunteers, or the partially paid.

At competitions like the World Cyber Games I was often struck by this professionalization-in-the-making around e-sports reporting. The event provided much in the way of standard accommodations for journalists—press passes that gave some additional access, Internet connections to facilitate filing reports, communications reps to liaise with, press conferences, and a special room with snacks, beverages, even swag. In this way the structure certainly tried to support the work of journalism.

And while you would regularly see a handful of reporters at the actual matches (typically in areas the public could not access) whose faces you would come to recognize over the course of the event, the scale did not ever seem to quite match the infrastructure provided. I was, for example, surprised to regularly turn up to postmatch press conferences and not see any consistent representation by e-sports sites. While final matches always drew a crowd to interview the participants, on-site journalists only spottily attended lesser competitions. Perhaps this is simply because many of the writers had direct access to the athletes so would get their quotes or coverage outside the formally organized press conferences. Nonetheless, it seems to stand in some contrast to traditional sports press conferences.

Journalists at tournaments also sometimes do double-duty. We saw this, for example, in the way a well-known commentator actually spotted a problematic game play move and brought it to the referees' attention. I have also seen a journalist be called on to act as translator for a player at a press conference. At one postmatch press conference for Stork, the South Korean player mentioned earlier, no official translator was present (fairly surprising in and of itself), so a journalist from the *Game Riot* website stepped in. At one point Stork was asked if he read any English sites. Despite replying no, that he didn't read English, he was then asked by the questioner to say "I love Team Liquid.net" (a popular e-sports website) on camera. The journalist-translator conveyed the request and Stork complied, essentially filming an impromptu promo. Everyone laughed and the press conference moved on. But I was struck by how odd this exchange was and I think it belies the continuing liminal state of e-sports. The journalist who steps in to function as translator to move the press conference along is on the one hand performing a helpful job for the rest of the press corps, yet is also perhaps undermining the ability of their organization to get a scoop based on access. The lack of endorsement gatekeeping to one of the top athletes on the scene at that time was also remarkable, especially in the case of a Korean star who is very used to having sponsorships. The blurry line defining everyone's professional roles came across strongly. One can certainly not imagine Michael Jordan granting an impromptu endorsement during a postgame press conference. And yet it is the case that e-sports stars still need the e-sports press to continue to grow, and maintain, the space. Perhaps this more equitable power balance is reflected in these informal arrangements and the ways professionals may slide between varying roles as needed.

Video on Demand, Replays, and Streaming Media

While newsites and forums provide rich areas for sustaining fans, it is in video on demand (VoD), replays, and demos that the roots of the community lie. Being able to rewatch matches, especially ones that simply can't be attended by the vast majority of fans, is a crucial part of e-sports. Regular competitive titles, including *Counter-Strike*, *Warcraft*, and *Starcraft* (to name just a few), actually have embedded within them the functionality for any given match to be recorded, saved, and reviewed. Watching matches this way is something done by fans and pro players alike and forms one of the core activities of the scene.

Henry Lowood (2005a, 2005b, 2007) has described the history of capturing game footage and its importance to game culture. He argues that these early videos form the basis of the much larger phenomenon known as machinima, whereby computer game engines are used for creative purposes well beyond the original intent of the designers. These videos became early platforms for skill demonstration and eventually a distribution mechanism for new tactics and patterns of play in games.

For fans, VoD provides a basic opportunity to spectate they would not have otherwise. In many ways e-sports echoes a trend in traditional sports media where match recording, rebroadcasting, and on-demand services now form an important part of sports consumption. Major League Baseball has particularly innovated in this area with their use of mobile devices and, notably here, the PS3 game console to provide baseball coverage. Within e-sports entire websites are dedicated to hosting collections of matches. While replays typically require the game to view them, as they are simply files with bits of data recompiled and rendered via the game engine, with the advent of YouTube and other streaming media systems the distribution of matches has become much easier. Interested spectators can simply go to a website, type in the name of their favorite player or game, and get a substantial list of matches to watch. For players these match videos and replay files are key training tools, providing the opportunity to review opponents' tactics and play styles in advance of competitions. Much like the use of prior game film in traditional sports, VoD and other archived games form a core component of a practice regime for players.

Several games also allow for a real-time spectator mode where the viewer can cycle through any number of player views, allowing them to take in the whole playing field but through the eyes of the user whose view they "pop" into. Perhaps unsurprisingly, spectator modes within the technology itself are one of the most discussed issues when it comes to growing the e-sports community. While some games (fighting games and *FIFA* for example) are considered fairly easy to spectate due to the singular field of play or basic mechanics, commentators, players, and fans alike have long struggled with good ways to spectate and archive their performances. Some game companies like Valve, Blizzard, and id, have been more attuned to this than others and have built into the system the needed functionality. But having a robust spectator mode continues to be something e-sports struggles with across a number of titles.

Another issue facing videos is the growing use of live streaming for events. With the growth of fast bandwidth and real-time video technology more and more tournaments are providing fans with opportunities to watch matches in real time. While a critical mass is regularly out of reach in terms of on-site fan participation, real-time streaming allows for broadening and building the e-sports fan base. Organizations like the MLG and ESL now regularly provide real-time commentated online coverage of their tournaments. Major events hosted by Blizzard (like Blizzcon and the Worldwide Invitational) have started offering an entire track of live video coverage of their event competitions (via DirectTV and online streaming).

Just as notable, however, are the ways smaller competitions and fans themselves are using streaming technology to distribute matches more broadly. Using software developed by Valve, websites like HLTV.org (Half Life TV) have long offered gamers a means of broadcasting matches via their centralized hub (with preference given to larger competitions). And as discussed previously, sites like UStream, Justin.tv, and Stickam, which allow users to easily pipe video through the site for live streams, are also allowing greater ease in broadcasting matches.[5] Broadcasting a competition was prohibitively expensive in the past, but with the widespread growth and ease of video streaming the possibilities for creating an audience have certainly grown.

The Roar, and Whisper, of the Crowd

While there is a long history of pro gaming tournaments being mediated through the Internet, via video captures of matches that fans watch after the fact, there has always been a nascent offline tournament component and this has grown dramatically in recent years with the rise of more leagues and regular events. A majority of early tournaments were held at LAN parties with an official set of competitive games for some prize. At these events players, some of whom were fans of pro e-sports but some who were not, would bring their own computers to a shared location, set up local area networks, and over the course of several days plays games, share files, and hang out with each other. Often in a back room or some set-off portion of the venue there would be professional players and teams also competing. Especially in the early days the line between the LAN players and the pros could be fluid. This structure worked well in continuing to support the player community while also creating viable financial venues for pro competitions and beginning to seed the aspirations of amateur players. The current state of tournaments can be broken down into several categories: grassroots and/or regional, LAN-hybrid and pro-am, exhibition matches, midprofile and national, developer-focused, and recurrent high-profile international tournaments.

Grassroots and Regional

Pro tournaments in these venues can at times have a very raw feel, much like I describe in Chapter 1. They are often organized by a regional committee, who may be trying to break into the tournament business, or by a fan website. They are typically held at a local net café or a random location with a makeshift play area and improvised infrastructure. Overall the feel can be very do-it-yourself. With homemade ladder charts that get progressively filled with handwritten names (or perhaps a website updated after every match), a volunteer admin and refereeing (if any) work force, and makeshift barriers marking tournament from nontournament space, these events stand as interesting bridge moments between the player culture that gave birth to pro gaming and the increasing attempts to professionalize it.

It is very rare to see any nonplayers at such events, though nonplayer girlfriends do sometimes show up. This level of tournament generally does not pay much consideration to spectatorship, belying a framework in which there is only the pro player and the hardcore player—not anyone just engaged in watching. Even if held at a net café the competition area is often blocked off to the patrons and there may be no meaningful way for them to access the event (if they even realize it is happening at all). On occasion there may be some kind of small audience area with a competition feed being piped out to it, but typically there is none or it is poorly maintained. Venues like this rarely have professional commentators unless they are being used for the production of a broadcast that will then go online. Given the fairly robust set of e-sports websites, the outcomes of these tournaments are still generally publicized. Though tournaments at this level typically don't have any well-considered notion of on-site spectatorship, if you speak to organizers they regularly talk in sophisticated ways about how crucial viewership is to pro gaming rising as a legitimate sport. For them it resides, however, in primarily online or recorded forms.

LAN-hybrid/Pro-am

Pretty closely tied to the grassroots model is the LAN-hybrid or the pro-am venue. Events like DreamHack, a 14,000+ person "digital festival" in Sweden, are a good example of this kind of space. While the bulk of the event is focused on non-e-sports activities, there will often be a special area dedicated to professional play and matches. These types of events are generally well organized and may have a long history. They sometimes struggle with integrating e-sports into their program, signalling an ambivalence in their community between what is considered a more authentic or grassroots feeling of the event and the inclusion of commercialized or elite play elements. One way this is sometimes ameliorated is by the introduction of pro-am components into the program whereby amateur players are allowed to compete in matches that reflect varying skill levels or allowed to qualify online in pre-event matches.

The e-sports space at these venues will typically be located in a special area, though it may not be clearly marked. The flow of general event attendees to pro matches at these tournaments is uneven. Often regular participants either do not quite know what is happening with the e-sports events or, if they do have some interest, may find them quite hard to get into. As with many e-sports events, introduction to the scene remains opaque to the outsider.

Exhibition and Exhibition-Hybrid Matches

E-sports regularly turn up as a kind of special exhibition at general trade venues and fan conventions like E3, Games Con, Cebit, and the CES. These events are generally dedicated to technology or games promotion and provide convenient opportunities for established tournaments to hold a qualifier or midseason match (as in the ESL's involvement with Cebit). In these arenas pro players will sometimes compete against convention attendees in exhibition-style matches with no prize money at stake or against other pro players for prizes.

The novelty of e-sports is harnessed in these spaces to provide an image of the future of computer gaming or highlight passionate play. Matches will typically take place on a stage or arena, often with the help of an emcee explaining to the audience what is happening. There may also be "booth babes" in an attempt to glamorize the match. Because of the exhibition quality in this setting, spectatorship is actually attended to, though generally there may not be a lot of sophistication in terms of visually piping out the in-game action. These matches can often have a strong spectacle feel whereby the pro players are fashioned as novelties, either in terms of their head-to-head competition with other pros or via their virtuosity in demolishing amateurs who try their hand against them. While on the one hand e-sports is given some prime space and attention in these venues, it also tends to stand alongside a range of convention show spectacles like massive demonstration booths, booth babes, swag, and other PR materials and activities.

Midprofile and National

Somewhere between the grassroots LANs and the high-profile international tournaments sit the midprofile matches. These may be national matches or fairly constrained to a special league or genre of games. They typically do not draw a large international pool of players, journalists, or spectators and tend to not be quite as large as the major e-sports events. This does not mean they are any less significant: indeed some key longstanding tournaments would fit into this category. But they do tend to cater to a fairly narrow slice of the e-sports scene, whether in terms of regionalism, game disciplines, or overall scope.

A typical example of this is the Eurocup XIII I attended in 2006. Like the WCG event, it was also held in Aarhus, and was quite interesting in that it was completely staged for broadcast with a competition set that looked straight out of a slick television poker tournament. Though the event was small in scale and located in a fairly nondescript media building outside the center of town, it strove for some polished production values. With multiple cameras, lighting effects, on-site commentators, and a full production team this event, though locally based, was geared toward a larger broadcast audience. One thing that was most striking about it, however, was the strange gap between what was being filmed and how it felt off camera. As I sat on a small tier of black painted wooden stands built for the audience, surrounded by very young guys (most of whom were competitors, not outside spectators), it felt at times you could simply turn your gaze from set to audience to traverse the world of professional to fan/

player in one sweep. Production coordinators were regularly coming by to remind people to throw away soda cans, stop going in and out while filming was occurring, and hide away extra keyboards and mice. It did not have the grassroots feel of the prior event I attended in Aarhus, but it also was not nearly as well produced nor massive in scope as, say, the World Cyber Games Grand Finals.

More polished but still fairly national in orientation are outfits like Major League Gaming (MLG) and annual fighting game tournaments like Evolution (Evo). MLG is a somewhat difficult case given it is surely one of the more stable pro outlets yet primarily focuses on the United States (though they've now branched out to Canada). Unlike grassroots or LAN-based productions, however, it has a very well-developed organizational structure and tournament circuit that mixes online and F2F competitions throughout the year. It contracts players and has notable sponsorship deals with advertisers outside of the standard technology products. Though historically focused on consoles, which sidelines them a bit from traditional e-sports, the rise of the console as a strong gaming platform and the league's inclusion of titles like *World of Warcraft* and *Starcraft 2* is broadening their profile to capture even hard-core e-sports aficionados. Their focus on North America, while likely a smart business move, does limit their profile (though the online presence may mitigate this some).

As e-sports grows, the inclusion of fighting games is worth mentioning. In this regard fairly well-established tournaments like Evo (started in 1995) provide the fighting game community important platforms for annual tournament competitions.[6] These events are focused on a specific genre (with a handful of titles), though they do draw players from not only North America (typically the United States) but also Japan. They are increasingly moving to pull in larger audiences via streaming broadcasts, commentating, and promotion within an e-sports (versus just gaming) frame. Though historically these tournaments have been deeply tied to the grassroots fighting game community (complete with coastal rivalries between the U.S. east and west coasts), the hit e-sports took in 2008 has lead to many giving these venues, and genres, more serious attention.

Developer-Focused Conventions

There are only a couple entries into this category—Quakecon and Blizzcon—but they are notable both in terms of their scope and in the way they show fairly rare examples of game developers being actively engaged in integrating pro gaming into their official view of how their products circulate among consumers. As previously discussed Quakecon, launched in 1996, is one of the oldest large-scale LAN parties around and id Software, developers of a number of popular e-sports titles, has been active in supporting high-level competitive play from the beginning. Though Quakecon was not initially launched by id, the game developer has grown to be a key supporter of the event.

Similarly, Blizzard has taken an active role, especially in the last several years, in showcasing elite play at their very popular Blizzcon and Worldwide Invitational events. Drawing upward of 20,000 attendees, e-sports is regularly given demonstration space through either the showcasing of matches or live raiding by a prominent guild. One of the notable things about a venue like Blizzcon or the Worldwide Invitational is that so many people attend who have no prior exposure to e-sports or high-end competitive play. While certainly the demographic of people at this kind of convention leans toward the hard-core fan of a particular game, these venues nonetheless provide e-sports a generally very polished presentation to spectators. Though Blizzard titles like *Starcraft* and *Warcraft* have played a major role in the scene, it is often through *World of Warcraft's* arena and elite raiding activities that players unfamiliar with e-sports first get a glimpse of formal competitive play.

High-Profile International Tournaments

Whether it is one of the Grand Finals for the World Cyber Games or matches by the CPL or ESWC (Electronic Sports World Cup), large-scale venues make up an important part of e-sports tournaments. These events often (though not necessarily) present a range of games for competition, draw a broad international player base, are widely covered in the e-sports (and sometimes mainstream) press, have significant sponsorships, take place in a fairly well set-up environment, and employ commentators.

The World Cyber Games are a particularly interesting example as one of the oldest tournaments of this sort and one that aspires to create a professional atmosphere. Fashioning itself as an "Olympics of e-sport," the WCG holds regional qualifiers throughout the year, which culminate in a World Final held in a major host city (for example, Los Angeles in 2010, Chengdu, China in 2009, and Cologne, Germany in 2008). Launched in 2000 (then named the WCG Challenge), the WCG Grand Final marks a key event on the pro circuit.[7] While regional qualifiers may vary in quality and size (ranging from highly orchestrated events to small grassroots tournaments), the World Final is the most polished public face of big-tent e-sports.

WCG events typically bring together players from a variety of countries (450 players from 58 countries in 2010, 600 from 65 countries in 2009, and 800 from 78 in 2008), not counting all of the ancillary team managers, coaches, supporters, and journalists from participating countries.[8] While the World Final generally also bills itself as a "computer festival" (as a way of drawing in a broader audience from the local host city), the core remains centered on high-stakes competition. The 2009 Grand Final in China boasted 82,000 spectators while the 2010 Los Angeles finals had 32,000 in-person spectators over the course of the event. Broadcasts (both online and television) and replays of the events raise the numbers dramatically. Prize money (2009 and 2010) ranged from $1,000 to $25,000 USD (for the team) depending on the game.

Spectatorship: The Still Unsolved Challenge

While I have detailed a fairly broad range of tournament types, the dual themes of imperfect support of on-site spectatorship and deep insider culture are consistent across all formats. This goes to the heart of the ways e-sports are still very much a work in progress and how the actual location of the audience is yet to be settled. The networked nature of the games, the fact that the playing field is often distributed over multiple devices, and the way computation is interwoven with human action has produced a complex formulation of spectatorship, one not easily grounded in traditional forms. With this laid on top of the general immaturity of the scene as a sports form, you find real challenges in shifting the domain to a broader set of participants.

I noticed this immediately at the first smaller events I attended. It was always awkward to turn up. On one level it was simply the way physical space is organized at e-sports events. No or little signage is common. I can't count the number of times I've entered a building or space completely unsure if I was in the right spot—the only clue typically being a handful of young men hanging around out front to have a cigarette between matches. The lack of clear demarcation of tournament space signals how closely tied to insider culture e-sports events often remain. People can walk by a spot completely unaware that just inside some of the best computer game players in the world are competing for money.

My experience of what it feels like once you are there also speaks to the insider/outsider culture. I was not a player, I was not a girlfriend or mother of any player, I was not staff. Who was I? A journalist perhaps? Quizzical looks only seemed to subside when, after starting to talk to people, it became clear I was a researcher. Attending events alone probably did not help. E-sports subculture is deeply social and communal. Being there with friends and people you know, participating because you are already a part of the community, is the norm. Unlike many traditional sports venues that can support a solitary yet collective form of participation, e-sports events (aside from the largest scale ones) still very much have a feel of wandering into a room full of friends.

This lack of attention to outsiders and spectators looks slightly different in various venues. Take, for example, a tournament I attended in 2009, the Arbalet Cup. Held at Inferno Online, a popular net café in Stockholm, this competition offered a pretty serious prize package ($37,000 USD) but was held at a fairly secluded venue. Though historically notable and an active space for e-sports—indeed on one wall was proudly displayed Schroet Kommando's winning CPL summer 2003 prize check—there was a strange feeling of disconnect for me between the tournament and the activity of the café. The matches were held at the back in a cordoned-off area. Though the café was constantly filled with teenage boys, many of whom were playing the same game as the pros (*Counter-Strike*), there was very little back-and-forth between the competition and the café patrons. There was a clear sign posted that the tournament area was off limits and though certainly some of the patrons knew what was going on, there was surprisingly little actual physical interplay between the spaces. Café visitors, if they were following the match at all, were doing so online, mostly via the website, which provided updates on who had won various rounds.

This event did not purport to be open to the general public nor did it have any ambitions about supporting on-site spectators. It had the feel of a hard-core, in-group tournament held for those in the know. In the e-sports community this translates to people who follow the scene avidly, know the variety of websites to visit to get to the video feeds (there is no single site that serves up everything, though there are some major ones), and know how to find the tournament info as it is updated. Dedicated e-sports fans actually do a tremendous amount of labor to piece together their fandom across a range of sites and technologies. But you have to know where to go to get the info you want, you have to know how to set up your machine to view matches or watching streaming video, and you have to know how to interpret what you are seeing. Being an outsider is simply not viable for tournaments like this.

We could compare this with the topmost level, something like the Grand Finals of the World Cyber Games. As mentioned, it bills itself as a computer festival more generally and tries to publicize events within a local city to at least bring in some spectators from outside the pool of players, owners, coaches, and sponsors.[9] Unlike many smaller events, when you go to a WCG Grand Final you will see a clearly marked entrance and can find good basic information online about attendance, pricing, and planned events. Grand Finals take an approach to spectatorship many tournaments do not by providing stages, broadcast screens, and audience seating. Yet far too often a nuanced handling of spectatorship is not followed through.

The first WCG Grand Final I attended was at Monza in Italy. While on the one hand a large main stage was set up for spectators to watch major matches, and several side rooms provided quarter or semifinal matches spectators could watch, much of the venue seemed to ignore that non-players would be roaming around. Though it billed itself as a computer festival and had some demo booths, the fact that it was held outdoors and it rained for large portions of the event proved disastrous. The location (the famous Autodromo Nazionale racetrack known for the Grand Prix) was hard to reach except by bus and even then included a walk. The Monza year was widely seen as one of the most disastrous by regular attendees. The fact that nearly the entirety of the finals and spectator area was outdoors (albeit tented) in the cold and the rain showed the local organizers' deep lack of attunement to the needs of the event. Players themselves were not thrilled with competition conditions for many matches either, often finding themselves sitting outside in the cold or wrangling with buggy machines. The final closing ceremony was staged entirely for the cameras such that the hosts onstage had their backs to us, the crowd actually present. Because the local organizers of such events may have only a tangential (if at all) relationship with the e-sports community, in the worst cases there is a fundamental misunderstanding of the special conditions tournaments such as this require.

While the second Grand Final I attended was held at a much more accessible location (the conference center at Seattle's QWEST Field, where the Seahawks football team plays), it also did something quite similar to the Monza event—physically separating large swaths of the competition space from areas the public could access. While final or semifinal matches were held on a large stage at both events, hours and hours of often exciting competition were carried out in secluded player/press-only areas of the venue, with games occasionally broadcast to smaller viewing areas. There is a very odd gap produced by this kind of setup between a front and backstage. Spectators often can't see the players firsthand (they are frequently cordoned off in another area) but instead only watch feeds of the game being played except at final or showcased matches. The draw of watching bodies at play, and indeed the interrelation between what is happening on screen and "in the chairs," is entirely overlooked in these moments. The irony is that capturing spectators at the event is something the cameras present are always doing. Playing up the spectator aspect of these events is common, with cameras regularly turning to the audience to capture their cheering.

A significant amount of the problems with how major events are run is tied to the deep ambiguity not only about who the e-sports audience is, but where they should actually be engaged. Tournaments of this scale try to make themselves appealing to their host city by situating themselves as something more than a very niche, hard-core activity. Terms such as "computer festival" or general gaming convention thus often get introduced. These large tournaments know they are going to have significant numbers of players and staff on site who will only be playing for a fraction of the time so will need entertainment more generally. There is also often an animating vision of e-sports as "sport," complete with stadiums and spectators, and that shapes how the space and activities are constructed.

E-sports organizations are simultaneously deeply aware of the roots of the community both online and situated within very specific media properties so tournaments of this scale are also seen as media productions. While the camera feed may pipe out to a screen for the on-site spectators, it is mostly there to capture the event for off-site distribution. The majority of spectators are not, in fact, at the tournament in person but distributed globally via many different websites, IRC channels, and perhaps (in the case of places like South Korea) specialty TV stations. Whereas traditional sports have worked hard to harness the duality of spectatorship in their domain (fostering and using the on-site participants to feed into televised productions), e-sports continues to struggle with this aspect.

I must pause for a moment here and foreground how this is tied to actual geographic and physical conditions. Traditional spectatorship at baseball parks, college football fields, or city soccer stadiums is deeply rooted in the relationship between geography and fandom. This gets tied at an economic level to the way sports stadiums are often built through public financing and subsidies. Local team owners have powerful incentives to build and maintain fandom among the voting population whose goodwill they rely on. E-sports have a radically different context. While there are examples of regionalism shaping the identity of a team (the CGS experimented with this some and certainly the WCG is predicated on national teams), the underlying structure of the scene is not based in locality. As one prominent commentator put it, "Our region is the globe." Constructing fandom (and thus spectatorship) looks quite different when the team is not actually from anywhere and when it has no host or sponsoring city (or university). The history of e-sports spectatorship is fundamentally shaped as a product of the Internet, and indeed an assemblage of networks (websites, IRC, video archives, and so on). The jump from digital spectatorship to fostering physical spectatorship is not trivial and the gaps and imperfections I have seen over the years as tournaments try and attune themselves for both models reflects the ambivalence and ambiguity of the task.

We can here fruitfully pull in work on "mediasport" as one method of situating the deep interrelation in e-sports between media, technology, and sport (Kinkema and Harris 1998, Real 1998, Wenner 1998). Whereas traditional athletics have morphed over decades into having decidedly transnational media components (think about events like the World Cup and the Olympics, or the global media distribution of sports like racing, cycling, and skiing), e-sports has encoded in its very nature a deep rooting in both technology and media. There is no actual performance of e-sport outside of computation and media (Hutchins 2008). It is co-constructed through human and machine action.

So far, much of e-sports (at least in North America and Europe) has leaned on the primarily "media technology" equation of things, focusing mostly around online spectatorship and the digital playing field. But the embodied, collective experience of watching high-end computer gameplay is compelling. There is an energy that circulates between audiences and competitors at live events that cannot be overlooked. The physical space of tournaments and the interactions there actually shape how play unfolds. This requires us to conceptualize the e-sports playing field as not residing solely in the virtual space, but in the hybrid of digital and corporeal. What the implications are for spectatorship given this foundation remains one of the areas still very much under construction, where stakeholders experiment and debate how to best construct and facilitate audience and fandom.

Broadcast Media Challenges

While a large part of e-sports spectatorship has been constructed online though VoD and websites, there have been several attempts to bring pro computer gaming to traditional broadcast media in North America and Europe. It is not unusual now to find a specialty cable channel showing select matches (ESPN and G4 in the United States, Eurosport2 in Europe). But anyone attempting to produce a televisable e-sports product confronts a range of technological and interpretative challenges.[10] Altheide and Snow wrote back in 1978 that,

> The concerns of television and of sports as a game are quite different. Television is concerned with making an economic profit, while the game of sports for players and fans is a matter of action/drama, skill at a highly problematic task, and the outcome of a contest. The fact that professional sports is a business does not in itself alter the character of the game. However, when television enters the relationship, the character of the game changes (190).

This remains very much the case. Because television reformulates spectatorship by including audiences not present at the event and potentially not even involved in watching it live, it very often steps in to alter the formulation of the game itself. This is not simply about the demands or constraints the medium may make, but the ways in which televisual technology may open up possibilities that weren't there before.

South Korean e-sports broadcasting has had much greater success than either European or North American initiatives. With several cable channels devoted to games and e-sports, it has managed to make a jump many have only dreamed of. Full-time regular coverage of competitive computer gaming is the norm there and broadcasters have done an impressive job weaving together television, entertainment, sports, and computer gaming into a recognizable genre. In North America though, e-sports broadcasting continues to come in fits and starts, with very little clear genre definition. One of the first attempts I recall seeing of a mainstream broadcast of e-sports was that CBS Sports Spectacular on a Sunday. Though it was anchored in a legitimate e-sports tournament (the WSVG), the way the matches were framed were odd and out of step with what you would typically see at that type of event. For example, a *Guitar Hero* match (an unconventional title for e-sports to begin with) also featured a panel of judges who evaluated player creativity and performance. Though the show was anticipated by many e-sports fans, it was largely a disappointment in conveying the heart of professional play.

At a basic level are the varying conditions of play different games provide, the predictability of game scenarios, and specific constraints broadcast presents. As one well-established e-sports commentator said, regarding the challenges in particular titles getting broadcast, "You won't see *Warcraft 3* in CGS on TV because you cannot guarantee anyone that two guys won't sit down and their match will be over in eight minutes. That match could last 52 minutes and then what happens? The TV is fucked." And though South Korea has managed to bring titles like *Warcraft* to broadcast, he wisely notes an important structural difference in the possibilities available there versus in North America or Europe, "Well, that's because they've got a channel you know. Scratch that, they've got three channels dedicated to gaming competitions where they've spent the last nine years perfecting that. We're in year two now of attacking like four completely different games and you know, we have an hour and a half program."

While traditional sports have spent years refining the actual conditions of play (including rules) to suit broadcast, e-sports is in its infancy in trying to translate gameplay within a televised frame. The discussion is further compounded when thinking about the value of live events in a traditional sports context. As a broadcaster put it, "Another thing to take into consideration is that your gaming has to be live [...] It's going to be easier to get someone to watch the Super Bowl with you when it's on than it is to say, 'Hey, let's watch that Super Bowl from yesterday.'"

In addition to how the structure of various games lends themselves to television, transforming a raw game feed into something spectators can not only understand but really get into also presents unique challenges. Bryant and Holt (2006), drawing on McChesney's work (1989), note in their review of sports media in the United States that several factors coalesced in the 1960s to dramatically shape the growth of traditional media sports coverage: technological innovations (growing use of videotape and improvements to color technology), policy decisions (the Sports Broadcasting Act of 1961 that allowed for collective negotiations), "big-ticket" advertising, and the influence of innovative producers like Roone Arledge of ABC (who did everything from putting microphones on the field to developing the replay system and providing the now ubiquitous narrative frame for competition).

Within e-sports we can see similar themes. It is perhaps unsurprising that this step, from online subcultural consumption to mass media-savvy entertainment object, has proven one of the most vexing challenges. It has been such a historically fraught endeavor that some have contracted their ambition, suggesting that e-sports will likely only ever have an existence online. Much like traditional sports, the interweaving of technical, structural, and creative challenges weigh on the production of e-sports as mediasport product.

At one level this is a difficult technical issue. Most computer games were simply not architected to have their images broadcast out over television. As one commentator in the field noted, there is a tension between balancing who the imagined audience is with the expense of transforming computer games into a broadcast product.

> I know who my audience are [...] and that is the hardcore gamer. So when we are doing a tournament that is aimed specifically at the hardcore gamer we're going to go out on internet video and internet TV. [...] I don't have the money to spend on producing for a TV set and HD cameras. We have a staff of 20 people. We have a level of production which is probably about mid-90's lowkey cable television but that is fine for a little box that goes on a website.

For independent e-sports commentators and broadcasters, the financial costs of the tech (purchasing expensive signal scaling equipment, live production facilities, and the like) can be a large hurdle in working in any medium other than the Internet. The jump from displaying on a computer monitor, often in a small window with non-HD quality, to putting something on a massive television screen is significant.

Beyond these narrow technical constraints, though, is an issue about the overall production of the space. When you think about the "field" in e-sports and how it might be produced for viewers you confront some core issues even if you don't want to broadcast. It is visually difficult to capture the whole digital field in most computer games. Unlike the position a spectator may take sitting in the stands looking down at the pitch or the court, at this point there is generally no "outside" seat in e-sports. Kane quotes one sports producer who took on the challenge of broadcasting gaming as saying,

> *Counter-Strike* is hard for television because scoring can occur anyplace within the game [...] When you think about sports on TV, they're somewhat linear. A football team kicks off left to right. A batter hits the ball into the outfield. Cars go around in a circle. If anything, this is most like golf, where in eighteen holes you've got a lot of guys out there making shots and you've got to figure out where to cut it. Of course, *Counter-Strike* moves a lot faster. (2008, 221)

Computer games presume, at their very core, direct action and as such rarely conceptualize a spectator role. Some games provide a top-down view that assists in seeing the entire playing field. A handful of games do provide spectator modes but they are typically rooted in the nonplayer assuming the viewpoint of a player. By cycling through several views (either anchored in players or as static world cameras) one would get an overview of the playing field. In some games that collage of viewpoints may not produce a comprehensive overview if fog of war mechanics are turned on—in other words, if the player doesn't see it, you the spectator don't either.

This lack of complete information can undermine e-sports spectatorship. For example, it can sometimes be difficult to easily tell how many players, or characters (such as troops in an RTS), are even still alive. If you can imagine how perplexing it might be to look at the football field but somehow not actually know how many people are still in the game you can begin to get a sense for how much we take for granted in watching traditional sports. The issue of intelligibility of the playing field is huge for e-sports. A core question about spectatorship of any particular title circulates around its overall accessibility. As one commentator put it about *Dead or Alive* (a fighting game used in the CGS), "It has the 'I could do this factor,'" which he notes football also has (the "I've played it in the park" angle).[11] Fighting games are often discussed as a good genre to bring people into the scene given their visual and gameplay accessibility (typically two characters fighting with dramatic moments, clear health bar readouts, and easy to see win/lose conditions). With a long history in computer gaming, it can be much more likely someone would have actually played a fighter versus, for example, a complex RTS game.

One important caveat is necessary here. Far too often we assume that traditional sports don't face similar problems, that things are always obvious or intuitive in soccer or basketball. This is clearly not the case. A novice soccer spectator will be just as confused as a novice *Starcraft* spectator if they have not had any experience playing or watching either game. Some research has suggested, for example, that people tend to prefer to spectate games whose genres they are familiar with and play themselves (Game Research 2002). But what about just following the ball? Surely anyone can do that? Perhaps. But training one's vision to catch fast-moving objects (think about the hockey puck whizzing along the ice) is not trivial. Indeed, the development of televisual techniques (digitally colored balls, annotated fields, graphical overlays) to assist spectators in viewing traditional sports speaks to this challenge. There is a fine-grained level of detail that accomplished sport spectators master to follow, and interpret, what is happening on the field and we should be cautious in overstating the ease of traditional sports spectatorship versus computer gaming.

Computer games prompt considerations about how the fundamental nature of spectatorship could be altered in relation to the technology. Viewing a game within the digital space itself could lend to an extreme customization of experience. For example, Marten Otten, software developer at Valve and creator of the Half Life TV functionality for many of their titles has written,

> Each spectator should be able to choose for himself how active or passive he wants to be while watching a game. A completely passive spectator just wants to lean back and enjoy the game without any further interactions. He assumes he will get a perfect show, seeing all important events from interesting viewpoints. At all times, he expects to have a clear understanding of the current situation provided by additional comments and visual information (scores, time, inset map, etc). A more active spectator, on the other hand, would choose the camera views on his own, might want to move freely throughout the virtual environment, and might want to track his favorite players or browse complex game statistics. Both kinds of spectators should be supported, even if the active and more sophisticated spectator will initially be a minority. (2001, 4)

In many ways this approach mirrors an attention to the active choices of players. Here, spectators are seen as the best constructors of their own experience and offering customizable views that may vary person to person is a fascinating goal.

Traditional sports have now had decades to polish the information space they afford spectators access to. Scoreboards, statistics, replays, high-resolution, extreme zoom cameras, audio feeds from the field, visual overlays to indicate important game markers, sophisticated graphics to augment the action on the field, the mundane yet crucial issue of visual recognition and distinction of players/teams (for example, team uniforms), and any number of other factors go into making a traditional sport spectator—and indeed media-spectator—friendly. Top it all off with sports commentators who are key in weaving the entire package together and you have an information-rich milieu for nonplayer participation. The oddity of e-sports actually lies in the fact that that while the underlying computational basis at least theoretically affords a total information space, in practice it is anything *but* for spectators. The holy grail for those wanting to produce spectator-friendly e-sports broadcasts that can reach an audience beyond the narrow segment that plays the game passionately will be to transform a fairly esoteric set of games into something that makes sense on television.

E-Sports as Entertainment: CGS Case Study

The trip I made to Southern California to visit the CGS offices included attending the World Final at their television studio competition space housed in a small hanger at the Santa Monica airport. On first walking in I simply felt as if I had entered a large warehouse with a number of offices constructed on one end. There were several rows of long tables where a smattering of people sat. Though I had come in the front door after getting

Figure 5.6
CGS World Final 2008, Santa Monica, California.

my press pass, it was entirely unclear where to go and where the match was being held. After aimlessly wandering around for a bit I finally clued into the way the entire center of the building was actually blocked off by black walls, a kind of room within the room. I made my way through, looking for the interior room entrance, until I emerged into the actual match studio space.

As I entered the studio area I found an entire competition set and spectators already filling up the seating. It was a somewhat shocking contrast to the otherwise nondescript space it all sat in. While the building was vast with an unpainted interior and with only the barest-bones makeshift furniture, this interior studio space clearly signaled it was made for television. Vibrant colors, dramatic theatrical lighting, elaborate tiered stages, and clear spaces for audience and players gave the overall impressive of excitement and energy. Coming into the space did not, however, remind me of what it feels like when you enter a sports stadium. This was something different. It was unfamiliar as a sports venue. But it did resonate with another domain, television. At first glance it was wrestling meets poker meets game show.[12]

I sat in the press box, which was situated above one side of spectator bleachers. The World Final was organized such that two teams—the San Francisco Optx and the Birmingham Salvo—were going head to head for first place. The CGS organized competition in an unusual way for e-sports—teams (franchises of the league) collectively accumulated points across several games (*Forza Motorsport 2, FIFA 08, Dead or Alive 4, Counter-Strike: Source*) during a match to produce a winner.

The competition area was organized so each side cheered for a team. The audience was not made up of hard-core e-sports fans but a mix of people interested in computer games or being involved in a television production. Free passes to the event helped guarantee an audience. Given their inexperience with e-sports their participation was quite malleable. Several times I saw people moved by production assistants from one side of the "stadium" to the other to help balance out the numbers, thereby changing the team they were supposed to cheer for. Audience members were given "thunder sticks" and a lot of coaching by the emcee about how to cheer, when to cheer, and what to chant. Rather than this being a sporting event where the fans had their own set of practices, this was a studio audience being led through the script. While traditional sporting events also give participation prompts (organ music to start a song or "Get up and shout!" messages on the Jumbotron) the quality was quite different here. Though enthusiastic participants, it was clear at the outset this was as much a television production as a sports event. A comedian warmed up the crowd while the emcee let people know how the program would go and led them through practice runs of their cheering. Simultaneously, a variety of production assistants moved and adjusted the spectators. Eventually a rehearsal for the players' entry began. Competitors came out of a special entrance on the side of the stage, bounding down as announced to take their place on their team's side. After a second take the production was off and running.

The various games were staged around specially constructed stations and each match typically launched with not only a referee's official call but with the appearance of a scantily clad woman, costumed in some way thematic to the game being played.

One of the things the CGS worked hard to innovate was the televisual rendering of the actual gameplay itself and the moments surrounding it. Given they were also working with live broadcasts, this was no small feat. One of the key actors in this process was producer Mike Burks, who brought experience as an Emmy award-winning producer with the NFL, NBA, NHL, and Olympics. He was particularly astute at the challenges the

Figure 5.7
FIFA match with Michael "Bazza" Barrett of the Birmingham Salvo.

endeavor faced, noting that "When you play a game your proximity is 18 to 24 inches from a screen. When you watch television it's 10 to 12 feet away. So what appears on a PC console to be adequate in a graphic sense would no way make it at home" (Personal communication, 2008). Visually translating the otherwise very personal graphical space of gameplay into something that works on a television involves a number of steps. At a core level there is a consideration of which games will actually work for spectatorship and broadcast. Factors involved at that level range from the popularity of the game to whether it will work on a TV screen to if it supports some kind of spectator function. For example, the CGS hit an unfortunate snag when a title they had used in a previous season, *Project Gotham Racing,* was updated and the spectatorship module was actually removed.

How accessible the core gameplay mechanic is to spectators also played a role in the CGS's choice of titles. Burks noted, for example, that nonlinear games or games with "stuff happening all over the place" can be tricky to convert into a broadcast form. He, and many others, contrast more mechanically or visually complex games with fighting games where there's a beginning, a middle, and an end.

Technically there are also significant challenges to broadcasting computer games. Burks pointed out, "The games are not stable and many of the games are not stable in the broadcast sense. You know their signals can be weak and have to be reamplified and the audio can be really complicated because it's the point of view of the gamer and not necessarily that of the audience. So the gamers want to hear one thing, you want to deliver 5.1 sound to the audience so it's very complicated and that was a huge mountain to climb and no one but us has ever done it" (Personal communication, 2008).[13] For example, the CGS team had around 130 people, which, when compared to the 80-person team Burks used for NFL broadcasts, speaks to the kind of technical complexity they faced.

Where possible, games were modded so that in-game characters wore the team jerseys of their corresponding players. Clear information about the win status and accumulated points of teams was presented. The presentation of the actual in-game play was often positioned alongside other visuals to help situate the multilayered nature of the data. Some of these

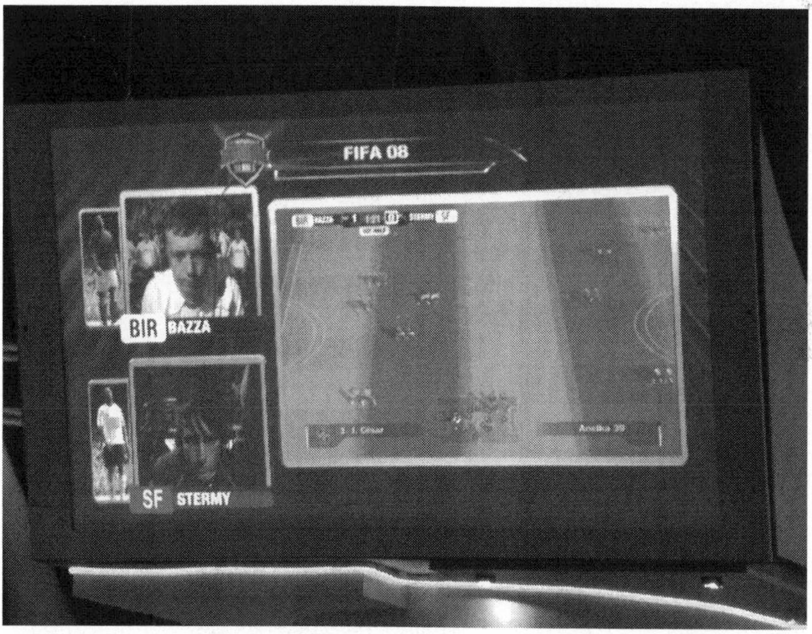

Figure 5.8

Overhead display showing both the in-game view and real-time images of the players with their avatar next to them.

innovations are quite impressive and speak to a nuanced understanding of the relationship between sport, information, and spectatorship.

The CGS was also good at staging drama and playing up the competitive and personal aspects of the games. The narrative of competitive individualism (Whannel 1999) and teamwork that dominates traditional sports was being interwoven into e-sports. The elevation of the player storyline aspect of the final production would be familiar to any fan of U.S. televised sports. This focus on player stories was echoed throughout the CGS as a core frame. As Burks put it,

> And you know what it really comes down to is that people get hung up a little bit on this sport or that sport. I always say it's not about the sport, it's about the people that play the sport. So my approach is always in that regard—that those people are the people you may get emotional attachment to as a viewer and you either like them or you don't like them. Sometimes not liking them is enough to make you watch them. If you don't care, you won't watch. So to do that well, then you have to be a good storyteller. You have to be, you have to know how to tell a story. You have to know the elements of drama. What's at play. You just don't point cameras at things and then they happen. (Personal communication, 2008)

The CGS shows regularly had player profiles interlaced with the games to help personalize the matches and give some dramatic hooks to the setting. Of course, for some this felt a bit contrived. Kane (2008) presents a vignette of several top e-sports players being prepped and guided through shooting some promo segments for the Championship Gaming Invitational. He recounts their unease; one hesitating at being coached how to say something because he thinks he'll "sound like a prick," another when being asked to boast remarking "I don't normally do that but . . ." and overall a feeling of being awkward in front of the camera. Yet it is very clear that part of what the CGS was actively doing was bringing known (American) sports broadcast tropes to bear on e-sports, for better or worse.[14] As Burks put it, "You know our mantra, if we have a mantra, is to treat it like a sport, treat the gamers like athletes." At times this particular public performance of a professional athletic identity, however, sits uneasily within e-sports.

As the event proceeded, with each game (called "disciplines" within the organization, mirroring traditional athletic language) moving forward and the winners garnering points, the presentation of the event was constructed to build dramatic tension. Lighting and set design were central, as was the theatricality to how the players and general managers were presented.

Figure 5.9
Counter-Strike battle, the heart of many tournaments.

I want to be cautious here to not disparage this aspect. Traditional sports are deeply theatrical as well and their televised broadcasts are, especially in the United States, tied to this tradition. The performance and the personas of coaches and players are part of the overall package. The public demonstration of effort, teamwork, elation, or disappointment are all also core aspects of how fans now interface with sports. These elements are woven into the actual production of spectatorship as an interplay between the actors on the field and passions of the fans in the seats. The CGS's deployment of this approach is at least partially anchored in traditional sports tropes.

The second referent commonly invoked for this approach was poker. It brought a set of aesthetic and dramatic conventions that were often seen within the CGS as productive guides for e-sports. As an emerging broadcast game (and one with immense popularity), poker speaks to the up-and-coming status of e-sports. The mix of technology (the lipstick camera), focus on players, and dramatic stories around them (old-timer with years of experience going up against a newly found Internet hotshot no one has heard of before) were not infrequently cited in my conversations with those developing the broadcast side.

What is not clear, however, is how much the CGS overstepped the line and moved their production out of the tonal range that we recognize and associate with legitimate sport into the realm of theater more along the lines of wrestling. The actual competition and outcomes of CGS games were certainly not predetermined but the glitz and staging of the events did not look authentic to some. For those invested in legitimizing computer game play as sport and serious endeavor, the approach the CGS took in visualizing e-sport play was at times off-putting.

This issue of legitimacy, and its symbolic representation, is not trivial. The CGS was often positioned as both potential savior and villain for e-sports. On the one hand it had an impressive amount of money at its disposal. Given the grassroots and volunteer nature of prior tournaments—not to mention the thin margins most e-sports organizations run on—it gave many hope that things would finally be "done right." The CGS hired a serious crew of executives, a number of whom had experience in tradi-

Figure 5.10
Final ceremony and awarding of Mountain Dew-sponsored (and branded) trophy to the Birmingham Salvo.

tional sports broadcasting and development. They gave players real contracts, hired team general managers, brought in experienced e-sports commentators, and in general attempted to put a professional polish on things.

At the same time, they scooped up a large chunk of the major talent on the scene, which often had a devastating effect on the diversity of competition available. Depending on your view of consolidation, you interpreted this move as simply a part of inevitable growth or as downright damaging. They also made formatting choices, ones tied to the ability to make e-sports intelligible to the larger public, that many regarded either with skepticism or outright hostility. The version of *Counter-Strike* they opted for, *Source*, was generally not seen as the best version from a play perspective and has not been the one most widely used in the scene (that would be *1.6*).[15] They brought in games that are often thought of as marginal among the most hard-core fans (*Dead or Alive 4*, a fighting game). And because the team franchise was put forward as the core fan anchor point, they operated a match structure that cumulated points among all the game competitions for an overall score to determine the final team winner. This is in stark contrast to the norm in e-sports, which is to have separate game title matches that conclude in distinct Grand Final winners. For many this undermined the seriousness of achievement within the various games and reduced the competition to a washed-out collective effort.

Given the key decisions made in the construction of the actual competition, the aesthetic choices do not appear as harmless as they might otherwise but instead got tied to a deeper overall impression about what the CGS initiative meant for e-sports in terms of representation and future. For the most cynical it was a kind of selling out, an undermining of e-sports authenticity. For the more optimistic it was typically seen as not ideal but needed, a step in trying to translate the subculture out to a broader audience and once and for all get it some real television coverage.

While I was at the Grand Final, and during my site visit where I spoke with a number of the executives in charge, I had no idea that it would be the last production the organization made. Within four months the CGS had folded, citing unprofitability yet simultaneously reaffirming their own visionary role in e-sports. I scrambled to archive bits from their website before it came down, adding it to the pile of their DVDs and glossy press folders. While the demise of the CGS was a blow to a particular imagined future of televised e-sports, it also prompted hard-nosed evaluation about the future of the endeavor.

Commentators: Making Expertise Visible

Leading that conversation in the wake of the CGS closure were the commentators and broadcasters who, having grown up with the scene from its earliest LAN days, now evaluated its future. Perhaps one of the most important new breed of professionals I have met over the course of my time researching e-sports is this group.

I first encountered one at DreamHack 2004. Walking around the venue I ran across several pro teams there to play exhibition matches. Set up at a small lectern and providing audio commentating to the matches as they went out over the Internet was one of these "shoutcasters" (an old term that harkens back to some of the first software they used to carry out broadcasts). Being a fairly new observer and listening to him was eye-opening. With the fast cadence of a traditional sports announcer he provided play-by-play analysis of a heated match. The sound of his commentating reminded me of listening to a radio broadcast of a baseball game. I couldn't see the action with my own eyes but followed it through

Figure 5.11
Popular commentators Marcus "djWHEAT" Graham and Nick "Tasteless" Plott covering a *Starcraft* match at the WCG Grand Final 2007, Seattle.

his voice. Game moves that were otherwise opaque to me became clear. He wasn't just commentating, but narrating, making the action real and intelligible to an audience. However, as I stood there I noticed that I was only one of a couple on-site spectators. What he was doing was streaming his comments out online, to a distributed fanbase.

This form of e-sports commentating taps into its origins. Going back to the earliest guys who overlaid commentary on already recorded matches or piped audio out online via programs such as Winamp as people watched a tournament, e-sports commentating has its roots not in staged in-person games but in bringing the scene to online spectators. Though commentating has grown well beyond this and now reaches audiences in a variety of venues, the close link between commentators and the online hard-core fan community is an important starting point in understanding the shape of the profession. Even though they may perform professional objectivity while commentating, broadcasters are often still very much fans at heart. Backstage you can regularly find them cheering on a favorite player as they watch a video feed coming in, and the close friendships they often have with players form an important affective aspect of their professional lives.

As with much of e-sports where jobs that are now undergoing professionalization originate in enthusiastic fan communities, the earliest e-sports broadcasters were themselves often former players who remained passionate about competitions after their own playing careers had ended. Whether for financial or skill-limit reasons, we see over and over again people who transfer their playing passion into some other sector of e-sports as a way of staying connected. One of the most highly respected and earliest commentators described to me his own transition from player to commentator:

> Over the course of time I really found myself saying, "I've got a choice to make here—to practice for eight to ten hours a day and put everything else in my life aside or to continue to remain involved as much as I can." And for me, I just knew that I wasn't going to be able to maintain being a player. I had to work a full-time job, I was living on my own, I was just like, I couldn't do it. I sort of passed that age where I had the comfort of "Oh, I'm at mom and dad's house, I can just play games." So I made a conscious effort that I was going to stay in competitive gaming but I would just kind of continue on with my life. And in doing that, I still remained a very active part of my team and one of the things that I used to do for my team is that I would watch their demos and I'd watch the, like, replays of their games and I would record an audio file for them over it. And so I would watch the game, "Okay guys, I'm going to talk about your game [...] and I'm going to try and explain

to you guys what I felt you did wrong, where I felt we need to improve. And so I was really using it almost as a coaching technique.

This progression, from player to commentating for a small team audience, to broadcasting more widely, is a common trajectory.

The roots of the commentator scene were also heavily built on voluntary or low-paid labor. The people who were breaking ground in this area were coming from inside e-sports, often as former players, and were deeply passionate and committed to the community. As this commentator noted, "I mean, we were volunteers. There was nothing [...] We were a happy-go-lucky group of people that were like, 'Wow, look at the great things we're doing for gaming.'" The sense of doing something for gaming was a consistent thread in my conversations with e-sports commentators. While they were serious about transforming their love of gaming into a career, there was also always an element of a larger good at work, a sense that computer games and the community could be grown and supported by them. It was often a commitment not just to e-sports, but to bringing gaming to the mainstream more generally. Using whatever technologies were at hand, they innovated what it meant to be an e-sports broadcaster. In many ways they were the preeminent bricoleurs of the scene in assembling a range of technologies and practices to sustain e-sports.

Like many of the professionals trying to carve out a living in e-sports, broadcasters typically do not live a financially lucrative life and often face key decision points where they have to weigh the necessity of a steady income (often to help support a family) against being able to be work in an area they are passionate about. While the CGS provided some popular broadcasters steady work, since its demise there has been a return to more piecemeal and event-based contracting spread out across a number of different tournaments. Many are deeply entrepreneurial, having set up their own media companies to provide full-service support to events, but the financial and structural struggles often remain. While they may occasionally have a director or producer involved, for the most part commentators regularly fill a number of roles, from seeding tournament ideas to editing and processing their own productions. At tournaments they are not simply "on-screen" talent who appear, do their shtick, and then leave, but often work incredibly long days that can start with setting up broadcast systems at a technical level, transition into actual commentating as the event goes on, and conclude with postproduction work.

The issue of what it means to be a pro player in terms of specialization is something broadcasters also confront within their field. The pressure to be competent across game disciplines is even greater for broadcasters.

Unlike most players, who stick to one game title (or genre) for the duration of their career, commentators often have to skill up very quickly with a new game to be able to work a tournament. Aside from a few exceptions (*StarCraft* commentators, for example, seem to remain some of the most specialized), broadcasters regularly commentate well outside their preferred game of choice. Though they often have a favored genre, knowing a range of games becomes key. This means not only playing them but having the broader knowledge to be able to speak comparatively. One broadcaster explained how he consciously worked on skilling himself up to be a pro commentator, telling himself, "'Okay, this is how I'm going to do this job. I'm going to prepare properly, spend time checking out all the players before I go, make files, I'm going to collect statistics. I'm going to learn the games properly. I'm going to learn more games. Make myself more valuable to any tournament who wants to use me.' And I got more tournaments."

This is, of course, radically different than how commentating works in traditional sports, where people generally stick to one discipline. For those who have a long history in e-sports and a desire to foster it, broadening their expertise has been key. One commentator found himself thinking about this development as he returned from a major tournament in South Korea. He recounted a pivotal moment to me:

> I was exclusively a *Quake 3* broadcaster. It was like my only game and of course that didn't mean I wasn't interested in the other games, but *Quake 3* was definitely the game that got me involved. And it was actually after [the tournament], I was flying home and obviously, it was fantastic. The event was great and I was just sort of thinking about what had led me to this point and why I was there. And I said to myself, "I need to stop being such a fan boy myself and start embracing what professional gaming is all about." And at that point, that's when I said, "I'm going to start learning *Counter-Strike*. I'm going to start looking at *Starcraft*. I'm going to start playing *Warcraft 3*. Every time a new game comes out that could be considered a competitive title, I'm going to play it. I want to look into it. I want to know which players are playing it." And it was really at that point where I sort of said, "If I want to be..." I was definitely [a] *Quake 3* broadcaster, but if I wanted to be [a] gaming broadcaster, then I had to learn to look at any game that professional gaming might throw at me.

For many commentators learning a variety of games is actually only one step in the process. As we have seen among top players, learning to play a game and understand it inside and out is also deeply connected with being engaged in the community practice of the game. One commentator clarified this point nicely when discussing how he was prepping for a *World in Conflict* tournament. He would spend hours a day playing (usually involving a three-hour session in the morning followed by an afternoon session). He noted though, "Then I spend time on community forums. I try and not just understand how I play the game but how the pros play the game, how different it is. There always seems to be some kind of language with every game [...] It has its own little language and it's important you recognize that and use it appropriately when you commentate otherwise you'd look like an idiot." Making this connection to how a game is actually circulating in the e-sports scene (and indeed often in the larger game culture), how it is being played on the ground, the language around it, and the conventions and practices that have organically emerged is something pro commentators do with incredible acuity.

Commentators, like some of the experienced journalists, are also often the sole history-keepers for the community. Because e-sports have not been institutionally stabilized, their constantly shifting terrain poses vexing problems for situating them historically. This is something I have certainly struggled with while doing the research for this book. Tournaments have come and gone over the years, often leaving no traces as their websites get taken down. I have scrambled to archive sites like the CGS or the WSVG because once the tournament or league is closed, its website quickly follows, thus erasing years of data and history. This is an instructive tale not only about e-sports, but for those of us undertaking research on the Internet more generally. The looming ephemeral nature of e-sports (and much online culture) affects not only researchers, but the community itself.

Players may come and go, as do teams, leagues, and tournaments. And if any are revived it is often under entirely different management with little investment in maintaining continuity beyond the brand name. Several tournaments have closed over the years only to reappear with new investors. But those tournaments also often originally left the scene on bad terms, typically in the form of unpaid prize winnings. More often than not the new management team works hard to distance themselves from the prior version of the organization and, aside from using a known brand name (like the CPL or ESWC), there is rarely investment in maintaining any meaningful historical archive.

In marked contrast, the handful of top commentators that have now been around since nearly the beginning provide impressive historical context for players, teams, and tournaments. As one noted though, this is no minor feat: "We've been fairly slack as a community because no one has built any kind of statistical records that date back to 1995. So if you want to find out who won a Deathmatch Tournament in 1995 for *Quake 1*, good luck with that. Good luck finding that information out. And even CPL records from four years ago, I can't find anything. And I know where I'm looking." He continued, imagining being queried by someone new to e-sports,

'What is the history? Who are the great players from ten years ago?'
'Oh, Fatal1ty, he's pretty good.'
'Oh, what's [sic] his stats?'
'I don't know, he won a few tournaments here and there. And he won a bunch of money.'
'Oh, how much?'
'Oh, I don't know, I have no idea.'
'Really??'
That's bad. Now here's what I know, even primitive sports are recorded in some way. Why haven't we done the same when we have the technology and the Internet, I don't know. Ridiculous.[16]

The issue of the elusive history of e-sports hits several areas. It certainly poses challenges to commentators who value situating any given game within a larger statistical story and history. Indeed, to fill the gap one commentator has actually made his own program to track tournament outcomes, any that he can get his hands on, for the last fifteen years. This type of archiving work is important because it is also a genre convention when it comes to linking e-sports with traditional sports, where statistical analysis and contextualization are prime forms of engagement. Stats and history are key hooks for part of the work commentators do, that of storytelling. As one puts it,

More than anything else I believe my role as a commentator is to tell a story. I'm a storyteller, nothing more than a glorified storyteller. And so to tell a story I need to know the background, I need to know the history, I need to know where they came from, where they're going, and what they've been through to get there. And I can't do that without history. I can't do that without records. Without validity.

The lack of history can also prove confusing, and sometimes worrisome, to new people who come around and are curious about investing either time or money but unsure of the prospects. While there have been some attempts to pull together a kind of central repository of e-sports data (such as the Got Frag wiki), for the most part it remains distributed over various sites and is vulnerable to simply being lost when they go down. Long-time commentators thus prove invaluable archivists for the community.

This link between commentators and the player community remains strong and can be evidenced in everything from them still playing for fun online with both fans and pros alike, to the use among broadcasters of gamer nicknames, like Paul "Redeye" Chaloner, Marcus "djWHEAT" Graham, or Nick "Tasteless" Plott. Part of their legitimacy comes from being known as dedicated gamers, from being committed to game culture and avid in their love of gaming.

Despite the hard work commentators do to polish and streamline their broadcasts, there is still an amazing tension at work between the roles they assume as spectator and commentator. Part of this is driven by the technological struggles at work in the space. Unlike traditional sports where a commentator and spectators can take in a field of play with relative ease, the field of a competitive e-sports match is, for the most part, only constructed via multiple viewpoints. While the commentator may be operating the in-game spectator view and controlling what gets piped out to the audience, this is not always the case. Often there are a number of views of the field at work in a match: the game as seen by the player(s), the game as seen by the commentators cycling through player viewpoints or ghosting across the game space, and the game as seen by a camera-observer that is getting piped out to the audience. The work commentators do to synthesize the space highlights the core challenges to spectatorship in computer games. One put it, "If I spectate a *Counter-Strike* match, people don't want to see my view because I may switch back and forth between players so quick because my brain's trying to like, wrap around what's happening in this 3D space and what could happen and what has happened."

In computer games all of the fleeting, mundane, minute shifts in vision get distilled down into very rigid technological constraints when talking about spectatorship. The embodied action of seeing translates awkwardly. A top commentator noted, for example, that if you overlaid spectatorship onto one of the best RTS commentator's view, it would simply not work.

> A spectator cannot watch [his] screen. He does all sorts of crazy stuff. He like, he drags stuff with his mouse. He moves around really weird. But he needs that to tell the story. So he's got to have his own camera, but someone else has to be listening to him and going, 'Okay, he's talking about the main command center. Okay, now he's talking about this southeast expansion. Okay, now he's talking about this hydralisk attack over here.' [...] And in order for him to do his job, he has to be able to go down to that lower corner and see what's happening in that expansion. Or you know, go see how many minerals this player has, right? But because [he] is thinking about commentating and not thinking about what the audience is watching, someone else must listen and display that.

"Seeing" in competitive matches is thus an assemblage process, constructed from a variety of viewpoints and patched together on the fly.

Sometimes there is a wide range of people who are granted "eyeball" access, other times it is more constrained. As I heard a commentator say once during a match, "I wish the observer [person running the in-game cam] would go back down. I want to see what's happening there." Commentators are incredibly agile in how they actually see the field of play and in constructing a meaningful narrative across the fragmentation.

The level of detail in some games can also be overwhelming for spectators, and commentators serve to mediate that. Despite hearing an experienced commentator exclaim at one *Starcraft* match, "There is so much going on I can't even look at it all!" part of the valuable work commentators provide is synthesizing a coherent picture of the field, the status of play given a fragmented landscape, and the huge amount of information available (RTS games being notable in this regard). Commentators not only have to be able to provide a narrative or story around the player, their specific play in that competition, and some frame for how the game works for novice listeners, they also synthesize the entire field of play for the spectator. The amount of information and quick reactions commentators provide is impressive.

Though fairly polished commentating has been going on for a while now, it is still very much a profession in development, finding its bearings and sorting out what its practices should be. The commentators I've spoken with over the years are probably some of the most articulate people in e-sports about the overall professionalization of the space and how they are integrating this work into their lives, but there of course remain moments where their job is still either unknown or nearly unintelligible to many people they meet. One recounted a conversation he had with a woman on a plane, one any of us would recognize from our own lives where you are making small talk with a stranger to pass some time.

> Inevitably the conversation turns to "So what do you do?" so I sort of say, "Oh, I'm in TV." "Oh really, what do you do?" I said, "I'm a commentator." She said, "Oh right, what sport?" I said, "Video games" and she said, "Is that a sport?" That's the kind of reaction I didn't want so that's why I didn't tell you but then she's like "Okay, that's cool. I didn't know that was a sport, cool. But if you're making a job out of it, it must be."

This in-progress state that e-sports professionals inhabit is one they are always working hard to overcome. I was struck by this at the WCG in Monza while hanging out with the broadcast team backstage. Commentators generally just look like any other player or spectator with their jeans, t-shirts, and hoodies, but this event was experimenting with symbolizing their professional status a bit more. Much like the players who now regularly put on logo- and sponsor-emblazoned team shirts as a match begins, I couldn't help but smile as I watched one of the young broadcasters get ready to head out to commentate a tournament. He quickly put on a button-down shirt with tie and "official" sports jacket over his t-shirt. One of the fellow broadcasters pulled out a lint brush and, a bit jokingly, went over his colleague's jacket with it, both of them laughing at the somewhat improvisational transformation. It was clear that the idea of dressing up for the camera was still a bit of an awkward and a self-conscious performance on their part. As he walked off to the match, his shirt remained untucked, a small marker of the in-between status of this emerging profession.

How Spectatorship Alters the Game and Players

As I discussed in chapter 2, the porting of computer games into formal competitive tournament environments actually transforms how they are played through the altering of rule sets and the emergence of community practices that filter both from the bottom up and from the elite players down. We might similarly inquire, does spectatorship specifically alter gameplay and e-sports? Without a doubt, the answer is yes. Todd Harper presents us with one notion of how, suggesting that the symbiotic relationship between player and observers shapes fundamental notions of good play. He writes,

> In fact, it was the crowd's participation as observers that helped to best identify how different styles and forms of play were held up as good or desirable, compared to which ones were instead considered negative in some way. Watching for what events got a positive response or negative response from the crowd—cheering, booing, and other crowd activity—helped create a sense of how tournament participants performed being "good players." (2010, 162)

Spectators, especially when they form a core part of the actual play community, are a powerful force in shaping how that gaming unfolds (Lin and Sun 2011).

Looking at traditional sports we also easily see how the desire for spectators has led to a number of changes to how games are played over the years (often for purposes of speeding up the game or accommodating advertising).[17] Traditional sports rules undergo constant alterations involving things like changes in the time of play periods and breaks, allowable ball maneuvers and possession, and passing rules, not to mention constant alterations to the game produced by technology (be it equipment or broadcasting).[18]

The push to bring high-end pro computer game play to a wider audience, sometimes through traditional media, has produced similar developments. Among the most loyal of e-sports followers these changes are sometimes viewed with ambivalence, on the one hand regarded as necessary for the growth of the scene, on the other as pernicious to its core authenticity, where the most legitimate form of play is seen as deriving from within the hard-core subculture. To unpack the ways spectatorship alters gaming we can break it down into the following categories: content and mechanics, community, and phenomenological.

Content and Mechanics

The most obvious ways spectatorship alters gameplay are by adjusting either formal mechanics or elements of the game, regulating gameplay actions, altering the game visuals, or choosing one version of the game over another.

Perhaps one of the most interesting changes, and again one we've seen used in traditional sports as well to accommodate broadcast, is alterations to the internal workings of the game system to promote spectatorship. One very common form of this is mechanics changes that speed up gameplay. For example, Major League Gaming, a console league, uses a number of these. They have made modifications such as increasing the player's run speed to 110 percent, damage to 110 percent, and shield recharge rates set at 90 percent. Respawn times on rockets have also been increased to promote more movement around the map and spawn locations for things like weapons and power-ups have been placed to maximize player movement in the gamespace. While these changes are not specifically discussed by the MLG as tied to spectatorship, they are resonant with how traditional sports alters rules to help make the competition more compelling to spectators. This kind of change is not unique to MLG but happens all across the pro scene. *Counter-Strike* competitions can similarly have setting configurations to promote faster paced games than nontournament versions.

Beyond tweaking the game settings is the additional layer of rules imposed in tournaments. In chapter 2 I discussed the ways rules were (re) constructed—for example, how duck-jumping has been handled in *Counter-Strike* or the use of *FIFA* goal boundaries. Regulating maneuvers like duck-jumping also, however, intersect an aesthetic component. As one person remarked to me about the prohibition that it could look pretty weird, if not ugly, to see everyone constantly engaged in this technique. Making sure a game is pleasing to watch is a regular topic of conversation and evaluation.

Some tournaments have also experimented with altering the visuals of the game, though this is much less common. The most notable example is perhaps the way the CGS modded the in-game *Counter-Strike* avatars in their competitions so they were wearing the team's jerseys. Conversations about the aesthetic quality of games in relation to spectators abound (though often mechanics trumps aesthetics for the hard-core).

While not strictly in the domain of content and mechanics, the physical space of a tournament, complete with a loud crowd or announcers broadcasting live, can also shape play. A top player remarked about the difference between playing in your room versus a loud tournament, "It's actually a lot more fun to play like that [at a loud venue] because when you're sitting at home and you're playing, this is like really specific *Counter-Strike* stuff but everyone kind of agrees on this—you're sitting at home and you're playing in a quiet room, you can hear everything, you can hear every little footstep. But you go to these big events and everyone can't really hear that well so everything you do is faster-paced because you know they can't hear you coming. So it changes the game. You don't have to be so cautious and careful and the gameplay kind of changes and becomes a little more aggressive. It's fun."

Finally, and often perhaps the most controversially, is the way game choices get tied to spectatorship. Advertisers prefer big audiences and games that will bring those in are valued. Again if we turn to the CGS, one of their more controversial choices was that of using *Counter-Strike Source* rather than the older *1.6* version. Though the graphics of *Source* look more contemporary and are more suited to polished broadcast productions, for the community *1.6* was the preferred title. We've certainly also seen instances of tournaments picking up a title because it is sponsored or is thought of as a useful "bridge" game to a larger audience.

Community

Debates about game choices and mechanics highlight the ways competitive play is always situated within very specific social contexts. Game culture is fundamentally interwoven with the constructions of community we find there. Whether it is fans of a particular franchise or a genre, players have long formed powerful affective attachments not only to computer games, but to their fellow players through online forums and meet-ups. E-sports, and the pro scene that has developed, provide another powerful layer in the attachment people can have toward computer games.

While within pro gaming this commitment to e-sports makes sense to other fans, it is not unusual for players to find their passion not understood outside the community. In the same way being a dedicated computer game player can leave some nonplayers scratching their heads, e-sports spectatorship and fandom can be perplexing to the uninitiated. As one fan remarked, "Well, its always hard to say when someone asks, 'So do you have a favorite team?' and then when I say, 'Yeah, sure, Complexity.' They make faces [at] me because they only know about supporting a team in football. But actually it's the same thing as being a football fan. You cheer for them. Watch [their] matches. And even buy team shirts to support your team. Its a passion."

But as this interest in e-sports expands, so does the fanbase. One of the issues that is most struggled with in the community is how the growth of e-sports and its drawing in new spectators and fans is forcing what used to be an otherwise fairly small and tight group to open up and deal with potential new members. As one e-sports journalist put it, "I think the best way to describe it would be a shift from being a niche community where everybody really knows each other to a more mainstream community where now you have new people and they kind of, everything is kind of gets too big to maintain, you know? [...] And even like on a very personal level, you know, just the anonymity of the Internet and just not knowing people. There's just a little less responsibility I would say as well."

This shift can mean you get people joining the community who don't know the history and may not give old-timers the respect they feel they have earned and deserve. Newcomers may not quite know all the norms and informal rules. They may bring with them identities and gameplay preferences that don't seem hard-core enough. Given how closely e-sports fandom has tracked with the intensity of one's own play and engagement, it is perhaps unsurprising if there are some who bemoan a perceived dilution of the sport by either games, or fans, that seem a bit too casual.

For some fans the professionalization of e-sports has also put its authenticity at risk. A journalist I spoke with noted with some nostalgia that the trend of commercialization has "kind of separated people who miss the old days." Valorization of people who play simply for the "love of the game" (a not uncommon phrase in traditional sports) can be heard. Some express concern that sponsorship or a desire to make the scene more engaging to a broader audience is driving questionable choices. One study suggested that the ambivalence within game communities around professionalism is typically linked to "bigger pressure, growing commercialism/

bureaucracy/sponsor influence, too much focus on money, lower degree of loyalty between clans, less amusement, and also the higher amount of cheating and annoying gamers" (Game Research 2002, 24). Most subcultures confront the rhetoric of money corrupting authenticity, and e-sports are not unique. The conversation, though, is always mediated by a recognition that the players and people who have been toiling tirelessly to promote e-sports deserve some recognition, including financial.

At a fundamental level the introduction of new people as potential fans will unavoidably change the nature of e-sports and pro gaming. For some there will be tensions between maintaining a kind of authentic fan subculture and growing into a mainstream activity. For others the transition is simply a part of the normal evolution of becoming a "real" sport with institutional legitimacy.

Phenomenological

While we can map out how spectatorship alters the growth and construction of a professional sport, we might also ask at a more mundane level if the existence of pro gamers changes how we understand our own play and what the rest of us, as regular players, actually do. Professionals offer all gamers a powerful rubric of legitimation for their play, something along the lines of "If people can do this for real money, as a real job, it can't be all that bad." While computer gaming is increasingly being accepted as a mainstream leisure activity, it is not entirely without stigma, especially for those who are avid players. Because the pro domain so closely ties itself to a rhetoric of "sport" and all that entails (for example, healthy competition), it is no surprise that fans may internalize this meaning system and promote it.

Professional gaming provides average players ways to envision highly specialized forms of competency and understand their own ludic action in perhaps more expansive, meaningful ways. This interpretive frame gets supported by pro gaming offering everyday gamers strategies to perfect their own play. As previously discussed, players can download configuration files to customize their user interface and internal game settings to match those of the pros they look up to. Through watching recorded sessions of pro matches they can analyze and marvel over moves and tactics. Learning by watching someone better than yourself is a classic strategy and everyday gamers regularly use e-sports stars as a resource for imagining their own play. The aspirational aspect of watching a pro, as well as the potent moment where you picture yourself as that pro undertaking the action, speaks to the power of spectatorship. This spectating of others helps build up future possible agency and lends itself to average gamers internally reconfiguring their own models of action.

Circuit between Digital Games and Traditional Sports

Perhaps unsurprisingly all this development within e-sports and computer gaming has filtered back out into traditional sports in interesting ways. Sports computer games make up a massive part of the market, despite being severely underrepresented within game studies (Leonard 2006). Crawford (2005) has found not only a notable relationship between participating in sports and playing digital sports games, but that playing such games can actually be productive in building knowledge of a sport and creating fandom.

At the same time, when we watch traditional sports broadcasts we are presented with visual augmentations of play that resonate with digital gaming. As Mike Burks, the former CGS producer whose main professional identity resides in traditional sports broadcast, put it to me, "And you know what, if you think about the evolution of video games, at least the sporting games, they were copying television coverage. And nowadays you can easily make the argument that there are things in video games that have found their way back into television. Graphics, some graphics, for example. But it's like a dog chasing its tail" (Personal communication, 2008). The circuit of influence between traditional media, such as television and film, and computer games seems to be completing itself as computer gaming aesthetics and tropes cycle back out into traditional forms. Field markers, notations of a phase of play, digital enhancement, and the "datafication" of sports performance all speak to tropes common within computer games. There are also several examples of traditional sports broadcasts drawing on computer games to augment their coverage. ESPN, for example, used Electronic Arts's *Sports Virtual Playbook* to create an "augmented reality" experience whereby the in-studio broadcasters were able to occupy a virtual field with avatar-players, recreating plays. ESPN also used the Madden football series game to produce a kind of virtual replay system. As one article put it, "So, instead of just drawing X's and O's on a telestrator, ESPN anchors will be able to interact with the virtual players on camera to illustrate various football strategies and outcomes" (Yang 2008).

We also have glimpses of traditional sports athletes using digital games to reflect, and perhaps perfect, their own on-the-field play. Building on a much longer tradition of the military use of video games for training purposes, Lauren Silberman (2009) recounts, for example, how soccer and basketball players integrate video game playing into not only their social and leisure lives, but how that play actually works as training and reflective engagement with their actual techniques.[19] Sports games like *Madden NFL*, which increasingly tie in-game characters to specific and constantly updated stats and techniques, seek to bridge the gap between how digital play is handled and its actual formulation on the field. In a *Wired* article on athletes and video games Chris Suellentrop (2010) recounts an unexpected, edge-of-your-seat move by Broncos wide receiver Brandon Stokley. For Suellentrop the move echoed what you might see in video game play so when he got a chance to ask Stokley about it, he did.

> When I caught up with Stokley by telephone a few weeks later, I asked him point-blank: "Is that something out of a video game?" "It definitely is," Stokley said. "I think everybody who's played those games has done that"—run around the field for a while at the end of the game to shave a few precious seconds off the clock. Stokley said he had performed that maneuver in a video game "probably hundreds of times" before doing it in a real NFL game. "I don't know if subconsciously it made me do it or not," he said.

That players can now tie the specific tactics, strategies, and moves found on the field back into the "virtual" one, simulating and running through games and possibilities, speaks to an increasingly complex circuit between traditional sports and their digital incarnations.

6 Conclusion

Throughout this book I've sought to show the ways computer gaming is emerging as a new form of serious play and "sport." This is not a smooth or unproblematic development, but one in which the game, players, supporters, and fans all undergo a variety of twists and turns to facilitate this professionalization, at times ambivalently. On the one hand e-sports can certainly be relegated to a quirky niche of game culture that only a handful of people inhabit. But I would argue its growth tells us much more.

Echoing research in MMOGs, computer games are constantly worked over in the service of varying player demands. They do not exist in some rarified state but are part of a complex process by which a bit of software traverses a field of interest, being transformed along the way. As I've argued before, you can't just take a game off the shelf, analyze it, and understand actual play. Computer games are always situated as complex cultural artifacts for different sets of communities and stakeholders. In the case of e-sports we can see a variety of games moving through diverse fields in nuanced ways in the service of professionalization and the transformation of leisure.

Within the realm of rules and the actual negotiation of play we witness in e-sports how the artifact of the game is subject to complex social processes that mediate its competitive use. Communities come up with rule systems and play norms to facilitate the use of often buggy or insufficient pieces of software in the service of high-end competition. Computer games also wind up doing important labor in the construction of entirely new identities for players both as gamers and as athletes. Perhaps unsurprisingly we are seeing young people transform and push into the domain of serious engagement, commitment, and work activities that have thus far been relegated to fun and leisure. If the MMOG player who spends twenty hours a week raiding with their guild has caused us to pause when thinking about passionate engagement with computer gaming, pro e-sports competitors up the ante. They ask us to reckon with both a new form of play and, more broadly, our notions of the interrelation between meaningful human action and technology. And just as players are being transformed through their own high-end play, the rise of spectatorship and fandom illuminates often flawed assumptions about interaction and games, as well as extending the conceptual formulation of "mediasport." All this transformation has not gone unnoticed outside the player base and as the e-sports industry grows the financial, legal, and institutional structures that support it are themselves undergoing change, often with high stakes.

As is probably quite evident by now, for a researcher like myself this space has been an incredibly fertile area to explore. It is a big, emergent scene yet remains something most people know very little about. The stories we do hear tend to focus on the players or the nearly mythical South Korea, but the nitty-gritty has tended to remain hidden. Yet the meshing, and sometimes collision, of so many different stakeholders and interests is instructive for understanding not only the situated use of computer games, but the emergence of a new sport and the transformation of leisure. Within this evolution there are at least four major themes that I want to especially note as worth considering in terms of future developments: gamer identity, mainstreaming, global play, and serious leisure versus professionalization.

Gamer Identity

Despite games forming a core part of human experience, the last several decades have tended to link playing digital games with a special kind of identity, the geek who is typically also a young, white, middle-class guy. It's certainly understandable how such an image emerged. The earliest digital games were born in research labs that only a select few had access to. Even as they moved from the arcade to the home (via PCs and consoles) the gendering of technology played its own role in shaping possibilities for leisure around digital games. Though women have long been active computer gamers, the imagined identity of a gamer certainly rooted itself in the figure of a young man. And though consoles have broad demographic reach when you look worldwide, the classic stereotype of the young male geek, deeply fascinated by technology and focused on mastering it, has been a powerful cultural trope in discussions about gaming.

We are at an important crossroads with this stereotype. In addition to more and more research establishing the activity of women in digital game culture, the general rise of gaming into popular culture is eroding the geek gamer stereotype. Consoles like the Wii have brought in diverse new sets of players, games on phones allow for mundane integration of gaming into even the most transitory spaces, and the development of games for platforms such as Facebook (often dubbed "casual" but that term sloppily masks the amount of time and effort that can be spent playing) further extends who is playing digitally (Consalvo 2009, Juul 2010). With this broad diffusion of gaming into everyday life, and so visibly among communities typically not associated with digital play, the identity category of "gamer" comes into question. Consalvo (forthcoming) suggests that, "We must put to rest the concept of the 'gamer.' Games are ubiquitous, and this concept is more exclusionary than helpful in scholarly conversations, as well as in identifying how individuals envision games in their lives." If we are now all "gamers" the distinguishing identity term becomes meaningless.

There is real ambivalence around this shift within dedicated self-identified gamer communities. For many longtime players there has been a reclaiming of the notion of the geek and the gamer. Though the terms have often been used against people in the past as a way of establishing their marginality or outsiderness, for many they have been reabsorbed into the subculture and embraced, forming a core part of identity. Calling oneself a gamer becomes a way of framing your passion and signaling it to others. Being a "gamer" is often a method for constructing community. Dunbar-Hester notes in her in discussion of a radio enthusiast group that the adoption of the "geek" label, in line with other rhetorical moves within identity politics, becomes a way to "derive strength from a label that had once been injurious to them, and use it instead to highlight their own uniqueness from others and commonality with each other" (2008, 206). Much like Fincham's (2007, 2008) bike messengers who found that their occupation gave them an immediate community no matter where they went, gamer identity has worked the same way. Being a gamer has offered a convenient shorthand identifying a specific orientation to play and technology, helping people make connections to each other. It has been used as a community building term.

As gaming has gone mainstream you can watch gamer subculture wrestling with the implications. Listen to gaming podcasts or read fan websites and you will quickly hear echoes (and indeed sometimes the shouts) of people unsure about how all these new players are changing the space. Accusations and fears about dumbed-down games as a result of all the "casual gamers" flooding the market or concerns about "hypersensitivity" (to issues of gender, race, politics, sexuality) abound. There is regularly a sense that gamer culture is being infiltrated by the masses and the "real gamers" are not happy about it.

And yet, at the same time, there is a deep desire for legitimacy and belief that opening up the space to more people can only be good. Self-identified gamers are themselves more than happy to have the stereotypes broken. As many gamers age they find that their own play patterns shift, that new genres catch their interest, and that their more youthful formulation of what it meant to be a computer game player (when perhaps a certain posturing was the norm) is morphing. While some in the community wear the traditional tag "gamer" proudly as a core identity and social marker, others would be more than happy to see the label fall by the wayside and simply let gaming become just another everyday leisure activity.

Unsurprisingly, professional gamers are right in the thick of this shift. For so many their identity has been defined through their love of gaming and passion for it. They often embrace the term. Those that enter into pro gaming have sometimes undergone the scrutiny and disapproval of friends and family members as they started their career. Identification as not only a gamer, but a very hard-core one, has not been without some cost. The tag of "gamer" has provided not only an important identity marker, but a powerful anchor in their social lives as they travel and compete, meeting others with whom there is a baseline bond as fellow players. Yet at the same time they are circling around notions of "athlete" and "sports" as a second rhetorical vector upon which to organize their identity. The way in which "e-sports" as a term is not yet fully developed (and perhaps even more poignantly the way "cyberathlete" never quite caught on) speaks to the betwixt and between status of pro player identity in relation to "gamer." And as those in e-sports age, as they complete their careers as players and move onto other aspects of the business (or out of it entirely), they find themselves facing the question that more and more adults do—what does it mean to simply have computer gaming as an integrated form of leisure in an adult life? As the broader culture shifts its stance on computer gaming and embraces it as simply another everyday activity, what was once an important identity and community term also faces transformation.

Mainstreaming

This shift, and battle, around "gamer" can be heard from a different angle in the e-sports scene via those who are very focused on notions of "making gaming bigger." I encountered this idea time and time again in my conversations with e-sports professionals. Very often there was a sense that e-sports, and gaming more generally, needed to break out of their niche subculture and enter into the mainstream. A word that came up continually in my conversations with those involved with e-sports was their "passion" for gaming and the desire to share it. Both a pragmatism and a more ideological vision underpinned this desire.

Tournament organizations were regularly dealing with this issue, wanting to draw in large audiences for their events, which in part increases the value for sponsors. The CGS is probably one of the best examples of a league tackling the mainstreaming of e-sports via the construction of broadcast products meant to be recognizable to, and interpretable by, those who weren't necessarily hard-core fans. Those familiar with the business and money side of the scene regularly talk about the value of broadening the base of people involved.

Yet beyond any pragmatic financial issues, a general sense that growth is important often comes up in conversations. For many it is framed as, if this doesn't grow into a mainstream activity, something is wrong. For them, there is too much talent, too much passion, too much exciting and interesting engagement with games to not foster growth. The feeling can sometimes be "look at this amazing scene we have—the world should know, and knowing, want to join in!" There is also a sentiment that growing and moving to the mainstream is an important legitimizing step. The term "e-sports" is laden with this hope.

And yet, as with the related case of "gamer," there is a tension at work in the move to the mainstream. Trade-offs get made in the service of such a transition and for some in the community the costs are not only high, but cut into its authenticity. This is not an issue unique to e-sports. All subcultures or specialized activities face similar struggles as the community undergoes a process of redefining thresholds of authentic participation and identification. E-sports are still in the midst of a potential transition from niche to mainstream culture, and the benefits and costs of that move are often debated by its members.

Global Play

One of the interesting things about e-sports is the way it is constructed across national lines but still quite rooted and shaped by local contexts. Game culture more broadly is also located in this fashion. Game titles circulate within a global entertainment market, yet the specificities of regionality simultaneously help shape preferences and play. Neither one nor the other vector predominates but instead there is a complex interplay between a construction of the global and local.

It is certainly also the case that as governments turn to high-tech industries to help build their economies (often with an almost cure-all hope of what technology will bring), computer games not infrequently get called into service. National initiatives focused on technology and the creative industries regularly bring computer gaming into the frame, and traffic on imaginations concerning how local economies can get tied to global high-tech futures. The production of a technologically savvy populace engaged in "innovative production" dovetails evocatively with a mythical rendering of the e-sports player as tech-athlete, competing all around the world.

We can definitely identify the global flow of game products and the construction of transnational player communities that are formed as titles not only make their way from country to country, but are indeed often formally launched as coordinated transnational products. At this point *Counter-Strike* is without a doubt a game that has over the past decade managed to branch out into a number of countries, constructing along the way a global community of players who recognize some clear affiliation with each other through their shared engagement with the title. Perhaps even more significant, however, are games like *World of Warcraft,* with its massive global reach, or *FIFA*, with its long history building a multinational player base (far surpassing even *WoW*'s numbers). In each of these cases, and among titles with smaller but also globally distributed player communities, we can certainly recognize ways in which game culture has become constructed through a global rubric.

At the same time, the way nationalism is formulated within global play is also important. Rowe, McKay, and Miller note in their consideration of nationalism and sports that, "the nation is conjured up at those moments when an affective unity can be posited against the gain of structural divisions and bureaucratic taxonomies" (1998, 120). The reconstitution of nationalism within global digital play presents itself with some frequency, though often with varying force. Sometimes the markers are nearly trivial, as with the selection of a country flag icon that gets appended to your online profile. Such icons operate with a bit more strength when they are constantly appended to forum participants' profiles (not uncommon in e-sports), creating a persistent symbolic visual representation of national membership as everyday conversations unfold. And in venues like the World Cyber Games national affiliations (and fandom) form a core structuring mechanism for competition.

There are also on-the-ground realities that any overreaching rhetoric about the globalization of play must reckon with. National cultures have varying ways of dealing with the games themselves. Countries make decisions about both what constitutes violence in games and then how to handle that violence. Whether it is voluntary ratings schemes (as in the United States) or the formal regulation of play based on age (as in Germany), the local political context around digital games modulates any rhetoric about global gaming communities. These discussions not only affect access but content: for example, when game imagery is changed to accommodate national sensibilities and contexts. Both game developers and e-sports organizers are regularly engaged in negotiating (and advocating for) the specialized national context digital games find themselves in.[1]

How games are handled in situ is also shaped via local contexts. We could consider, for example, the availability of particular platforms or generation of a given technology. And while many titles are released in multiple countries there can be staggered release dates or, on occasion, no worldwide distribution. While the Internet itself is always facilitating disruptions to these structures (for example, players regularly pirate games to get around regional constraints), national considerations still help shape local game cultures. Regional regulation of content—where some content is variably available from country to country or where location segments play communities, as with regional servers in MMOGs—always plays an important role in the global distribution of gaming. Deeper infrastructural constraints to networks, such as ping times, additionally perform a significant role in the shaping of actual play communities and practices.

Finally are the ways the cultural constructions of leisure identity (intersecting everything from gender, race, and class) influence how people take up and inhabit gamer culture, or not. Women may have different access, both symbolically and concretely, to taking up games or in particular venues—net cafés are not universally gender-neutral territories but can vary in tone by country. The distribution of platforms can dovetail into broad socioeconomic structures (for example, consoles versus PCs in lower-income homes). And increasingly we find national governments wrangle with policy concerned with game "addiction." So while on the one hand computer games certainly occupy some identity as a global media and entertainment product—and e-sports are absolutely woven through with a multinational orientation—it is important we also recognize the ways national and regional structures influence, and modulate, any potentially utopic or overstated "global game community" idea.

Serious Leisure or Professional Play?

Perhaps one of the thorniest issues remaining in this domain is around the question of whether or not all the high-end formalized competitive play in e-sports simply constitutes serious leisure (Stebbins 1982, 2001, 2004) or is actually a form of professionalized play. The formulation of serious leisure provides some helpful footholds to understanding the cultures of commitment and practices of dedicated focus that can arise in a variety of domains. Making sense of play that can involve repetition, practice, personal and financial investment, and at times even work-like orientations is a crucial part of understanding e-sports. But when does it cross over into professionalization?

As it stands the current high-end e-sports scene is a mix of amateur, serious leisure, and professional orientations. There are a large number of players involved in either formal amateur leagues or informally organized, but nonetheless skill-stratified, communities of play. At the other end, professionalization is most clearly at work among a much smaller number of contracted players, the team owners, league operators, tournament organizers, and some parts of the broadcast/journalist domain who have managed to create full-time occupations out of supporting, and growing, professional computer game play. Not unlike the transformation baseball made from being simply a rudimentary child's stick game to its current incarnation that ranges from amateur to adult pro play, computer gaming is also undergoing shifts and transformations as it moves beyond its historically narrow demographic and subculture.

Within the various domains of the scene we can find the span from amateur to professional. Many pro players, for example, operate at what we might think of as a semi-pro level. They are engaged in competitions and winning tournament prize money, perhaps even traveling internationally, but may still maintain a day job or have a student life that subsidizes their ability to participate in the high-end scene. For some, pro play is a time-bounded form of serious leisure. They have a temporary intense dedication to it but have not entirely bought into the idea of e-sports forming their core occupational identity—after school, for example. And for a top-level slice of players, the ones who have managed to secure contracts and sponsorships, or have built up over a number of years a working identity as a pro gamer who makes their living by competing in tournaments, they perhaps most easily slot into an identity of a professional.

The designation is thus not simply about the development of a career trajectory, but also about how the person thinks about their activity and ties it to their identity. Given e-sports is still very much a work in progress, it is perhaps not surprising that we can find a wide range of stances among those passionate about competitive gaming.

Imagined Futures

This still-emerging identity for e-sports is fragile. The global economy's roiling in 2009 left e-sports shaking. Though in the context of defaulting home mortgages and bank crises computer games can seem a side concern, they nonetheless echoed the contractions within the financial system. The closure of a number of prominent tournaments, the tightening up of sponsorship and prize money, and a general sense of deep reassessment took hold.

For a while one sensed pessimism, or at least some bleakness, about the future of competitive high-end gaming. The sudden closure of the CGS in particular, which had so shifted the networks upon which the scene was built, left many people dismayed. One appraisal suggested that e-sports wasn't dying but that "it might just be growing up" (Andrews 2009). Slowly it seems things have begun to settle. A number of CGS players were reabsorbed into the larger e-sports system from which they came. Teams rebuilt and sponsors continued to put money in their hands. Tournaments kept being held. Fan sites, podcasts, and e-sports journalism continued to support, and build, interest.

It was always perhaps misguided to imagine e-sports would go away completely. The evolution of forms of leisure, from amateur to professional, casual to serious, certainly seems a persistent theme when we look at both sports and other "fun" activities. What is still quite unknown, of course, is the scale to which pro e-sports will grow. I make no predictions. The conditions under which South Korea's incredibly robust scene emerged are tied to fundamental policy, economic, and infrastructural supports. It is uncertain if Europe and North America will develop similar mechanisms to build their scenes. What is clear is that, from the birth of digital gaming, there has been an interest in serious competitive player-against-player matches and as long as that basic fact holds, e-sports will have some place in our culture.

Assemblage, Cultural Sociology, and Computer Games

There are a multitude of ways to tell the story of e-sports and professional computer gaming. I've tackled one version here and I hope it contributes to an area that will be developed by other researchers working in the field. When I began the project I had no strong framework for what would unfold, other than my own predisposition as a sociologist and ethnographer with an interest in understanding play in real, everyday, contexts. While I went into the field first and foremost because I was interested in the players themselves, something more than that emerged. When trying to explain e-sports in conversation with people who didn't know much about the scene, I found myself turning to stories of team owners or tournaments, rules or IP debates, and talk about fans and spectators as equally compelling areas to bring to life what I was seeing.

I also found myself drawn to the complex and diverse ways meaning-making was happening within this highly specialized segment of game culture. Professional players, and others involved in facilitating pro play, were engaged in complex conversations about the nature of their activity. While they didn't use the language game scholars typically invoke, they were nonetheless thinking through many of the same issues: the relationship between work and play, the nature of intensive computer gaming, what it means to be a gamer (and a highly skilled one at that), and the character of engagement in a sport that is so interwoven with technology.

These meta-conversations were always anchored in various sets of practices and social work, often built up over years within very specialized communities. E-sports was fascinating, though, because it wasn't simply about informal norms and ways of acting, but also about emerging modes of institutionalization and the formalization of those practices. The governance of professional play was being built not just by on-the-ground communities, but also in new organizations and in the adaptation of traditional ones. The way institutions formed a core part of sustaining a pro scene came to be an important part of the story.

And if that wasn't enough to try and wrap one's head around, underpinning it all was technology. E-sports is fundamentally constructed through complex relationships with computation and machines. As with all computer gaming, it is produced through a nuanced interplay between human and nonhuman actors. How systems operate in the wild, when situated in particular cultural contexts, came to the foreground as I watched expert communities integrate, and push, various games. The ways agency, expertise, and action are constituted and operate cannot be easily boiled down to a story of simply the human or the machine. The intersection of our corporeal bodies and the material world with computation provides a whole other layer for us to try and understand.

My approach in this work has been to simultaneously untangle, yet leave linked, the assemblage of actors (be they human, nonhuman, individual, communal, or institutional) and activities that help make up the domain of e-sports. We cannot understand serious professional play by simply looking at the construction of a particular game title nor can we capture it fully by only looking at how players behave. E-sports is not constituted out of only formal game properties or official forms of organization and governance. Nor are its grassroots beginnings or community the defining feature. The story of professional computer gaming is about the interplay of all of these.

I've written elsewhere about the assemblage nature of computer gaming and argued that it is only in trying to understand the interrelation between components that we actually get to the heart of the lived experience of play (Taylor 2009). From software to institutions to informal practices to meaning systems, gaming on the ground is constituted not through any one vector but the intersection of many. Of course, this poses huge methodological challenges. I do not want to argue that any given project needs to tackle everything (though admittedly my own exploration into e-sports led me down many paths). We should recognize the way our analysis of a domain is built through the *accumulation* of our projects *as a research community*. Taken together we can formulate a collective knowledge about not only computer gaming, but about its cultural implications.

Our best work will come through trying to understand the *interplay* of the various domains, the assemblage that makes up actual play. And it is this culturally situated interplay in *specific* context and domains, in *particular* historical moments, where we find our richest understandings of what computer game play is, and means. My hope is that this work contributes to our conversations on computation and action, on the formation of new leisure/work/sporting identities and activities, on the institutionalization of gaming, on the governance of play, and on what it means to be not simply players, but audiences for new forms of digital culture. E-sports, whatever it may end up becoming, is being forged through the interaction of these domains and understanding computer gaming is ultimately rooted in nuanced stories about this cultural work in progress.

Notes: This contract is reproduced with the original, uncorrected text. This contract includes insurance.

On signature:

□ signed originals to Club
□ signed originals to Player
□ signed copy to G7

STANDARD PLAYER CONTRACT

BETWEEN

1
2
3

(hereinafter called "CLUB")

and

4
5
6

(hereinafter called "PLAYER")

For the period

____________to ______________

The player is a citizen of

____

[1] Full official (legal) name of CLUB
[2] Official company number in order to identify the CLUB in public registry
[3] Official address of head office of CLUB
[4] Full name in accordance with name in passport
[5] Address and postcode as documented from identity card etc.
[6] Personal identity number (if applicable in home country)

Tick whichever of the following alternatives applies:

□ Article 10 shall not apply as this is an employment contract

□ Article 10 shall apply as this is a service contract.

PREAMBLE AND DEFINITIONS:

§ 1.

1.1 CLUB is an organisation existing under the laws of [[7]]. The main purpose of the CLUB is to organize and manage teams within e-sport in particular within online computer gaming.

1.2 PLAYER wants to participate in e-sport activities on a professional basis.

1.3 PLAYER wants to make a living as professional e-sport participate.

1.4 PLAYER does not have any obligation towards another e-sport club and/or team and is free to enter into this Contract. If the Player is transferred from another club this will be regulated in 1.5.

1.5 If PLAYER is transferred from another club it is the sole responsibility of the CLUB to clear the transfer with the PLAYERs former club.

1.6 PLAYER acknowledges that revenue from sponsors is an important part of the e-sport activities and that PLAYER has to support the sponsors as called for in this contract in order for the CLUB to succeed financially.

1.7 The purpose of the Contract is to set out the obligations and right of the CLUB and PLAYER allowing the CLUB to run e-sports business and allowing PLAYER to earn money from participating in e-sport.

1.8 For the purpose of this contract "e-sports" shall mean: "Any competitive gaming activity which is conducted through the use of a computer/gaming device in an organised way".

1.9 For the purpose of this contract "team" shall mean: "one or more players playing together in the same e-sport activity and competing as a team against other teams".

1.10 For the purpose of this contract "week" shall mean: Monday to Friday.

[7] The country where the Club is incorporated or where it has its main office.

E-sport activities:

§ 2.

2.1 PLAYER shall while representing the CLUB participate in the following e-sport activities: [[8]]

The e-sport activities are to be:

□ full-time job for PLAYER.

□ part time job for PLAYER and PLAYER shall be allowed to undertake the following activities besides playing for the CLUB:

2.2 All awards/titles/achievements/trophies of any kind won by PLAYER/the PLAYERs team are the property of the CLUB. PLAYER shall be entitled to keep any individual trophy.

PLAYERS obligations:

§ 3.

3.1 PLAYER shall throughout the term of the Contract show absolute loyalty towards the CLUB/the teams he participates in.

3.2 PLAYER shall participate in training sessions and training camps according to the Clubs instructions/agreements within the teams PLAYER is part of.

3.3 PLAYER shall submit to any decisions taken by his team leader/CLUB management concerning the composition of a team.

3.4 PLAYER shall not – after signing this contract – engage in e-sports activities outside the scope of this contract.

3.5 PLAYER shall participate in matches/tournaments according to the Clubs instructions.

3.6 PLAYER shall spend as a minimum [ ] hours per week on training and [ ] hours per week on matches.

3.7 PLAYER shall be allowed to take [ ] weeks off during a calendar year during which PLAYER is free from training and free from playing matches. The weeks shall be agreed with the CLUB and shall be planed at least 3 month in advance.

---

[8] Describe the types of e-games that the player shall participate in.

3.8 PLAYER must use any equipment provided by the CLUB including but not limited to computer equipment, software, voice-communication (head sets), internet-connection etc.

3.9 To the extent the CLUB does not provide equipment necessary for playing PLAYER shall at his own expense provide any necessary equipment in order to perform his obligation as a professional gaming player.

3.10 PLAYER shall make sure he is in good psychical shape and that he is living a healthy life. If the Club has issued guidelines on how to live a healthy life PLAYER is obliged to follow said guidelines.

3.11 PLAYER shall participate in game conferences, game fairs and/or events according to the Clubs instructions given a fair warning. If PLAYER cannot participate due to exams or other similar excuses PLAYER shall inform the CLUB at least 2 months in advance.

3.12 PLAYER shall participate in any sponsor event according to the CLUBS instruction it being on- or offline including but not limited to interviews, TV-appearance, endorsement of sponsor product, appearance in advertising for a sponsor unless the reasons for not participating in 3.11 applies.

3.13 PLAYER shall in all public appearance use CLUB/team clothing and equipment.

3.14 PLAYER accepts that he is a role model and therefore he shall not consume alcohol in public, or use drugs either in private or in public or engage in other activities which constitute a violation of criminal laws in the countries where PLAYER is domiciled or is acting on behalf of the CLUB.

3.15 Nor shall PLAYER engage in activities that will jeopardize or are likely to jeopardize his image as a role model.

3.16 PLAYER shall in all public appearance use and promote sponsored products/ services and shall observe clause 3.18 at all times.

3.17 PLAYER shall use and promote products produced by sponsors even if the PLAYER is not actually involved in promoting a product/service.

3.18 PLAYER shall throughout the term of this contract not use goods and/or services which compete with goods/services provided by the CLUBS sponsors including but not limited to: mouse pads, headset/head phone, teflon/glides, monitors, computers, game machines, mice, cloth, soft drinks, magazines and food.

3.19 PLAYER shall allow the CLUB – without special payment to PLAYER – to give the CLUB/team sponsor(s) permission to use PLAYER's image for advertising purposes with or without mentioning PLAYER's name. This shall not apply to products that are in direct conflict with PLAYER's religion.

3.20 PLAYER shall after the end of the duration of this Agreement allow the CLUB to distribute and/or promote products produced prior to the end of the Agreement including/showing/displaying the name and/or image of the PLAYER.

3.21 PLAYER shall inform the CLUB immediately if PLAYER due to illness is unable to train/play matches and or appear for the CLUB. The information to the CLUB shall include the nature of illness, the expected duration and in case the absence exceeds 4 days the CLUB shall receive a statement from a doctor evidencing that PLAYER is in fact ill and the expected recovery.

3.22 If the absence exceeds 2 weeks PLAYER shall be under an obligation to allow himself/herself to be treated by a doctor/specialist assigned by the CLUB provided that the CLUB pays the full cost of the treatment less any public payments that PLAYER may be entitled to.

3.23 PLAYER shall not in an unfair manner use any non-standard, 3rd party programs and/or in-game enabled tools to improve game play in an unfair manner. Nor shall PLAYER use any software including game software which has been obtained by infringing the intellectual property rights of the publisher of the software in question.

3.24 PLAYER shall at all times observe fair play and respect the rules of the e-sports activities conducted by PLAYER.

3.25 PLAYER may only have personal sponsors if the CLUB has given its prior written permission.

The CLUB's obligations

§ 4.

4.1 The CLUB shall throughout the term of this contract show absolute loyalty towards PLAYER.

4.2 The CLUB shall promote PLAYER and the team(s) he is playing in.

4.3 The CLUB shall pay PLAYER:

4.4 Compensation: [9]

---

[9] Here should the basic payment to the Player be stated.

4.5 Bonus: [10]

4.6 Personal benefits: [11]

4.7 Prize money: [12]

4.8 Unless otherwise agreed the compensation and other monies to the PLAYER shall be paid out by the CLUB in monthly payments with 1/12 of the agreed yearly amount.

4.9 The compensation (and other monies) shall be paid out in EURO to a bank account designated by PLAYER. PLAYER shall pay any and all transaction costs and exchange fees.

4.10 The compensation (and other monies) is the gross amount to be paid to PLAYER including pension, social contribution and any other amount levied on compensations.

4.11 PLAYER shall report and pay any local taxes levied on the compensation. The CLUB shall be entitled to withhold and report any local taxes in the country where PLAYER is domiciled or any other country where PLAYER has become tax liable.

4.12 The CLUB shall be entitled to withhold or reduce any payments to the PLAYER if the CLUB has rendered the PLAYER a 1,5 month notice that PLAYER is not performing at all (becoming inactive) or performing substantial below the normal level.

4.13 The CLUB shall make it possible for PLAYER/the team he is playing for to participate in online tournaments and matches with relevant opponents and exposure by paying fees or taking other relevant measures to make participation possible.

4.14 The CLUB shall make it possible for PLAYER/the team he is playing for to participate in on site tournaments and matches with relevant opponents and exposure by paying fees and taking other relevant measure to make participa-

[10] If no bonus state N/A – otherwise be sure to state bonus events, whether bonus in monthly, annually etc. and the amount of bonus.

[11] Tax treatment not regulated. Examples of benefits: Free Internet connection, free computer, upgrade in travel and accommodation, free magazines, mobile phone, paid mobile phone. Make sure that it is clearly stated that the Player shall return any goods upon termination of contract.

[12] Split in prize money should be clearly stated. If player shall receive more or less than is part of prize money won this should be stated.

tion possible. PLAYER shall bear the risk of not being able to get visa or other necessary travelling documents.

4.15 The CLUB shall distribute any prize money won by PLAYER or the team he is playing for among the players in equal shares less the share that the CLUB is entitled to unless otherwise agreed.

4.16 The CLUB shall be entitled to keep all sponsor money received from CLUB sponsors.

4.17 The CLUB shall assist PLAYER in getting the best possible deal on an internet connection where PLAYER is domiciled but PLAYER shall at all time pay for his own Internet connection unless otherwise agreed.

4.18 The CLUB shall pay PLAYERS expenses for travelling, accommodation and living costs if and when PLAYER is travelling on behalf of the CLUB unless otherwise agreed. The level of payment is set out in the expense policy of the CLUB.

4.19 If the PLAYER accepts to use own money to pay for expenses mentioned in 4.18 reimbursements shall take place as soon as the PLAYER presents the CLUB with a valid invoice/receipt. No reimbursement can be claimed more than 30 days after the expenses has been paid by PLAYER.

4.20 The CLUB is only committed to furnish PLAYER with gaming equipment if the equipment is sponsored but shall at its own discretion be entitled to furnish PLAYER with any sort of gaming equipment.

4.21 The CLUB shall have an obligation to secure that the PLAYER can represent any national team at least ? week a year including practise session. Any representation on national teams shall be announced to the CLUB at least 3 month in advanced. If the CLUB has a significant interest in the PLAYER playing for the CLUB the CLUB can reduce the time of availability of the PLAYER of the national team.

TRANSFER

§ 5.

5.1 The CLUB shall be entitled to negotiate a transfer of PLAYER to another club against a transfer fee.

5.2 PLAYER can request to be transferred to another club before the term of this contract expires. If the CLUB agrees to transfer PLAYER the CLUB shall be entitled to a transfer fee per year left of the term of the Contract.

NEGATIVE COMPENSATION:

§ 6.

6.1 PLAYER shall pay a compensation to the CLUB in the following events:

6.1.1 Failure on part of PLAYER to participate in training, matches and/or sponsor activities with-out due reason.

6.1.2 PLAYER acts disloyal against the CLUB or the teams/other team members.

6.1.3 The level of the compensation to be paid shall be decided by the CLUB management. The compensation shall as a minimum amount to [[13]] EURO per day and to a maximum of [[14]] EURO per day the failure on part of PLAYER has existed.

6.1.4 Failure on part of PLAYER to comply with 3.14 shall trigger payment of a compensation equals two months of compensation paid by the CLUB according to clause 4. If repeated the CLUB shall be entitled to terminate the contract without warning and without any further payments to PLAYER.

6.2 The compensation to the CLUB shall be deducted from the monthly compensation paid by the CLUB or any other payments due to PLAYER.

CONFIDENTIAL:

§ 7.

7.1 PLAYER shall at all times also after termination of the Contract keep any and all information received from sponsors strictly confidential.

7.2 For the duration of the contract and for a 2-years period after the termination of the con-tract PLAYER shall not speak in a negative manner about sponsors and/or there products.

7.3 PLAYER shall restrain from saying or writing anything negative about the CLUB or PLAYER's team during the term of this contract and for a period of 5 years after the contract has terminated.

7.4 PLAYER shall never be entitled to use any information about the CLUB that is not public known in interviews or books or on the Internet or in any other form likely to be distributed to the public.

---

[13] Minimum amount in EURO
[14] Maximum amount in EURO

7.5 PLAYER may only – during the term of this contract – give interviews with the prior written approval of the CLUB. The CLUB shall have the right to be present during the interview.

7.6 The CLUB shall not be allowed to state anything negative about PLAYER or use personal information about PLAYER in any public announcement unless PLAYER has given his written permission or unless it is necessary to protect the reputation of the CLUB.

INSURANCE:

§ 8

8.1 The CLUB shall take out and keep in force an International Health Insurance which gives PLAYER access to free basic medical treatment within [15]

DURATION/TERMINATION

§ 9.

9.1 This contract comes into force on [[16]] and shall expire on [[17]] unless it is prolonged by mutual agreement.

9.2 During the term of this contract it cannot be terminated by either party unless provided for in this contract.

§ 10

INDEPENDENT CONTRACTORS

10.1 It is expressly agreed that the CLUB and PLAYER are acting hereunder as independent contractors, and under no circumstances shall any employees of one party be deemed the employees of the other for any purpose. This Contract shall not be construed as authority for either party to act for the other party in any agency or other capacity or to make commitments of any kind for the account of or on behalf of the other except to the extent and for the purposes expressly provided for herein.

[15] The countries where Player shall be entitled to basic medical treatment. (Make sure the insurance covers these countries.)
[16] Date of first service/working day.
[17] Date of last service/working day.

OTHERS:

§ 11.

11.1 If any provisions or part of any provisions of this Contract is determined by a court or a body of competent jurisdiction or by the below Tribunal to be invalid or unenforceable, such determination shall not affect the validity or enforceability of any other part or provision of this Contract.

11.2 If this Contract is signed on behalf of a minor PLAYER the person signing has – under domestic law – the full and legal capacity to sign on behalf of the minor and the person signing the Contract has obtained acceptance from PLAYER to sign and the person signing has explained – in detail – the consequences of this Contract to PLAYER.

11.3 The minor PLAYER accepts and acknowledges that he will have to resign this Contract when he – under domestic law – is no longer a minor and has obtained power to sign for himself. Unless otherwise stated under domestic law the minor will have to resign this contract when he has reached the age of 18.

CHOICE OF LAW and VENUE:

§ 12.

12.1 This contract is regulated by international principals of bono and equity and by international principles applying in major sport disciplines.

12.2 PLAYER waiver to the extent possible any protection under his domestic national law protecting employees.

12.3 In the event of a dispute between the parties the dispute shall be settled by negotiations. If negotiations have not settled the dispute with one month each party may request mediations. If mediation has not settled the dispute within 2 months after the request has been made each party may refer the dispute to arbitration.

12.4 The mediator shall be appointed by CAS – the Court of Arbitration for Sport and the rules of said body on mediation shall be applied.

12.5 The cost for the mediation shall be paid equally by PLAYER and the CLUB.

12.6 The arbitration shall be conducted by a single arbitrator according to the ICC rules. The arbitrator shall be appointed by the ICC unless appointment can be made by the Court of Arbitration for Sport.

12.7 The arbitrator shall apply international principals of bono and equity and shall use principles form other international sports games such as football when deciding the dispute at hand. The case law of the Court of Arbitration for Sport shall apply where applicable.

12.8 When deciding the case the arbitrator shall take into consideration the expectations of the parties and the stage of development of e-sport when the contract was entered into.

12.9 An award should be rendered no later than 12 month after the tribunal has been established.

12.10 The cost for arbitration shall be shared equally by PLAYER and the CLUB regardless of the outcome of the award.

12.11 English shall be the official language of this Contract and of the dispute and any negotiation and dispute resolution shall be conducted in the English language.

Signature:

--ooOoo--

....

Notes

Chapter 1

1. "E-sport" (or "eSport," short for "electronic sport") has become the prevalent term within the global community of formalized, competitive computer gaming, though its origination is not easily placed. It overtook the word "cyberathlete" in common usage, a term that originated in the 1990s and was most popularized, and apparently trademarked, by Angel Munoz and his Cyberathlete Professional League. Wagner (2006) suggests that a 1999 press release from the Online Gamers Association is perhaps one of the earliest appearances of the "eSports" formulation. Though uncoupled from "athleticism," it retains a link to a serious competitive pursuit via "sports," yet also signals it is something other than traditional physical activity through that simple "e." The legitimating work the term does for the community is important and is something I will discuss in more detail throughout the book. Situating playing computer games within the frame of sports has been an important rhetorical move for many.

2. This may be a surprising detail given that *Space Invaders* (1978) is typically credited with the first high score function in a digital game (Poole 2000), but screenshots from *Sea Wolf* indicate a different history (see, for example, http://www.arcade-museum.com/game_detail.php?game_id=9459).

3. For a nuanced story about the transformation and demise of arcade halls, one that weaves together not just technology but cultural attitudes, read J. C. Herz's *Joystick Nation* (1997). See Steven Poole's *Trigger Happy* (2000) for a slightly different account of the growth of computer gaming.

4. Henry Lowood also recounts some of these early roots of e-sports in his article "'Beyond the Game': The Olympic Ideal and Competitive e-Sports" in *Play and Politics: Games, Civic Engagement, and Social Activism*, Douglas Thomas and Joshua Fouts (eds.), forthcoming.

5. For a good account of that first Quakecon, see King and Borland's (2003) *Dungeons and Dreamers*.

6. Though not as widely known, the Deathmatch '95 tournament, cosponsored by Microsoft to help promote Windows 95 gaming, is certainly just as significant given it was perhaps one of the first competitions to be built around regional qualifiers (via the DWANGO system) and culminating in a national tournament. That final match, held at the Microsoft offices in Washington, awarded the title of "World's Best Deathmatch Player" (King and Borland 2003).

7. Not to be confused with the short-lived Professional Gamers League (PGL), whose first commissioner was Nolan Bushnell, founder of Atari. That organization launched in 1997 on the heels of Dennis Fong's success and e-sports getting some of its earliest popular press coverage (King and Borland 2003).

8. ESPN is one of the few traditional sports outlets whose presence has been constant in e-sports. The network has long been involved in sports deemed too marginal for the "Big 3" U.S. networks (ABC, NBC, and CBS) and they seem to be always keeping an eye on competitive computer gaming, watching to see if it is ready to break big. See Wood and Benigni (2006) for some discussion of cable TV, ESPN, and sports coverage more generally.

9. One of the most controversial articles to come out about the CPL was authored by Tonya Welch (2010), a former employee. In her multiseries installment she made allegations of questionable business practices, as well as duplicity by the organization and several of its' executives, who continued in e-sports after leaving the CPL. The article was widely read and commented upon within the e-sports community. Kane's 2008 *Game Boys* book also presents allegations of shady dealings and never-paid prize money.

10. For those surprised and skeptical that Angel Munoz would walk away from e-sports after having invested so many years, in September 2010 it was announced that his company NewWorld had entered into an arrangement with the CPL's newest owners, WoLong Ventures, to provide content via his *Adrenaline Vault* Website.

11. Jin's book, *Korea's Online Gaming Empire* (2010), is particularly helpful in developing the full picture of the South Korean model.

12. Jin and Chee help frame the issue, writing, "To put quantity into perspective, there were only 100 PC cafés in Korea during 1997; however, by May 2002 this had rapidly increased to 25,000. In 2005 there was a decrease in the number of cafés to about 20,000 because of market saturation and the growing access to broadband services in the home" (2008, 48).

13. More recently, this is shifting with the growing use of microtransactions as a primary model for online games.

14. There was also a desire to expand South Korean gaming from simply playing online games (where the market is well developed) to playing console-based games (where significant growth was envisioned). The Institute identified some challenge

in this, however, given the rich culture of online guilds and communities. The perceived solo play aspects of consoles, and the limitations on text communication, and a general notion that consoles were not going to be as socially rich posed concern. They note somewhat pessimistically that, "Despite diverse efforts, however, it will not be easy to convert Koreans into video gamers since they are already accustomed to online games" (Korea Game Development and Promotion Institute 2003, 12).

15. This has been undertaken to some degree in Singapore as well with the creation of its CyberSports Association (CSA) and "Team Singapore" (Wai-Leng 2006a). As noted in The Straits Times, "Mr. Thomas Lim, the Infocomm Development Authority's director for education, learning, digital media and entertainment, said a national team 'will not just help increase awareness of online gaming in Singapore but also augment Singapore's position as a digital games hub'" (Wai-Leng 2006b). Government initiatives for the game industry have also been undertaken in places like Ireland (for more see Kerr 2006).

16. As Lowood (forthcoming) notes, however, the WCG has followed a particular formulation of the Olympic ideal whereby professional, versus amateur, athleticism finds a home in the competition. The cash prizes certainly support this, though I would shade in a slight nuance. Many countries send national players to the WCG who do not compete on par with the top signed e-sports players, and would probably better fit into the semi-pro, if not amateur, category.

17. Aside from a fair amount of discussion about the WCG in later chapters, this book will not delve into the intricacies of the South Korean model much further. To do so would take a degree of language competency and on-site research that would form a whole project on its own. For work on Korean game culture more broadly see, for example, Chee 2006.

18. The first event was held at Stanford University in May 2009 and information about it can be found at http://www.stanford.edu/group/htgg/cgi-bin/drupal/?q=node/967. The second was held at the IT University of Copenhagen in May 2010 and information about it can be found at http://esportseuropeanedition.wordpress.com.

19. A small note about this multidisciplinary engagement: I have tried when possible to situate some of my arguments and findings in at least an initial conversation with research communities outside game studies. This is no small undertaking as domains such as the sociology of sport now have several decades of research upon which to base conversation. There is a distinct trade-off I've made here. In the service of getting this research out so as to help move a game studies conversation forward, I've had to forego mastery of areas that, if I knew them better, would certainly lend to the theoretical work here. I've tried to split the difference, finding hooks into those bodies of literature but leaving fuller exploration for later work by myself and, hopefully, others.

Chapter 2

1. Wagner, in his article "On the Scientific Relevance of eSports," proposes the following definition: "eSports is an area of sport activities in which people develop and train mental or physical abilities in the use of information and communication technologies" (2006, 438).

2. For a more definitional consideration of the issue, as well as several potential models that would then follow, see Jonasson and Thiborg (2010).

3. There is useful companion work on this thread to be found within Internet studies, in particular virtual worlds and embodiment. See, for example, Biocca 1997, Boellstorff 2008, Dibbell 1998, Sundén 2003, and Taylor 2002.

4. See, for example, Johnson 1996 and Sheridan 2006.

5. He also has a line of components meant to give the average gamer a full high-end experience in their own home. Computers themselves are complex material artifacts within computer gaming generally and in the high-end competitive scene in particular.

6. As one reviewer noted about the *Rock Band* gaming setup on the WCG Ultimate Gamer TV show, "Being someone who plays a ton of *Rock Band 2*, I know that playing *Rock Band* on an uncalibrated TV is like playing *Counter-Strike* with backwards interp (for the uninitiated out there, imagine shooting at an enemy in an FPS who is on your screen in one position, but actually about ten feet away from that position, causing your bullets to miss them). If you watch the band challenge portion, every drummer misses the green note on the drum fills, causing them to miss overdrive (or star power). It's a tell tale sign of bad calibration. I don't know if it's cause of the Samsung TVs, because I have heard specific complaints about Rhythm Games [sic] with Samsung, but something was up and I feel pity for the players" (Hicks 2009).

7. Though I will not discuss it in detail, we should keep in mind that as software products computer games are not exempt from the normal technological problems all such artifacts have. Newman reminds us that, "Moreover, the system may behave in an unpredictable manner unintended by the game designers due to imperfections in the code or unanticipated emergent contingencies" (2008, 124). This has certainly been echoed in my conversations with, for example, virtual world and multiplayer game designers. The best are all too aware of the contingent nature of the system.

8. It is important to remember the caveat Salen and Zimmerman provide in sketching out this structure when they say that the schema is not meant to be a "definitive explanatory typology" but is "a framework for identifying, analyzing, and solving design problems as they arise in your game" (2004, 134). We should be cautious in picking the formulation up as a way of explaining *actual* games and their play in everyday contexts.

9. The article in full presents a nuanced handling of the discussion of contingency, specifying various forms.

10. For another close read of a play scenario see Conway's 2010 article analyzing a session of *Pro Evolution Soccer* among friends.

11. For an entertaining collection of cheating within traditional sports see Zimniuch 2009.

12. This session of *Starcraft* continued to be particularly fraught. After rewinning the round between himself and iP.Ex, some argued that Stork began to throw his matches against Ra because he wanted a second place position (rather than first), which would keep him from having to face another member of the South Korean *Starcraft* team in one of the brackets (thus bettering the team's chances for more members to advance to the finals). This resulted in a prolonged three-way round robin cycle between Stork, Ra, and iP.Ex during which everyone spectating and refereeing essentially knew what was going on and was pretty openly discussing it. As the journalist Mahmood Ali (2007) put it, "When a player like Stork wants to lose, it's blatantly obvious." After several hours of delays between the bug issue and allegedly thrown games, Stork finally beat Ra and the bracket round continued.

13. There remains much rumor and speculation about what actually happened to cause what was seen by many as a reversed decision. Ali (2007) wrote that "a Korean S-VIP and VIP stepped in and told the head referee that the match needed to go to a one map decider." But a referee commented on this particular news account of this decision writing, "I was a CS ref at this year's WCG and the VIPs and SP did not choose to play the third map it was the idead [sic] of an MYM player. You are getting a lot of info wrong in this post" (Ali 2007). Allegations and rumors played a big role in most discussions of the event.

Chapter 3

1. Despite how catchy it is to think about a nine-year-old pro, one study put the average age of professional gamers at twenty-one (Game Research 2002). This matches my own sense of the demographics.

2. In the *60 Minutes* piece Fatal1ty was reported to have won $300,000 in total prize money, $150,000 of that from a single Cyberathlete Professional League tournament (though Kane's 2008 book *Game Boys* presents a darker side of the story, with the prize money payout quite delayed). When e-sports hit a fairly bumpy patch in 2009 the tone of these popular press stories shifted. Witness the *New York Times* article entitled "Virtual Leagues Fold, Forcing Gamers to Find Actual Jobs" complete with an image of a former gamer now employed at a big box store (Goldberg 2009).

3. There is one important slice of e-sports that goes against this story and that is the fighting game scene where arcades still formed an important space for building a competitive community and where players went to hone their skills.

4. LAN parties aren't just about game matches but can also involve file sharing, demos, showing off customized PCs, general partying, and just building a community. See Fetscherin, Kaskiris, and Wallenberg 2005, Hertzberg Johnson 2000, Jansz and Martens 2005, Jörissen 2004, Nordli 2003, and Swalwell 2006, 2008, and 2009 for more on LANs generally.

5. There are a few examples of top players or e-sports professionals publishing companion materials to the private lessons some also give. Danny Montaner's (2008) *The Art of fRoD* and Paul Chaloner's (2009) *So You Want To Be a Shoutcaster?* both come to mind.

6. Technicity is infused in many discussions with e-sports people. Players regularly talk about wanting to "keep working with computers" or technology in general when their pro career has run its course. Even broadcasters and journalists tie into this more general professional identity, often maintaining day jobs in tech and info sectors.

7. I was curious about this issue of intuition and actually asked if this was something players talked to each other about or if some things you keep to yourself (as a kind of competitive advantage). He remarked, "We don't, me and my teammates sometimes don't even talk about our full intuition. We just know the product of everyone's intuition. We know everyone's play style, their definitive play style, and what they're good at. But we don't always talk about all of our thought processes."

8. Stald, in her 2001 paper on *Counter-Strike*, made one of the earliest comparisons between the game and soccer and concluded what is often echoed by the players of e-sports—that the motivations, work, and pleasures of playing these games often closely align to traditional sports.

9. With an even longer historical frame, Morris notes of baseball that the earliest players viewed it "primarily as a recreation rather than as a competition" (2006, xxiii) and though this (quickly) changed, it highlights the shifting meaning of our leisure, and sporting, activities.

10. Perhaps the most common exception concerns the youngest of kids playing sports. We are all certainly familiar with the scenario of the adult or coach standing on the sideline being overly harsh or imposing more structure than is warranted for the age of the players. In these instances the ideal of good or healthy play is overridden by the notion that organized sports, and their practice, offer important moral, and indeed civilizing, lessons. See Siegenthaler and Gonzalez 1997 for a critical consideration of the notion of serious leisure applied to organized youth sport.

11. They do note that pursuing the hobby for profit is not seen as appropriate, something that markedly distinguishes it from e-sports.

12. There is potentially an interesting comparison with how guilds in MMOGs very often adopt similar language around family, new bonds, and connections through the game they are passionate about.

13. See Silverman 2007 for an application of Stebbins to the MMOG domain and power gamers.

14. Fincham (2007, 2008), who notes a link between his own work and that of people like Howard Becker (1963, 2008), often uses the term "subculture" to help anchor his analysis. This is something I've mused over myself when it comes to these particularly hardcore segments of game culture. It can at times seem a fairly fitting designation.

15. I was struck by a powerful counter story from one player I talked to. As he transitioned from being an ice hockey player to a pro CS player his mother also shifted from driving him to those competitions to e-sports tournaments. This is mirrored in Nicholas T. Taylor's (2009b) work on the Major League Gaming organization, where he occasionally found mothers turning up at competitions to watch their teenage sons play.

16. Though Turkle (1984) has been critiqued for over-essentializing gender in her early handling of technologists, her discussion of what it means to have one's everyday life so interwoven with computation is still some of the most interesting work on what we'd now identify as geeks and gamers. Ellen Ullman's book (1997) is another poignant examination on the complex relationship between ourselves and computation, on being "close to the machine."

17. Consalvo (2003) critically unpacked one of the few domains in which traits like aggression and violence get wound up in the (media) image of the geek/gamer—that of the "monsters next door" in the form of Dylan Klebold and Eric Harris (the perpetrators of the Columbine High School massacre). The media panic around violence and gaming is perhaps one of the more fascinating disruptions of an otherwise anodyne image of geekdom.

18. The malleability of what counts as masculinity (particularly within the intersectionality of class) is nicely summarized and historicized by Segal 1990.

19. In addressing the complicated, and common, use of the term Pascoe notes, "The fag epithet, when hurled at other boys, may or may not have explicit sexual meanings, but it always has gendered meanings. When a boy calls another boy a fag, it means he is not a man but not necessarily that he is a homosexual" (2007, 82). Nonetheless, as one team owner put it to me about the e-sports scene, "The level of homophobia is, like, unimaginable."

20. Events like the Hip Hop Gaming League are, I think, a terrific example of attempts to walk this kind of razor's edge line (though the racial component complicates the analysis even further).

21. For an interesting contrast and comparison see Mennesson's work (2009) on men in dance and Chimot and Louveau's (2010) research on boys in rhythmic gymnastics.

22. See Fausto-Sterling 1985 and 2000, Laqueur 1990, and Tavris 1992 for just a few interventions on the myths and imaginaries of biological difference constructed via "science."

23. In Baasanjav's (2010) recent paper about women chess players online she notes a fascinating twist on how gender is interpreted in the chess world. Quoting Jennifer Shahade (an international chess master), she notes that "Contrary to a common notion of girls being less aggressive when they play games, Shahade argues that a 'girl move' in chess nowadays means more fierce and aggressive because of the ways many female players play chess in male tournaments."

24. See Lawler 2002 for an account of pleasures women can find in violent sports.

25. In Chimot and Louveau's article on boys who participate in rhythmic gymnastics, which are often coded as feminine, boys encounter similar challenges and undertake compensatory moves. They write that, "Adults (parents and other family members) as well as peers exert pressure on boys taking part in rhythmic gymnastics to conform to traditional masculine norms" and that "These young men implement strategies in order to reconcile the different images of masculinity they are confronted with and to construct their identity: that of a man playing a feminine sport" (2010, 436).

26. The one notable exception I've found to this is on *World of Warcraft* arena teams. This is surely tied to the growing, and widespread acceptance of, women in the MMOG genre.

27. See Hargreaves 1994 and McDonagh and Pappano 2008 for a broader sports context for this issue.

28. Though not focused on pro gaming specifically I do want to mention the work of Leonard (2006, 2008) who has given important consideration to the issue of race and computer games. He argues that games regularly serve as spaces in which traditional white masculinity is afforded an opportunity of "racialized play, fantasy, and pleasure," (2008, 91) trafficking in the complex and often problematic representations of black men vis-à-vis tropes of sports star, thug, and "urban" persona.

29. We could perhaps similarly tie in a discussion concerning the level of comfort women typically have with modding or whether or not they are the primary owner of their gaming device and thus are authorized to tweak it.

Chapter 4

1. While I am not going to focus on it here in any detail, there is certainly an important conversation to be had about how notions of industry invoke crucial conversations about labor (see, for example, Dyer-Witheford and de Peuter 2009). The nature of labor in digital games, often short-handed as "playbour," while outside the scope of this book, could be fruitfully considered. As I will discuss later, this

angle perhaps comes into even sharper relief when we confront cases of e-sports players going unpaid.

2. The Danube-University Krems, Austria in 2004 even offered a several-week course (for 1,950 euros) on "E-Sport Consulting" that included sessions on marketing, PR, and business development. Lecturers were drawn from both academia and e-sports (most notably SK Gaming).

3. For a solid journalistic account of the rise of the CGS and the personalities involved see Kane's 2008 book *Game Boys*.

4. For a particularly critical handling of the commodification of lifestyle sports and building of consumerist youth culture see Rinehart 2008.

5. Unfortunately the nitty gritty financial details remain a mystery to many people, though there is some speculation that the economics of the sponsor deals were perhaps not as rosy as they appeared on the outside. See, for example, Cole 2008.

6. CEO and commissioner, lawyer Andy Reif, came from a strong entertainment (ICM and Paramount Pictures) and sports background, having been instrumental in building the AVP Pro Beach Volleyball Tour. Kieve Huffman, senior vice president of business development, also came from an entertainment background, having worked in licensing and mobile content. The first general counsel, Michael J. Widman (formerly VP of business development with Disney) came with expertise in entertainment and global brands. Others like Geoff Stevens (COO) brought an MBA and a background in Internet services vis-à-vis search services at Yahoo!. Mike Burks, producer, brought years of experience in working with televised traditional sports (from the NFL to the Olympics). Rachael McLean, one of two women on the executive team (the other being Jennifer Costa, the second general counsel), came from MTV and mobile online development. A few on the team, lawyer Jason Katz (VP of global marketing) and Scott Valencia (senior VP of operations), had computer games in their background, though Katz brought significant marketing experience with traditional brands like M&M/Mars. Scott Valencia was perhaps the person on the executive team with the most e-sports experience, having been involved with a number of ventures including the World Series of Video Games.

7. They also provided me a number of PDFs via e-mail after my visit with additional details about various events, and the like.

8. Founders include Jens Hilgers (CEO, now chairman, b.1975), currently in China undertaking new ventures; Ralf Reichert (founder and managing director, b. 1974), also one of the cofounders, along with his brothers of SK (1997–2001), was also managing director of CPL Europe 2000–2003; Alexander T. Müller (b. unknown), now managing director of SK Gaming; Jan-Philipp Reining (director of product design, b. 1975); and Björn Metzdorf (director of IT, b. 1978).

9. E-sports outfits do not typically benefit from one of the major sources of revenue traditional sports do—TV licensing. As one executive noted, even if it reaches this

stage it will not be quite the same as in traditional sports. "When the point in time comes that that is a big income stream then actually I think the publishers will get a significant amount of money or a share of that for the work they did on the games."

10. Other quoted amounts you can find for MLG contracts include about $83,000 a year per player ($1,000,000 for a team of four over three years) for top Halo teams (MLG Admin 2006a). The current construction of payment to top players is perhaps not what we think of with traditional contract formulations.

11. With a few exceptions the scope of "world" in e-sports is still typically made up of the United States; Canada; central, southern, and northern Europe; South Korea; occasionally Brazil; and increasingly China. Despite computer gaming being big in Japan, e-sports players from there are still noticeably absent from the traditional e-sports circuit.

12. I am specifically not including something like the CGS's general managers, given they were salaried to managed a franchise owned by the league, but there are many overlaps and indeed, several CGS general managers were previously independent owners and returned to that position once that organization folded.

13. Nor is there any phalanx of doctors and physical therapists, lawyers, agents, or union representatives similarly intervening in the player/owner relationship.

14. He is here using the term "coach" but clarified in other parts of our conversation that he does not act as a traditional coach. In this case "coach" is a kind of substitute word for "owner/manager."

15. This could alternatively be more provocatively formulated along the lines Connor takes in situating athletic exploitation as rooted in the surplus of available play labor. He argues that, "Elite athletes have become mere widgets, interchangeable and individually irrelevant in modern corporatized and spectacularised sporting endeavours" (2009, 1369).

16. The company's commitment to e-sports perhaps makes even more sense when you know that Kim Rom, their chief marketing officer, is heavily involved in the scene. Once a player himself, he now facilitates and supports e-sports from the sponsorship side.

17. For a helpful review of the range of issues in this domain see Lastowka's (2010) book, *Virtual Justice: The New Laws of Online Worlds.*

18. This branch is now known as the Ministry of Culture, Sports, and Tourism.

19. The linked article no longer goes to a document in which the quote can be found. After looking at the Blizzard website I cannot find any document, in English or Korean, with the quote.

20. Rumors continue to swirl about SC2 and LAN functionality with speculations about future competition packs that will allow it. As of June 2010, Blizzard was still

not confirming any such plans. Though they have stated they will "address the needs of location-based pro tournaments" in a post-patch launch, many do not expect this to include LAN functionality reappearing (Kuchera 2010).

21. The only time I have heard e-sports ever mentioned at the annual Game Developer's Conference was, in fact, in a 2008 talk by Rob Pardo, vice president of game design at Blizzard, when he actually put e-sports in one of his slides when talking about the future of games.

22. The World Series of Video Games (WSVG) was an interesting example of a tournament that allowed a preapproved mod but I was always unsure of Blizzard's stance on this. Unfortunately Della Bitta was not able to recollect this specific example and so could not comment on it.

23. Instances of third-party gold sellers, character auctioning, or contentious commercial software "add-ons" like WoWGlider offered similar skirmishes, however (Dibbell 2006, Grimmelmann 2006, Lastowka 2010).

24. As one team owner said to me regarding the sometimes perplexing difficulty in negotiating broadcast licenses: "I was laughing at how ironic it can be. Right now we have trouble getting developers to sign off on TV rights. I mean like it takes months, and lawyers, and to me it's like, if I had a video game and a company comes up like, 'we want to put your video game on TV' I'd be like, here you go, how can I help you? All these companies are whoa, whoa, you've got to talk to our lawyers."

25. KeSPA has drawn criticism from fans and players over the years for the ways they themselves assert a tremendous amount of authority over how e-sports are handled in South Korea. They are definitely not seen as an innocent party but often heavily criticized for overextending their control and management of South Korean e-sports. For example, in a post at Gosu Gamers, a popular *Starcraft* and *Warcraft* website, the assertion is made that KeSPA actually prohibited some *Starcraft 2* exhibition matches from being broadcast and regularly seeks to regulate where its registered players compete (XATMO8G 2009). Anecdotes like this abound and at the minimum the reputation of KeSPA is mixed in the community.

26. The disputes around the copyrighting of yoga moves are particularly fascinating. See, for example, Susman 2004.

27. In addition to the sidelining of KeSPA, it is also unclear what will happen with tournaments and broadcasts that have taken place via outlets like OnGameNet and MBCGame, also longtime organizers in the South Korean scene. There is speculation that Gretech-GomTV will cut subsidiary deals with these outlets.

28. See Ernkvist and Ström (2008) for an analysis of Chinese governmental action in developing their online gaming industry.

29. The original founding teams were 4Kings, Fnatic, Made in Brasil, Mousesports, Ninjas in Pajamas, SK Gaming, and Team 3D. As of August 2010 the current member

teams are Fnatic, Made in Brasil, Mousesports, SK Gaming, Complexity, and Team EG. Craig Levine is listed as an "individual" member.

30. The ESWC's founder Matthieu Dallon, in an interview at Fragster.se, stated, "Even though I have no personal liability in that process of payment, I do my best to make it happen. I help the liquidator to find the best new business owner. I help him to give the best values to all the company's assets. Then, in the best scenario, two possibilities: the liquidator directly pays the prizes with the money gathered at the end of the liquidation, or the new business owner pays the prizes as single debt of ESWC to cover" (Donschen 2009).

31. Often this is due to a tournament default on prize payouts making its way down the food chain, though as one owner commented to me, "The fact that they're using tournament money commissions to pay bills is not illegitimate but means that they're in a funding crunch. That's what it tells me."

32. In addition to salary problems, there are also sometimes quite fraught, acrimonious labor disputes between teams over players. In a particularly well-publicized dispute—between the two G7 members Fnatic and SK Gaming no less—we could see the contentious fight for a player unfold not only on various e-sports news sites, but on the team websites themselves.

Chapter 5

1. White (2006) raises a similar issue for Internet studies, prompting a consideration of ways to bring notions of watching and spectatorship back into the conversation.

2. We could go even further back and think about pinball machines and the same dynamic at work.

3. Perhaps the most notable exception to the Internet being the sole locus of fandom in e-sports is found in South Korea where professional computer gaming magazines can be found.

4. As one pro *CS* player put it to me, the loudness and intensity of his fellow players made them engaging for spectators while "You look at the *World of Warcraft* players and, no offence, but a lot of the time they're just quiet little kids that get angry at each other and don't know how to be a team."

5. In an interesting twist on what happens with this functionality, though, is the issue of the regulation of game broadcasting. Fans have been known to bypass rules about broadcasting, piping out a competition via one of these sites and allowing other viewers access to a match they should not have been able to view. This happened most recently at an ESL demonstration event, where KeSPA did not want the match with one of its top players being broadcast back into South Korea (Motion 2010). The trend is also occurring within English Premier League football, resulting

in skirmishes between spectators, clubs, and broadcasters (see Birmingham and David 2011).

6. Devastation, started in 2005, is another event with a strong fighting game component though they have included a number of other titles such as *Quake Live, Call of Duty,* and even *Madden NFL*. For a close read of the fighting game culture see Harper 2010.

7. I am somewhat torn about using the term "circuit" in the context of e-sports since there is not much large-scale coordination between tournaments (outside of regional qualifiers). As one long-time broadcaster noted to me about the diversity of approaches to how things are done and the general heterogeneity in the scene, "I don't think there is a pro circuit as such. I think we are getting closer to Grand Slams." Nonetheless I will here use the term to indicate a collection of higher-level tournaments that very often the same handful of teams fly around the world to participate in.

8. The 2010 Grand Final boasted a total of 400 "media representatives" at the event, for example.

9. This often leads to odd choices of entertainment between matches including theatrical dance pieces or comedy routines meant to entertain a broad audience. I can't count the number of times I've watched top players and e-sports participants chuckle in amusement at these strange turns of event planning.

10. Game Research (2002) sketched out some of the basic issues as well, noting that the difficulties of third person views and complex visual fields (including icons) create spectatorship challenges.

11. Perhaps ironically, however, *DoA* is sometimes a contested fighting title within the scene. As one e-sports commentator put it, "It's a little bit of an older game. It's not really the most popular fighter. There are certain aspects of it that make it a little less technical. And it's like, it's basically like the countering system which is if you throw a mid-punch I can do something to counter that and it'll hurt you instead obviously. And at that point it really becomes a guessing game. You know, are you going to throw a mid-punch or a low kick? So it's almost like, there's not as much technical skill involved as it is knowing your opponent. That, combined with it being a little older game, so it's a little frowned down on by like, the hardcore within the fighting community."

12. Kane in fact suggests that DirectTV envisioned "something glitzy in mind, something more like a game show. They wanted a set to echo *Who Wants to be a Millionaire* with gamers facing each other in seats on elevated stages. They envisioned a crowd-stirring emcee and player entrances through smoke and lights, like a smaller-scale *WWE Fight Night SmackDown!* But with the dust-up inside computers instead of in a wrestling ring" (2008, 210). Reading this with an eye on my fieldnotes I'd stay they about nailed it.

13. It is, of course, worth noting that South Korean game broadcasters have tackled these same challenges.

14. Given some negative feedback I'd heard from Europeans about the CGS and its setup, I queried whether they felt there were any cross-cultural limits to the way the CGS was staging the matches. Burks's take on it was, "I thought about that when I was in the early stages of this. I talked to a lot of people about it because I was concerned about, you know, cross-culture [...] And the conclusion with most everyone I talked to is that American culture is devoured overseas. So don't try and overthink this thing. Use it just like you will produce it and you know, Levi's doesn't make different Levi's for Asia or Fender doesn't make different guitars for Asia" (Personal communication, 2008).

15. Interestingly there is an initiative, the *CSPromod*, that is trying to address these challenges. As their website states, "The objective of *CSPromod* is to improve the graphical quality, feature set, and spectatorship of *Counter-Strike*, while preserving the title's beloved gameplay, and in doing so provide community [sic] with the assurance of unlimited gameplay longevity." A number of people involved in the project have deep ties to the pro scene.

16. The only irony here, one the commentator is certainly aware of, is that because Jonathan "Fatal1ty" Wendel has been so active in building himself as a brand he is probably one of the few players there is actually any detailed history on.

17. See Rader 1984 for a particularly critical account of the influence.

18. For an in-depth consideration of baseball's evolution, for example, see Morris 2006 or Goldstein 1989.

19. In one of the more interesting twists on what happens as athletes integrate digital gameplay into their lives, Etkowicz (2008), jumping off the example of Detroit Tigers pitcher Joel Zumaya being unable to compete because of an injury from playing *Guitar Hero*, speculates about the potential inclusion of computer gaming on the list of prohibited activities clauses in pro player contracts.

Chapter 6

1. For a discussion of the variety of ways player communities are themselves involved in this dance between globalization and localization, see Benjamin Wai-ming Ng's 2009 piece on Japanese combat games in Hong Kong.

Bibliography

Aarseth, Espen. 1997. *Cybertext: Perspectives on Ergodic Literature.* Baltimore: Johns Hopkins University Press.

Adams, Ernest, and Andrew Rollings. 2007. *Fundamentals of Game Design.* Upper Saddle River, NJ: Pearson Prentice Hall.

Ali, Mahmood. 2007. "World Cyber Games 2007: International Disgrace at the Grand Finals." *Global Gaming League,* October 9. http://wire.ggl.com/e-sports/world-cyber-games-2007-international-disgrace-at-the-grand-finals.

Altheide, David L. and Robert P. Snow. 1978. "Sports versus the Mass Media." *Urban Life* 7 (2): 189–204.

Andrews, Stuart. 2009. "Does Professional Gaming Have a Future?" *Bit-Tech.net,* April 10. http://www.bit-tech.net/gaming/2009/04/10/the-future-of-professional-gaming/1.

Bambauer, Derek. 2005. "Legal Responses to the Challenges of Sports Patents." *Harvard Journal of Law and Technology* 18 (2): 401–433.

Baasanjav, Undrahbuyan. 2010. "Chess for Girls – Revisited Online". Paper presented at *The Association of Internet Researchers (AoIR) Conference,* Gothenburg, Sweden.

Bayliss, Peter. 2007. "Notes Toward a Sense of Embodied Gameplay." In *Situated Play: Proceedings of the Digital Games Research Association (DiGRA) Conference 2007,* ed. Akira Baba. Tokyo. http://www.digra.org/dl/db/07312.19059.pdf.

Becker, Howard. 1963. *Outsiders: Studies in the Sociology of Deviance.* New York, N.Y.: The Free Press.

Becker, Howard. 2008. *Art Worlds.* Berkeley and Los Angeles: University of California Press.

Beyond the Game (film). 2008. Dieptescherpte.

Bigham, Lucas. 2007. "Starcraft: Controversy in Group F." *GotFrag,* October 5. http://www.gotfrag.com/star/story/40190.

Biocca, Frank. 1997. "The Cyborg's Dilemma: Progressive Embodiment in Virtual Environments." *Journal of Computer-Mediated Communication* 3 (2). http://jcmc.indiana.edu/vol3/issue2/biocca2.html.

Birmingham, Jack, and Matthew David. 2011. "Live-streaming: Will Football Fans Continue to be More Law Abiding than Music Fans?" *Sport in Society* 14 (1): 69–80.

Blizzard. 2010a. "World of Warcraft Terms of Use Agreement." *Blizzard.com.* http://www.worldofwarcraft.com/legal/termsofuse.html.

Blizzard. 2010b. "World of Warcraft Subscriber Base Reaches 12 Million Worldwide." *Blizzard.com.* http://us.blizzard.com/en-us/company/press/pressreleases.html?101007.

Boellstorff, Tom. 2008. *Coming of Age in Second Life.* Princeton: Princeton University Press.

Bolin, Anne, and Jane Granskog, eds. 2003. *Athletic Intruders: Ethnographic Research on Women, Culture, and Exercise.* Albany: State University of New York Press.

Boyden, Bruce E. 2010. "Games and Other Uncopyrightable Systems." *Marquette Unviersity Law School Legal Studies Research Paper Series,* Research Paper No. 10-11. http://ssrn.com/abstract=1580079.

Brand, Stewart. 1972. "Spacewar: Fanatic Life and Symbolic Death Among the Computer Bums." *Rolling Stone,* 7 December.

Brower, Jonathan J. 1977."Motives for Owning a Professional Athletic Team." *Journal of Sport and Social Issues* 1 (17): 17–51.

Bryant, Jennings, and Andrea M. Holt. 2006. "A Historical Overview of Sports and Media in the United States." In *Handbook of Sports and Media,* ed. Arthur A. Raney and Jennings Bryant, 22–46. New Jersey: Lawrence Erlbaum.

Bryce, Jo, and Jason Rutter. 2002. "Killing Like a Girl: Gendered Gaming and Girl Gamers' Visibility." In *Computer Games and Digital Cultures (CGDC) Conference Proceedings,* ed. Frans Mayra. Tampere: Tampere University Press.

Bucholtz, Mary. 1998. "Geek the Girl: Language, Femininity, and Female Nerds." In *Gender and Belief Systems: Proceedings of the Fourth Berkeley Women and Language Conference,* eds. Natasha Warner, Jocelyn Ahlers, Leela Bilmes, Monica Oliver, Suzanne Wertheim and Melinda Chen. Berkeley, CA: Berkeley Women and Language Group.

Bucholtz, Mary. 2002. "Geek Feminism." In *Gendered Practices in Language,* ed. Sarah Benor, Mary Rose, Devyani Sharma, Julie Sweetland, and Qing Zhang, 277–307. Stanford, CA: CSLI.

Burrill, Derek A. 2008. *Die Tryin': Videogames, Masculinity, Culture*. New York: Peter Lang.

Butler, Judith. 1990. *Gender Trouble: Feminism and the Subversion of Identity*. New York: Routledge.

Cahn, Susan K. 1994. *Coming on Strong: Gender and Sexuality in Twentieth-Century Women's Sports*. Cambridge, MA: Harvard University Press.

Caillois, Roger. 2001. *Man, Play, and Games*. Translated by Meyer Barash. Urbana: University of Illinois Press.

Call of Duty (game). 2003. Infinity Ward.

Caoili, Eric. 2009. "Major League Gaming Picks Up $7.5M For Competitive Gaming." *Gamasutra*, January 12. http://www.gamasutra.com/view/news/21817/Major_League_Gaming_Picks_Up_75M_For_Competitive_Gaming.php.

Cassell, Justine, and Henry Jenkins, eds. 1998. *From Barbie to Mortal Kombat: Gender and Computer Games*. Cambridge, MA: MIT Press.

Chaloner, Paul. 2009. "So You Want to Be a Shoutcaster?" *The Shoutcaster*. http://www.theshoutcaster.co.uk/site/index.php/so-you-want-to-be-a-shoutcaster.

Chasing Ghosts: Beyond the Arcade (film). 2007. Men At Work Pictures LLC.

Chee, Florence. 2006. "The Games We Play Online and Offline: Making Wang-tta in Korea." *Popular Communication* 4 (3): 225–239.

Chimot, Caroline, and Catherine Louveau. 2010."Becoming a Man while Playing a Female Sport: The Construction of Masculine Identity in Boys Doing Rhythmic Gymnastics." *International Review for the Sociology of Sport* 45 (4): 436–456.

Choi, Jennifer. 2002. "No Room for Cheers: Schizophrenic Application in the Realm of Right of Publicity Protection." *Villanova Sports and Entertainment Law Journal* 9: 121–153.

Chosun. 2007. "Korean Navy to Launch Online Game Team." *The Chosun Ilbo*, July 2. http://english.chosun.com/w21data/html/news/200707/200707020011.html.

Chung, Peichi. 2009. "The Dynamics of New Media Globalization in Asia: A Comparative Study of Online Gaming Industries in South Korea and Singapore." In *Gaming Cultures and Place in Asia-Pacific*, ed. Larissa Hjorth and Dean Chan, 58–81. New York: Routledge.

Cianfrone, Beth A., and Thomas A. Baker III. 2010. "The Use of Student-Athlete Likenesses in Sport Video Games: An Application of the Right of Publicity." *Journal of Legal Aspects of Sport* 20: 35–74.

Clement, Annie. 2000. "Contemporary Copyright and Patent Law and Sport." *Journal of Legal Aspects of Sport* 10 (3): 143–153.

Cole, Corin. 2008. "The Fall of CGS." *Cadred.org*, December 2. http://www.cadred.org/News/Article/45243.

Collins, Harry. 1990. *Artificial Experts: Social Knowledge and Intelligent Machines*. Cambridge, MA: MIT Press.

Collins, Harry, and Martin Kusch. 1998. *The Shape of Actions: What Humans and Machines Can Do*. Cambridge, MA: MIT Press.

Connell, R. W. 1995. *Masculinities*. Cambridge, UK: Polity Press.

Connell, R. W. 2001. "The Social Organization of Masculinity." In *The Masculinities Reader*, ed. Stephen Whitehead and Frank Barrett, 30–50. Cambridge, UK: Polity.

Connell, R. W., and James Messerschmidt. 2005. "Hegemonic Masculinity: Rethinking the Concept." *Gender and Society* 19 (6): 829.

Connor, James. 2009. "The Athlete as Widget: How Exploitation Explains Elite Sport." *Sport in Society* 12 (10): 1369–1377.

Consalvo, Mia. 2003. "The Monsters Next Door: Media Constructions of Boys and Masculinity." *Feminist Media Studies* 3 (1): 27–45.

Consalvo, Mia. 2007. *Cheating: Gaining Advantage in Videogames*. Cambridge, MA: MIT Press.

Consalvo, Mia. 2009. "Hardcore Casual: Game Culture Return(s) to Ravenhearst." In *Proceedings of the 4th International Conference on Foundations of Digital Games*, ed. R. Michael Young. Orlando, FL: ACM Press.

Consalvo, Mia. Forthcoming. "The Future of Game Studies." In *Media Studies Futures*, ed. Kelly Gates. Malden, MA: Blackwell Publishing.

Conway, Steven. 2010. "'It's in the Game' and Above the Game." *Convergence* 16 (3): 334-354.

Coombe, Rosemary J. 1998. *The Cultural Life of Intellectual Properties: Authorship, Appropriation, and the Law*. Durham, NC: Duke University Press.

Copier, Marinka. 2005. "Connecting Worlds: Fantasy Role-Playing Games, Ritual Acts and the Magic Circle." In *Changing Views: Proceedings of the Digital Games Research Association (DiGRA) Conference 2005*, eds. Suzanne de Castell and Jennifer Jenson. Vancouver: University of Vancouver.

Costikyan, Greg. 2010. "Fluxus Games." *Playthisthing.com*, October 5. http://playthisthing.com/fluxus-games.

Counter-Strike (game). 2000. Valve Corporation.

Crawford, Garry. 2005. "Digital Gaming, Sport, and Gender." *Leisure Studies* 24 (3): 259–270.

Crawford, Garry, and Jason Rutter. 2007. "Playing the Game: Performance in Digital Game Audiences." In *Fandom: Identities and Communities in a Mediated World*, ed. Jonathan Gray, Cornel Sandvoss, and C. Lee Harrington, 271–281. New York: New York University Press.

Crawford, Garry, and Victoria K. Gosling. 2009. "More Than a Game: Sports-Themed Video Games and Player Narratives." *Sociology of Sport Journal* 26: 50–66.

D'Agostino, F. 1981. "The Ethos of Games." *Journal of the Philosophy of Sport* VIII: 7–18.

De Paoli, Stefano, and Aphra Kerr. 2010. "The Assemblage of Cheating: How to Study Cheating as Imbroglio in MMORPGs." *Fibreculture*. http://sixteen.fibreculturejournal.org.

Dead or Alive (game). 1996. Team Ninja.

Dibbell, Julian. 1998. *My Tiny Life*. New York: Henry Holt.

Dibbell, Julian. 2006. *Play Money: Or, How I Quit My Day Job and Made Millions Trading Virtual Loot*. New York: Basic Books.

DiSalvo, Betsy James, Kevin Crowley, and Roy Norwood. 2008. "Learning in Context: Digital Games and Young Black Men." *Games and Culture* 3: 131–141.

DiSalvo, Betsy James, Kevin Crowley, Roy Norwood, Mark Guzdail, Tom Mcklin, Charles Meadows, Kenneth Perry, Corey Steward, and Amy Bruckman. 2009. "Glitch Game Testers: African American Men Breaking Open the Console." In *Breaking New Ground: Innovation in Games, Play, Practice and Theory: Proceedings of the 2009 Digital Games Research Association conference*, eds. Barry Atkins, Helen Kennedy, and Tanya Krzywinska. London.

Doom (game). 1993. id Software.

Donschen, David. 2009. "Interview with Matthieu Dallon." *Fragster*, May 11. http://www.fragster.de/de/esport/szene/artikel/09/05/interview-with-matthieu-dallon-games-services-has-almost-always-lost-money_szene.html.

Douglas, Susan. 1999. *Listening In: Radio and the American Imagination*. New York: Times Books.

Dovey, Jon, and Helen W. Kennedy. 2006. *Game Cultures: Computer Games as New Media*. New York: Open University Press.

Dreyfus, Hubert. 1972. *What Computers Can't Do*. New York: Harper & Row.

Dunbar-Hester, Christina. 2008. "Geeks, Meta-Geeks, and Gender Trouble: Activism, Identity, and Low-Power FM Radio." *Social Studies of Science* 38: 201–232.

Dyer-Witheford, Nick, and Greig de Peuter. 2009. *Games of Empire: Global Capitalism and Video Games*. Minneapolis: University of Minnesota Press.

E-@thletes (film). 2008. Magnus Caput Productions.

Eglash, Ron. 2002. "Race, Sex, and Nerds: From Black Geeks to Asian American Hipsters." *Social Text* 71, 20 (2): 49–64.

Ernkvist, Mirko, and Patrik Ström. 2008. "Enmeshed in Games with the Government." *Games and Culture* 3 (1): 98–126.

Etkowicz, Jonathan M. 2008. "Professional Athletes Playing Video Games: The Next Prohibited 'Other Activity?'" *Villanova Sports and Entertainment Law Journal* 15: 65–101.

EverQuest (game). 1999. Sony Online Entertainment.

Fausto-Sterling, Anne. 1985. *Myths of Gender: Biological Theories About Women and Men.* New York: Basic Books

Fausto-Sterling, Anne. 2000. *Sexing the Body: Gender Politics and the Construction of Sexuality.* New York: Basic Books.

Fetscherin, Marc, Charis Kaskiris, and Frederik Wallenberg. 2005. "Gaming or Sharing at LAN-parties: What Is Going On?" In *Proceedings of the First International Conference on Automated Production of Cross Media Content for Multi-Channel Distribution*, eds. Paolo Nesi, Kia Ng, and Jaime Delgado. Florence, Italy: Firenze University Press.

FIFA (game). 1993. Electronic Arts.

Fincham, Ben. 2007. "'Generally Speaking People Are In It For the Cycling and the Beer': Bicycle Couriers, Subculture and Enjoyment." *The Sociological Review* 55 (2): 189–202.

Fincham, Ben. 2008. "Balance is Everything: Bicycle Messengers, Work and Leisure." *Sociology* 42 (4): 618–634.

Frag (film). 2008. Cohesion Productions.

G7. 2009a. "G7 Teams Working to Resolve Prize Money." *G7*, September 11. http://www.g7teams.com/page/news/39.

G7. 2009b. "G7 Teams Pursuit of Prize Money Update." *G7*, November 16. http://www.g7teams.com/page/news/41..

G7. 2009c. "G7 Teams Launch Online Petition To Collect Owed Prize Money." *G7*, December 23. http://www.g7teams.com/page/news/47.

G7. 2010a. "About G7." *G7*. http://www.g7teams.com/page/aboutg7.

G7. 2010b. "G7 Teams Announce ESWC 2010 Action Plan." *G7*, June 30. http://www.g7teams.com/page/news/48.

Game Research. 2002. "Pro Gamers: United States, United Kingdom and the Nordic Countries." *Game Research*. http://www.game-research.com.

Gaudiosi, John. 2007. "Is Pro Gaming the Next Poker?" *ESPN.com*, April 24. http://sports.espn.go.com/espn/print?id=2848261&type=story.

Geertz, Clifford. 1973. *The Interpretation of Cultures*. New York, NY: Basic Books.

Giddings, Seth. 2007. "Playing with Non-humans: Digital Games as Technocultural Form." In *Worlds in Play: International Perspectives on Digital Games Research*, ed. Suzanne de Castell and Jen Jensen, 115–128. New York: Peter Lang.

Giddings, Seth, and Helen Kennedy. 2008. "Little Jesuses and *@#?-off Robots: On Cybernetics, Aesthetics, and Not Being Very Good at Lego Star Wars." In *The Pleasures of Computer Gaming*, ed. Melanie Swalwell and Jason Wilson, 13–32. Jefferson, N.C.: McFarland.

Gillespie, Dair L., Ann Leffler, and Elinor Lerner. 2002. "If It Weren't For My Hobby, I'd Have a Life: Dog Sports, Serious Leisure, and Boundary Negotiations." *Leisure Studies* 21: 285–304.

Goffman, Erving. 1959. *The Presentation of Self in Everyday Life*. New York: Anchor Books.

Goldberg, Ryan. 2009. "Virtual Leagues Fold, Forcing Gamers to Find Actual Jobs." *New York Times*, April 1.

Goldstein, Warren. 1989. *Playing for Keeps: A History of Early Baseball*. Ithaca: Cornell.

Griffith, Wm. Tucker. 1997. "Beyond the Perfect Score: Protecting Routine-Oriented Athletic Performance with Copyright Law." *Connecticut Law Review* 30: 675–730.

Griggs, Gerald. 2011. "'This Must Be the Only Sport in the World Where Most of the Players Don't Know the Rules:' Operationalizing Self-refereeing and the Spirit of the Game in UK Ultimate Frisbee." *Sport in Society* 14 (1): 97–110.

Grimmelmann, James. 2006. "Virtual Borders: The Interdependence of Real and Virtual Worlds." *First Monday*. 11 (2). http://firstmonday.org/htbin/cgiwrap/bin/ojs/index.php/fm/article/view/1312/1232.

Gruneau, Richard. 2007. "Problems of Agency and Freedom in Play, Games, and Sport." In *The Sport Studies Reader*, ed. Alan Tomlinson, 36–41. London: Routledge.

Halberstam, Judith. 1998. *Female Masculinity*. Durham: Duke University Press.

Half-Life (game). 1998. Valve Corporation.

Hargreaves, Jennifer. 1994. *Sporting Females: Critical Issues in the History and Sociology of Women's Sports*. London: Routledge.

Harper, Todd. 2010. *The Art of War: Fighting Games, Performativity, and Social Game Play*. PhD Dissertation, Ohio University.

Hertzberg Johnson, Birgit. 2000. "The Internet Generation and 'The Gathering.'" Workshop paper for *Doomed to Free Choice* workshop. Dubrovnik, May 22–28. http://publications.uu.se/journals/1651-0593/114.pdf.

Herz, J. C. 1997. *Joystick Nation: How Videogames Ate Our Quarters, Won Our Hearts, and Rewired Our Minds*. New York: Little, Brown and Company.

Hicks, Bobby. 2009. "WCG Ultimate Gamer." *Complexity Gaming*, March 17. http://www.complexitygaming.com/index.php?c=news&id=610.

Hills, Matt. 2002. *Fan Cultures*. New York, NY: Routledge.

Hjorth, Larissa, and Dean Chan. 2009. "Locating the Game." In *Gaming Cultures and Place in Asia-Pacific*, ed. Larissa Hjorth and Dean Chan, 1–18. New York: Routledge.

Hornby, Nick. 1995. *High Fidelity*. New York: Riverhead Books.

Hruby, Patrick. 2007. "So You Wanna Be a Professional Video Game Player?" *ESPN.com*, October 7. http://sports.espn.go.com/espn/page2/story?page=hruby/071008.

Hughes, Linda. 2006. "Beyond the Rules of the Game: Why are Rooie Rules Nice?" In *The Game Design Reader*, ed. Katie Salen and Eric Zimmerman, 504–517. Cambridge, MA: MIT Press.

Hunh, Jun-Sok. 2008. "Culture and Business of PC Bangs in Korea." *Games and Culture* 3 (1): 26–37.

Hutchins, Brett. 2008. "Signs of Meta-change in Second Modernity: The Growth of E-sport and the World Cyber Games." *New Media and Society* 10 (6): 851–869.

Hutchinson, Rachael. 2007. "Performing the Self: Subverting the Binary in Combat Games." *Games and Culture* 2 (4): 283–299.

Hyun-cheol, Kim. 2010. "StarCraft Rigging Scandal Hits e-Sports Industry." *Korea Times*, April 15. http://www.koreatimes.co.kr/www/news/tech/2010/07/129_64247.html.

I Got Next (film). 2011. Mattoid Entertainment.

International E-Sports/Entertainment Festival. 2008. "News Centre." http://www.e-ief.com.

Iszatt-White, Marian. 2007. "Catching Them At It: An Ethnography of Rule Violation." *Ethnography* 8 (4): 445–465.

Jakobsson, Mikael. 2007. "Playing with the Rules: Social and Cultural Aspects of Game Rules in a Console Game Club." In *Situated Play: Proceedings of the Digital*

Games Research Association (DiGRA) Conference 2007, ed. Akira Baba. Tokyo: University of Tokyo.

Jakobsson, Mikael. 2011. "The Achievement Machine: Understanding Xbox 360 Achievements in Gaming Practices." *Game Studies* 11 (1). http://gamestudies.org/1101/articles/jakobsson.

Jansz, Jeroen, and Lonneke Martens. 2005. "Gaming at a LAN Event: The Social Context of Playing Video Games." *New Media and Society* 7 (3): 333–355.

Jenkins, Henry. 1992. *Textual Poachers: Television Fans and Participatory Culture*. New York, NY: Routledge.

Jin, Dal Yong. 2010. *Korea's Online Gaming Empire*. Cambridge, MA: MIT Press.

Jin, Dal Yong, and Florence Chee. 2008. "Age of New Media Empires: A Critical Interpretation of the Korean Online Game Industry." *Games and Culture* 3 (1): 38–58.

Jin, Dal Yong, and Florence Chee. 2009. "The Politics of Online Gaming." In *Gaming Cultures and Place in Asia-Pacific*, ed. Larissa Hjorth and Dean Chan, 19–38. New York: Routledge.

Jin-seo, Cho. 2008a. "Hanbit Founder Fades into Twilight." *Korea Times*, May 21.

Jin-seo, Cho. 2008b. "*StarCraft* Losing in Gaming League." *Korea Times*, May 19.

Johnson, John W. 1996. "In the Groove? The Legal War over Golf Clubs." In *Sports and the Law: Major Legal Cases*, ed. Charles E. Quirk, 97–110. New York: Garland Publishing.

Jonasson, Kalle, and Jesper Thiborg. 2010. "Electronic Sport and Its Impact on Future Sport." *Sport in Society* 13 (2): 287–299.

Jörissen, Benjamin. 2004. "Virtual Reality on the Stage: Performing Community at a LAN Party." In *Envision: The New Media Age and Everyday Life*, ed. Patrik Hernwall, 23–40. Stockholm: Stockholm University.

Juul, Jesper. 2005. *Half-Real: Video Games Between Real Rules and Fictional Worlds*. Cambridge, MA: MIT Press.

Juul, Jesper. 2010. *Casual Revolution*. Cambridge, MA: MIT Press.

Kafai, Yasmin, Carrie Heeter, Jill Denner, and Jennifer Y. Sun, eds. 2008. *Beyond Barbie® and Mortal Kombat: New Perspectives on Gender and Gaming*. Cambridge, MA: MIT Press.

Kane, Michael. 2008. *Game Boys: Professional Videogaming's Rise from the Basement to the Big Time*. London: Viking/Penguin Books.

Katz, Jackson. 1999. *Tough Guise: Violence, Media, and the Crisis in Masculinity*. Northampton, MA: Media Education Foundation.

Kay, Tess. 2003. "Sport and Gender." In *Sport and Society*, ed. Barrie Houlihan, 89–104. London: Sage.

Kelly, William H. 2002. "Training for Leisure: Karaoke and the Seriousness of Play in Japan." In *Japan at Play: The Ludic and the Logic of Power*, ed. Joy Hendry and Massimo Raveri, 152–168. London: Routledge.

Kendall, Lori. 2002. *Hanging Out in the Virtual Pub: Masculinities and Relationships Online*. Berkeley: University of California Press.

Kennedy, Helen. 2005. "Illegitimate, Monstrous, and Out There: Female Quake Players and Inappropriate Pleasures." In *Feminism in Popular Culture*, ed. Joanne Hallows and Rachel Mosley, 183–201. London: Berg.

Kerr, Aphra. 2003. "Women Just Want to Have Fun: A Study of Adult Female Players of Digital Games." In *Level Up Conference Proceedings*, eds. Marinka Copier and Joost Raessens. Utrecht, NL: Universiteit Utrect.

Kerr, Aphra. 2006. *The Business and Culture of Digital Games: Gamework/Gameplay*. London: Sage.

KeSPA. 2010. "[Update] KeSPA Speaks Out On Intellectual Property Rights." *Team Liquid*, May 4. http://www.teamliquid.net/forum/viewmessage.php?topic_id=123275.

KeSPA. n.d. "Purpose of Business." *KeSP.* http://www.e-sports.or.kr/about/Eng/about_20.kea?m_code=aboute_20.

Kieff, F. Scott, Robert G. Kramer, and Robert M. Kunstadt. 2008. "It's Your Turn, But It's My Move: Intellectual Property Protection For Sports 'Moves.'" *Santa Clara Computer and High-Technology Law Journal* 25: 765–785.

King, Brad, and John Borland. 2003. *Dungeons and Dreamers: The Rise of Computer Game Culture From Geek to Chic*. New York: McGraw-Hill.

King of Chinatown (film). 2010. Psycho Crusher Productions.

King of Kong (film). 2007. LargeLab.

Kinkema, Kathleen M., and Janet C. Harris. 1998. "MediaSport Studies: Key Research and Emerging Issues." In *MediaSport*, ed. Lawrence A, Wenner, 27–56. London: Routledge.

Kline, Stephen, Nick Dyer-Witheford, and Greig De Peuter. 2003. *Digital Play: The Interaction of Technology, Culture, and Marketing*. Montreal: McGill-Queen's University Press.

Klosterman, Chuck. 2009. *Eating the Dinosaur*. New York: Scribner.

Kolko, Jed, Charles Q. Strohm, and Ayanna Lonian. 2003a. *Hispanics and Blacks Game More*. Boston: Forrester Research.

Kolko, Jed, Charles Q. Strohm, and Ayanna Lonian. 2003b. *Marketing To America's Ethnic Minorities*. San Francisco: Forrester Research.

Korea Game Development and Promotion Institute. 2003. *The Rise of Korean Games: Guide to Korean Game Industry and Culture*. Seoul, Korea: Ministry of Culture and Tourism.

Korea Times. 2004a. "Computer Gaming Looking to Become Sports Power." *Korea Times*, July 24.

Korea Times. 2004b. "Samsung Sees Long-Term Gains With WCG Sponsorship." *Korea Times*, October 8.

Korea Times. 2007. "Korean Gamers Look to Europe." *Korea Times*, February 5.

Kuchera, Ben. 2010. "Why Lack of StarCraft 2 LAN Play Still Matters." Ars Technica, October 10. http://arstechnica.com/gaming/news/2010/07/why-lack-of-starcraft-2-lan-play-still-matters.ars.

Kücklich, Julian. 2009. "A Techno-Semiotic Approach to Cheating in Computer Games: Or How I Learned to Stop Worrying and Love the Machine." *Games and Culture* 4 (2): 158–159.

Kukkonen, Carl A. III. 1998. "Be a Good Sport and Refrain from Using My Patented Putt: Intellectual Property Protection for Sports Related Movements." *Journal of the Patent and Trademark Office Society* 80: 808–829.

Lahti, Martti. 2003. "As We Become Machines: Corporealized Pleasures in Video Games." In *The Video Game Theory Reader*, ed. Mark J. P. Wolf and Bernard Perron, 157–170. London: Routledge.

Lambert, Bruce. 2007. "He's 9 Years Old and a Video-game Circuit Star." *New York Times*, June 7. http://www.nytimes.com/2007/06/07/nyregion/07gamer.html.

Landström, Catharina. 2007. "Queering Feminist Technology Studies." *Feminist Theory* 8 (1): 7–26.

Laurendeau, Jason, and Carly Adams. 2010. "'Jumping Like a Girl': Discursive Silences, Exclusionary Practices and the Controversy Over Women's Ski Jumping." *Sport in Society* 13 (3): 431–447.

Laqueur, Thomas. 1990. *Making Sex: Body and Gender from the Greeks to Freud*. Cambridge, MA: Harvard University Press.

Lastowka, Greg. 2010. *Virtual Justice: The New Laws of Online Worlds*. New Haven: Yale University Press.

Latour, Bruno. 2005. *Reassembling the Social: An Introduction to Actor-Network Theory*. Oxford: Oxford University Press.

Lawler, Jennifer. 2002. *Punch! Why Women Participate in Violent Sports*. Terre Haute: Wise Publishing.

Leonard, David J. 2006. "Not a Hater, Just Keepin' It Real: The Importance of Race- and Gender-Based Game Studies." *Games and Culture* 1: 83–88.

Leonard, David J. 2008. "To the White Extreme in the Mainstream: Manhood and White Youth Culture in a Virtual Sports World." In *Youth Culture and Sport*, ed. Michael D. Giardina and Michele K. Donnelly, 91–112. New York: Routledge.

Light, Jennifer. 1999. "When Computers Were Women." *Technology and Culture* 40: 455–483.

Lin, Holin. 2008. "Body, Space, and Gendered Gaming Experiences: A Cultural Geography of Homes, Cybercafes, and Dormitories." In *Beyond Barbie® and Mortal Kombat: New Perspectives on Gender and Gaming*, ed. Yasmin Kafai, Carrie Heeter, Jill Denner, and Jennifer Y. Sun, 67–82. Cambridge, MA: MIT Press.

Lin, Holin, and Chuen-Tsai Sun. 2011. "The Role of Onlookers in Arcade Gaming: Frame Analysis of Public Behaviours." *Convergence* 17(2) 125–137.

Loland, Sigmund. 2002. *Fair Play in Sport: A Moral Norm System*. London: Routledge.

Lotter, Aline H. 1978. "Keeping the Illusion Alive: The Public Interest in Professional Sports." *Suffolk University Law Review* 12: 48–96.

Lowood, Henry. 2005a. "High-performance Play: The Making of Machinima." In *Videogames and Art: Intersections and Interactions*, ed. Andy Clarke and Grethe Mitchell, 59–79. Bristol: Intellect Books.

Lowood, Henry. 2005b. "Real-time Performance: Machinima and Game Studies." *International Digital Media and Arts Association Journal* 1 (3): 10–17.

Lowood, Henry. 2006. "Community Players: Gameplay as Public Performance and Cultural Artifact." Paper for Symbolic Systems Forum, March 9. Stanford: Stanford University.

Lowood, Henry. 2007. "'It's Not Easy Being Green': Real-Time Game Performance in Warcraft." In *Videogame/Player/Text*, ed. Barry Atkins and Tanya Krzywinska, 83–100. Manchester: Palgrave.

Lowood, Henry. Forthcoming. "'Beyond the Game': The Olympic Ideal and Competitive e-Sports." In *Play and Politics: Games, Civic Engagement, and Social Activism*, ed. Douglas Thomas and Joshua Fouts.

Malaby, Thomas. 2007. "Beyond Play: A New Approach to Games." *Games and Culture* 2 (2): 95–113.

MacDonald, Clifford N. 2004. "Gamecasts and *NBA v. Motorola*: Do They Still Love This Game?" *North Carolina Journal of Law and Technology* 5(2): 329–349.

Madden NFL (game). 1988. High Score Entertainment.

Malkan, Jeffrey. 2009. "Rule-Based Expression in Copyright Law." *Buffalo Law Review* 57: 433–509.

Matzkin, Matthew G. 2000. "Getting Played: How the Video Game Industry Violates College Athletes' Rights of Publicity by Not Paying for Their Likenesses." *Loyola of Los Angeles Entertainment Law Review* 21: 227–252.

McChesney, Robert. 1989. "Media Made Sport: A History of Sports Coverage in the United States." In *Media, Sports, and Society*, ed. Lawrence Wenner. Newbury Park, CA: Sage.

McCrea, Christian. 2009. "Watching Starcraft, Strategy and South Korea." In *Gaming Cultures and Place in Asia-Pacific*, ed. Larissa Hjorth and Dean Chan, 179–193. New York: Routledge.

Mccutcheon, Anderson. 2010. "Blizzard Drops KeSPA, Seizes Control of StarCraft 2's Future." *SC2 Blog*, April 28. http://www.sc2blog.com/2010/04/28/blizzard-drops-kespa-seizes-control-of-starcraft-2s-future.

McDonagh, Eileen, and Laura Pappano. 2008. *Playing with the Boys: Why Separate is Not Equal in Sports*. Oxford: Oxford University Press.

Medler, Ben. 2009. "Generations of Game Analytics, Achievements and High Scores." *Eludamos* 3 (2): 177–194. http://journals.sfu.ca/eludamos/index.php/eludamos/article/viewArticle/66/127.

Mennesson, Christine. 2009. "Being a Man in Dance: Socialization Modes and Gender Identities." *Sport in Society* 12 (2): 174–195.

Messner, Michael. 1989. "Masculinities and Athletic Careers." *Gender and Society* 3: 71–88.

Messner, Michael. 1990. "Boyhood, Organized Sports, and the Construction of Masculinities." *Journal of Contemporary Ethnography* 18 (4): 416–444.

Miraa (Luis Mira). 2009. "I Fear for eSports." *Meet Your Makers*, August 18. http://www.mymym.com/en/article/943.html.

MLG Admin. 2006a. "MLG Awards $1.75 Million in Contracts for Top Pro Players." *Major League Gaming*, December 18. http://www.majorleaguegaming.com/news/mlg-awards-1-75-million-in-contracts-for-top-pro-gamers-2.

MLG Admin. 2006b. "MLG Secures $25 Million From Oak Investment Partners." *Major League Gaming*, December 15. http://www.majorleaguegaming.com/news/mlg-secures-25-million-from-oak-investment-partners.

MLG Admin. 2009. "Major League Gaming Secures $10 Million in Series A Financing from Ritchie Capital to Build World's First Professional Video Game League." *Major League Gaming,* May 8. http://www.majorleaguegaming.com/news/mlg-secures-10-million-in-series-a-financing-from-ritchie-capital-to-build-worlds-first-professional-video-game-league.

Moberg, Brent C. 2003. "Football Play Scripts: A Potential Pitfall for Federal Copyright Law?" *Marquette Sports Law Review* 14: 525–550.

Moeller, Ryan M., Bruce Esplin, and Steven Conway. 2009. "Cheesers, Pullers, and Glitchers: The Rhetoric of Sportsmanship and the Discourse of Online Sports Gamers." *Game Studies,* 9 (2). http://gamestudies.org/0902/articles/moeller_esplin_conway.

Montaner, Danny. 2008 *The Art of fRoD*. http://www.tao-frod.com.

Montola, Markus. 2009. "The Invisible Rules of Role-Playing: The Social Framework of Role-Playing Process." *International Journal of Role Playing* 1 (1): 22–36.

Morris, Peter. 2006. *A Game of Inches: The Stories Behind the Innovations that Shaped Baseball.* Chicago: Ivan R. Dee.

Mortensen, Torill Elvira. 2008. "Humans Playing World of Warcraft: or Deviant Strategies?" In *Digital Culture, Play, and Identity: A World of Warcraft® Reader,* ed. Hilde G. Corneliussen and Jill Walker Rettberg, 103–124. Cambridge, MA: MIT Press.

Motion. 2010. "Did KeSPA cancel TLO vs Nada at IEM?" *Team Liquid* forum post, August 21. http://www.teamliquid.net/forum/viewmessage.php?topic_id=146083.

MrHoon. 2010. "Match Fixing Players All Banned By KeSPA." *Team Liquid* forum post, June 7. http://www.teamliquid.net/forum/viewmessage.php?topic_id=129893.

Myers, David. 2010. *Play Redux: The Form of Computer Games.* Ann Arbor: University of Michigan Press.

Nakamura, Lisa. Forthcoming. "'It's a Nigger in Here! Kill the Nigger!': User-Generated Media Campaigns against Racism, Sexism, and Homophobia in Digital Games." In *Media Studies Futures,* ed. Kelly Gates. New York: Blackwell.

Newman, James. 2002. "In Search of the Videogame Player." *New Media and Society* 4 (3): 405–422.

Newman, James. 2004. *Videogames.* New York: Routledge.

Newman, James. 2008. *Playing With Videogames.* New York: Routledge.

Ng, Benjamin Wai-Ming. 2009. "Consuming and Localizing Japanese Combat Games in Hong Kong." In *Gaming Cultures and Place in Asia-Pacific,* ed. Larissa Hjorth and Dean Chan. New York: Routledge.

Nordli, Hege. 2003. "The Gathering Experience. A User Study of a Computer Party," *SIGIS Report*. http://pdf.textfiles.com/academics/sigis_d04_2.01_ntnu1.pdf.

Olsen, Lars "cYaN." 2009. "GosuCup number five." *GosuGamers*, February 3. http://www.gosugamers.net/starcraft/news/9524-gosucup-number-five.

Otten, Martin. 2001. "Broadcasting Virtual Games on the Internet." Unpublished paper. http://www.slipgate.de/download/BroadcastingVirtualGames.pdf.

Pascoe, C. J. 2007. *Dude You're a Fag: Masculinity and Sexuality in High School*. Berkeley: University of California Press.

Perrow, Charles. 1984. *Normal Accidents: Living with High Risk Technologies*. Princeton, NJ: Princeton University Press.

Poole, Stephen. 2000. *Trigger Happy: Videogames and the Entertainment Revolution*. New York: Arcade Publishing.

Prettyman, Keith A. 1976. "The True Story of What Happens When the Big Kids Say, 'It's My Football, and You'll Either Play By My Rules or You Won't Play At All.'" *Nebraska Law Review* 55 (2): 335–361.

Quake (game). 1996. id Software.

Quinn, James W., and Irwin H. Warren. 1983. "Professional Team Sports New Legal Arena: Television and the Player's Right of Publicity." *Indiana Law Review* 16: 487–516.

Rader, Benjamin G. 1984. *In Its Own Image: How Television Has Transformed Sports*. New York: The Free Press.

Rambusch, Jana, Peter Jakobsson, and Daniel Pargman. 2007. "Exploring E-sports: A Case Study of Gameplay in Counter-Strike." In *Situated Play: Proceedings of the Digital Games Research Association (DiGRA) Conference 2007*, ed. Akira Baba. Tokyo: University of Tokyo.

Real, Michael R. 1998. "MediaSport: Technology and the Commodification of Postmodern Sport." In *MediaSport*, ed. Lawrence A. Wenner, 14–26. London: Routledge.

Reeves, Stuart, Barry Brown, and Eric Laurier. 2009. "Experts at Play: Understanding Skilled Expertise." *Games and Culture* 4 (3): 205–227.

Rinehart, Robert E. 2008. "Exploiting a New Generation: Corporate Branding and the Co-optation of Action Sport." In *Youth Culture and Sport*, ed. Michael D. Giardina and Michele K. Donnelly. New York: Routledge.

Rowe, David, Jim McKay, and Toby Miller. 1998. "Come Together: Sport, Nationalism, and the Media Image." In *MediaSport*, ed. Lawrence A. Wenner, 119–133. London: Routledge.

Salen, Katie, and Eric Zimmerman. 2003. *Rules of Play*. Cambridge, MA: MIT Press.

Schiesel, Seth. 2006. "The Land of the Video Geek." *The New York Times*, October 8.

Schiesel, Seth. 2007. "Geek Heroes; South Korea Has the World's Biggest and Most Advanced Video Game Culture, and the Top Players Are Treated Like Rock Stars." *The Straits Times*, January 7.

Schott, Gareth, and Kirsty R. Horrell. 2000. "Girl Gamers and Their Relationship with the Gaming Culture." *Convergence* 6 (4): 36–53.

Segal, Lynne. 1990. *Slow Motion: Changing Masculinities, Changing Men*. New Brunswick, NJ: Rutgers University Press.

Sepso, Mike. 2008. "Episode 1 Basic Business Facts of MLG." *Major League Gaming*. http://www.mlgpro.com/content/link/205543/Episode-1-Basic-Business-Facts-of-MLG%5C/2

Shane, Jason. 2006. "Who Owns a Home Run? The Battle of the Use of Player Performance Statistics by Fantasy Sports Websites." *Hastings Communication and Entertainment Law Journal* 29: 241–258.

Shaver, Lea, and Caterina Sganga. 2009. "The Right to Take Part in Cultural Life: On Copyright and Human Rights." *Wisconsin International Law Journal* 27: 637–662.

Sheridan, Heather. 2006. "Tennis Technologies: De-Skilling and Re-Skilling Players and the Implications for the Game." *Sport in Society* 9 (1): 32–50.

Shu-ling, Ko, and Jimmy Chuang. 2007. "MOFA decries Chinese attack in Seattle," *Taipei Times*, October 10. http://www.taipeitimes.com/News/front/archives/2007/10/10/2003382462.

Sicart, Miguel. 2011. "Against Procedurality." *Game Studies*.

Siegenthaler, K. L., and G. Leticia Gonzalez. 1997. "Youth Sports as Serious Leisure: A Critique." *Journal of Sport and Social Issues* 21: 298.

Silberman, Lauren. 2009. "Double Play: How Video Games Mediate Physical Performance for Elite Athletes." In *Digital Sport for Performance Enhancement and Competitive Evolution*, ed. Nigel Pope, Kuhn Kerri-ann, and John Forster. Hershey, PA: Information Science Reference.

Silverman, Mark. 2006. *Beyond Fun in Games: The Serious Leisure of the Power Gamer*. Masters Thesis. Montreal: Concordia University.

Simon, Bart. 2009. "Wii Are Out of Control: Bodies, Game Screens and the Production of Gestural Excess." *Loading* 3 (4). http://journals.sfu.ca/loading/index.php/loading/article/view/65/59.

Sirlin, David. 2005. *Playing to Win: Becoming the Champion*. Lulu.com.

Si-soo, Park. 2010. "*StarCraft* Players Indicted for Game Fixing." *Korea Times*, May16. http://www.koreatimes.co.kr/www/news/nation/2010/05/117_65996.html.

Sniderman, Stephen. 2006. "Unwritten Rules." In *The Game Design Reader*, eds. Katie Salen and Eric Zimmerman, 476–503. Cambridge, MA: MIT Press.

Stald, Gitte. 2001. "Meeting in the Combat Zone: Online Multi-player Computer Games as Spaces for Social and Cultural Encounters." In *Proceedings of Association of Internet Researchers* Conference, ed. Leslie Shade. Minneapolis, USA.

Starcade (TV show). 1981. JM Production Company.

Starcraft (game). 1998. Blizzard Entertainment.

Starcraft 2 (game). 2010. Blizzard Entertainment.

Stebbins, Robert A. 1982. "Serious Leisure: A Conceptual Statement." *Pacific Sociological Review* 25: 251–272.

Stebbins, Robert A. 2001. *New Directions in the Theory and Research of Serious Leisure*. Lewiston, NY: The Edwin Mellen Press.

Stebbins, Robert A. 2004. *Between Work and Leisure: The Common Ground of Two Separate Worlds*. New Brunswick: Transaction Publishers.

SteelSeries. 2011. "About." http://steelseries.com/about.

Stenros, Jaakko. 2010. "Nordic Larp: Theatre, Art and Game." In *Nordic Larp*, eds. Jaakko Stenros and Markus Montola. Sweden: Fëa Livia.

Stenros, Jaakko, and Markus Montola. 2011. "The Making of Nordic Larp: Documenting a Tradition of Ephemeral Co-Creative Play." In *Proceedings of Digital Games Research Association Conference*, Utrecht: The Netherlands.

Street Fighter (game). 1987. Capcom.

St-Jacques-Gagnon, Thierry. 2008. "Duck Jump, The Controversy for CS," *XLAN*, March 19. http://www.xlan.co.nz.

Suchman, Lucy A. 1987. *Plan and Situated Actions: The Problem of Human-Machine Communication*. Cambridge: Cambridge University Press.

Sudnow, David. 1983. *Pilgrim in the Microworld: Eye, Mind, and the Essence of Video Skill*. New York: Warner Books.

Suellentrop, Chris. 2010. "Game Changers: How Videogames Trained a Generation of Athletes." *Wired* 18 (2). http://www.wired.com/magazine/2010/01/ff_gamechanger/all/1.

Sundén, Jenny. 2003. *Material Virtualities: Approaching Online Textual Embodiment*. Switzerland: Peter Lang.

Sundén, Jenny. 2009. "Play as Transgression: An Ethnographic Approach to Queer Game Cultures." In *Breaking New Ground: Innovation in Games, Play, Practice and Theory: Proceedings of the 2009 Digital Games Research Association conference*, eds. Barry Atkins, Helen Kennedy, and Tanya Krzywinska, London.

Sung-jin, Yang. 2001. "First World Cyber Games opens in Seoul." *The Korea Herald*, December 6.

Supernovamaniac. 2010. "GOM TV/Blizzard Sign Exclusive Broadcast Agreement." *Team Liquid*, May 27. http://www.teamliquid.net/forum/viewmessage.php?topic_id=127674.

Susman, Jordan. 2004. "Your Karma Ran Over My Dogma: Bikram Yoga and the (Im) Possibilities of Copyrighting Yoga." *Loyola of Los Angeles Entertainment Law Review* 25: 245–274.

Swalwell, Melanie. 2006. "Multi-player Computer Gaming: Better Than Playing (PC Games) with Yourself." *Reconstruction: Studies in Contemporary Culture* 6 (1). http://reconstruction.eserver.org/061/swalwell.shtml.

Swalwell, Melanie. 2008. "Movement and Kineasthetic Responsiveness: A Neglected Pleasure." In *Pleasures of Computer Gaming: Essays on Cultural History, Theory and Aesthetics*, ed. Melanie Swalwell and Jason Wilson, 72–93. Jefferson, N.C.: McFarland.

Swalwell, Melanie. 2009. "Lan Gaming Groups: Snapshots From an Australasian Case Study, 1999–2008. In *Gaming Cultures and Place in the Asia–Pacific Region*, ed. Larissa Hjorth and Dean Chan, 117–140. London: Routledge.

Swalwell, Melanie, and Janet Bayly. 2010. *More Than a Craze: Photographs of New Zealand's Early Digital Games Scene*. Available online at http://www.maharagallery.org.nz/MoreThanACraze.

Tavris, Carol. 1992. *The Mismeasure of Woman*. New York: Touchstone.

Taylor, Nicholas T. 2009a. *Power Play: Digital Gaming Goes Pro*. PhD Dissertation, York University, Toronto.

Taylor, Nicholas T. 2009b. "Where the Women Are(n't): Gender and a North American 'Pro-Gaming' Scene." In *Breaking New Ground: Innovation in Games, Play, Practice and Theory: Proceedings of the 2009 Digital Games Research Association conference*, eds. Barry Atkins, Helen Kennedy, and Tanya Krzywinska. London.

Taylor, T. L. 2002. "Living Digitally: Embodiment in Virtual Worlds." In *The Social Life of Avatars: Presence and Interaction in Shared Virtual Environments*, ed. R. Schroeder, 40–62. London: Springer-Verlag.

Taylor, T. L. 2006a. *Play Between Worlds: Exploring Online Game Culture*. Cambridge, MA: MIT Press.

Taylor, T. L. 2006b. "Does WoW Change Everything?: How a PvP Server, Multinational Playerbase, and Surveillance Mod Scene Caused Me Pause." *Games and Culture* 1 (4): 1–20.

Taylor, T. L. 2006c. "Beyond Management: Considering Participatory Design and Governance in Player Culture." *First Monday*, Special Issue 7. http://www.uic.edu/htbin/cgiwrap/bin/ojs/index.php/fm/article/view/1611/1526.

Taylor, T. L. 2008. "Becoming a Player: Networks, Structures, and Imagined Futures." In *Beyond Barbie and Mortal Kombat: New Perspectives on Gender, Games, and Computing*, ed. Yasmin B. Kafai, Carrie Heeter, Jill Denner, and Jennifer Y. Sun, 51–66. Cambridge, MA: MIT Press.

Taylor, T. L. 2009. "The Assemblage of Play." *Games and Culture* 4 (4): 331–339.

Taylor, T. L., and Emma Witkowski. 2010. "This Is How We Play It: What a Mega-LAN Can Teach Us About Games." In *Proceedings of the Fifth International Conference on the Foundations of Digital Game*, ed. Yusuf Pisan. Monterey, CA: ACM Press.

Tomlinson, Alan. 1993. "Culture of Commitment in Leisure: Notes Towards the Understanding of a Serious Legacy." *World Leisure and Recreation* 35 (1): 6–9.

Traweek, Sharon. 1998. *Beamtimes and Lifetimes: The World of High Energy Physicists*. Cambridge, MA: Harvard University Press.

Turkle, Sherry. 1984. *The Second Self: Computers and the Human Spirit*. New York: Simon and Schuster.

Ullman, Ellen. 1997. *Close to the Machine: Technophilia and Its Discontents*. San Francisco: City Lights Books.

Vikan, Jonas Alsaker. 2007. "Counter-Strike: Fnatic Flameout." *GotFrag*, October 6. http://www.gotfrag.com/cs/story/40191.

Wagner, Michael. 2006. "On the Scientific Relevance of eSport." In *Proceedings of the 2006 International Conference on Internet Computing and Conference on Computer Game Development*. Las Vegas, Nevada: CSREA Press.

Wai-leng, Leung. 2006a. "Cybergaming Gets Official Nod of Approval as a National Sport; Association Is Set Up to Select and Train Team Players for International Events under the Team Singapore Banner." *The Straits Times*, April 24.

Wai-leng, Leung. 2006b. "Make Us Proud, Cyber Team Singapore; Players Will Be Picked for a Permanent Cybergames National Team at This Week's World Cyber Games." *The Straits Times*, August 8.

Wajcman, Judy. 1991. *Feminism Confronts Technology*. University Park, PA: Pennsylvania State University Press.

Warcraft (game). 1994. Blizzard Entertainment.

WCG Ultimate Gamer (TV show). 2009. Granada America and World Cyber Games.

Wearing, Betsy. 1998. *Leisure and Feminist Theory.* London: Sage.

Weber, Bruce. 2009. *As They See 'Em.* New York: Scriber.

Weber, Loren J. 2000. "Something in the Way She Moves: The Case for Applying Copyright Protection to Sports Moves." *Columbia-VLA Journal of Law and The Arts* 23 (3/4): 317–361.

Weber, Max. 1949. *The Methodology of the Social Sciences.* New York: The Free Press.

Welch, Tonya. 2010. "Don't Be Fooled." Complexity, April 2. http://www.complexitygaming.com/index.php?c=news&id=1704.

Wenner, Lawrence A. 1998. *MediaSport.* London: Routledge.

Whang, Sang-Min. 2005. "Online Games Dynamics in Korean Society: Experiences and Lifestyles in the Online Game World." In *Proceedings of the Biennial General Conference of the Association of Asian Social Science Research Councils, Youth in Transition: The Challenges of Generational Change in Asia*, eds. Fay Gale and Stephanie Fahey. Canberra, Australia.

Whannel, Garry. 1999. "Sport Stars, Narrativization, and Masculinities." *Leisure Studies* 18 (3): 249–265.

Whannel, Garry. 2010. "Mediating Masculinities." Unpublished manuscript based on material originally published in "Sports Stars, Narrativization and Masculinities." *Leisure Studies* 18 (3): 249–265.

Wheaton, Belinda. 2004a. "'New Lads'? Competing Masculinities in the Windsurfing Culture." In *Understanding Lifestyle Sports: Consumption, Identity and Difference*, ed. Belinda Wheaton, 131–153. London: Routledge.

Wheaton, Belinda. 2004b. *Understanding Lifestyle Sports: Consumption, Identity and Difference.* London: Routledge.

White, Michele. 2006. *The Body and the Screen: Theories of Internet Spectatorship.* Cambridge, MA: MIT Press.

Whitson, David. 1998. "Circuits of Promotion: Media, Marketing and the Globalization of Sport." In *MediaSport*, ed. Lawrence A. Wenner, 52–72. London: Routledge.

Wilson, Douglas. 2011. "In Celebration of Low Process Intensity." Unpublished manuscript, last modified August 11, 2011. Microsoft Word file.

Witkowski, Emma. 2012. "Inside the Huddle: The Sociology and Phenomenology of Team Play in Networked Computer Games." PhD diss., IT University of Copenhagen, Denmark.

Wolfenstein 3D (game). 1992. id Software.

Wood, Chris, and Vince Benigni. 2006. "The Coverage of Sports on Cable TV." In *Handbook of Sports and Media*, ed. Arthur A. Raney and Bryant Jennings, 147–170. New Jersey: Lawrence Erlbaum.

World Cyber Games. 2006. *Press Kit*.

World Cyber Games. 2008. "About WCG: WCG Concept." *World Cyber Games*, March 20. http://www.worldcybergames.com/6th/inside/WCGC/WCGC_structure.asp.

World Cyber Games. 2009. "World Cyber Games Announces Official 2009 Tournament Rules and Player Regulations." *World Cyber Games*, http://www.wcg.com/6th/fun/news/news_view.asp?keyno=C09051110000.

World Cyber Games. 2010. "World Cyber Games Completes 10th Annual Grand Final in Los Angeles." *World Cyber Games*, http://www.wcg.com/6th/fun/news/news_view.asp?keyno=C10100410094&page=1.

World of Warcraft (game). 2004. Blizzard Entertainment.

XATMO8G. 2009. "Why the SC2 Matches Weren't Broadcasted." *Gosu Gamers* forum. http://www.gosugamers.net/starcraft/thread/423824-why-the-sc2-matches-weren-t-broadcasted.

Yang, Dennis. 2008. "If ESPN Can Replay Games With Madden '09, Let Us Do It Too." *TechDirt*, September 5. http://www.techdirt.com/articles/20080905/0032532176.shtml.

Yonhap News. 2010. "Blizzard to Cease Negotiations with KeSPA." Translated by Waxangel, *Team Liquid*, April 25. http://www.teamliquid.net/forum/viewmessage.php?topic_id=121471.

Zimniuch, Fran. 2009. *Crooked: A History of Cheating in Sports*. Lanham, MD: Taylor Trade Publishing.

Index

87619857R00198

Made in the USA
Middletown, DE
05 September 2018